Betty McLellan is a feminist ethicist, author, psychotherapist and committed activist of long standing. With a focus on both the personal and political, she successfully combines her work as a psychotherapist with a broader emphasis on feminist ethical analysis and activism.

BY THE SAME AUTHOR

Overcoming Anxiety (1992)

Beyond Psychoppression (1995)

Help! I'm Living with a ~~Man~~ Boy (1999, 2006)

Unspeakable

A FEMINIST ETHIC OF SPEECH

Betty McLellan

OtherWise Publications

First published 2010
by OtherWise Publications

PO Box 688, Townsville,
Queensland 4810
Australia

http://www.feministagenda.org.au/otherwise.html

© Betty McLellan 2010

This book is copyright. Apart from any use permitted under the Copyright Act 1968 and subsequent amendments, no part may be reproduced, stored in a retrieval system or transmitted by any means or process whatsoever without the prior written permission of the publisher.

Edited by Janet Mackenzie
Typeset by Palmer Higgs Pty. Ltd.
Cover design by Deb Snibson

Printed in Australia by
McPherson's Printing Group

National Library of Australia
Cataloguing-in-Publication data:

McLellan, Betty.
Unspeakable: a feminist ethic of speech
ISBN 9780646517780

1. Freedom of speech. 2. Feminism. 3. Ethics. 4. Feminist ethics.

CONTENTS

Acknowledgements	vii
Abbreviations	ix
Introduction	1
PART I FREE SPEECH VERSUS FAIR SPEECH	25
Chapter 1 │ Free Speech	27
Chapter 2 │ Fair Speech	51
PART II THE SILENCING OF WOMEN	81
Chapter 3 │ Silencing Women's Voices	83
Chapter 4 │ Silencing Dissenting Voices	123
Chapter 5 │ Women Silencing Women	163
PART III SPEAKING THROUGH THE SILENCING	197
Chapter 6 │ Speaking the Unspeakable	199
Chapter 7 │ Feminist Speech in the Twenty-First Century	219
References	241
Index	257

ACKNOWLEDGEMENTS

This is the book I've wanted to write for many years. Ethics is a challenging and exciting discipline. For radical feminist activists, it provides a framework for activism and reminds us that change is possible; that the feminist aim of transforming male-focused, unjust, violent cultures into communities where equality, justice and harmony prevail is possible.

In the writing of this book, I am particularly indebted to two women who read my work chapter by chapter several times over and whose comments and suggestions have helped shape it into a book I am immensely proud of: Coralie McLean, whose clear-thinking, insightful, challenging comments kept me on track and who advised me on more than one occasion about the importance of avoiding exaggeration and dogmatism in the interests of credibility; and Renate Klein who, with her wealth of knowledge and experience in feminist ethical analysis, challenged my thinking in so many ways, encouraging me time and again to broaden and deepen my analysis. Special thanks, too, to Susan Hawthorne for her invaluable input into several chapters dealing with issues where her expertise is second to none.

Continued nourishment of one's feminist spirit is crucial when one undertakes the somewhat lonely task of researching and writing and, for that, I thank my sisters on the Townsville Feminist Collective. Also, members of the feminist email discussion list, f-agenda, are a constant source of support and stimulation.

Finally, thanks to my colleagues on the Coalition for a Feminist Agenda – Coralie McLean, Chantal Oxenham and Joanne Baker. Words can never adequately express my gratitude to them for their constant love and support.

ABBREVIATIONS

ACTU	Australian Council of Trade Unions
ALRC	Australian Law Reform Commission
CALD	culturally and linguistically diverse
CATW	Coalition Against Trafficking in Women
FACT	Feminist Anti-Censorship Task Force
IMF	International Monetary Fund
IPA	Institute of Public Affairs
n.d.	no date
NGO	non-government organisation
RAWA	Revolutionary Association of the Women of Afghanistan
WEL	Women's Electoral Lobby
WESNET	Women's Services Network
WHO	World Health Organization
WLUML	Women Living Under Muslim Laws
WTO	World Trade Organization

INTRODUCTION

This book is about speech, and the silencing of speech. It is an analysis of who gets to speak and who does not, who is listened to and who is ignored. While there is wide agreement among citizens of all democratic countries that freedom of speech is a basic and universal human right, crucial questions remain unresolved: Do people have a right to free speech if it is not, also, fair speech? Can it really be said that people enjoy the right of free speech when what they say is most often ignored or when their life conditions are such that they are afraid to speak their thoughts?

More particularly, this book focuses on *women's* speech and the silencing of it. Attention to the speech of both sexes reveals that it is women who are most often the victims of free speech which is not fair speech and, also, that it is women whose speech is most often ignored or ridiculed and women who most often develop a fear of speaking their true thoughts. For these reasons, a feminist ethical inquiry into the concept and practice of freedom of speech is long overdue. It is undertaken here with a focus on the situation of women in personal and social arenas as well as in the arena of international relations.

Another major focus is the speech of feminists. From beginning to end, this book explores, both implicitly and explicitly, what is surely the greatest source of frustration experienced by radical political feminists in the twenty-first century: if radical feminism is a "feminism of dissent" as is widely claimed, what is the point of being a voice of dissent in a world where the feminist voice is of little or no consequence to the wider society?

A brief look at feminist literature from the past reveals that women's speech has always been a focus of feminist attention. Nineteenth-century feminism in the United States, known as the "woman movement", identified the inability to speak and be heard as central to the problems being experienced by women at that time. The 1848 Seneca Falls women's rights convention, attended by Elizabeth Cady Stanton, Lucretia Mott and others, identified areas where justice was being denied women. The right to vote and be involved in the political process was high on their list of demands. Also, they called for improved access to education and employment, dress reform, marital and property rights, and a situation where motherhood was "voluntary". Such reforms were deemed necessary and urgent if women's voices were to be heard alongside those of men.

Susan B. Anthony (1820–1906) worked tirelessly for women's suffrage, for women's right to have their say through the ballot box. Some of her often-quoted statements include:

> there never will be complete equality until women themselves help to make laws and elect lawmakers.
>
> Men their rights and nothing more: women their rights and nothing less.
>
> Failure is impossible.

The words of Elizabeth Cady Stanton (1815–1902), too, can still be heard today:

> We hold these truths to be self-evident: that all men and women are created equal.
>
> The moment we begin to fear the opinions of others and hesitate to tell the truth that is in us, and from motives of policy are silent when we should speak, the divine floods of light and life no longer flow into our souls.
>
> Because man and woman are the complement of one another, we need woman's thought in national affairs to make a safe and stable government.[1]

Believing that the Church was the institution most responsible for keeping women in a subordinate position and, therefore, the institution most in need of reform, Stanton and a group of committed women set about to "revise the Bible". Responding to criticism of their actions, Stanton wrote in the introduction to *The Women's Bible*:

> [some] say it is not politic to rouse religious opposition. This much-lauded policy is but another word for cowardice. How can woman's position be changed from that of a subordinate to an equal, without opposition, without the broadest discussion of all the questions involved in her present degradation? For so far-reaching and momentous a reform as her complete independence, an entire revolution in all existing institutions is inevitable [1898, p. 11].

The Revising Committee, as it was called, was made up of twenty women from the United States and five foreign members (one each from Finland, England, Austria, Scotland and France). Their aim was to address both the personal and political subordination of women and create a society where women would have the confidence to speak and where women's speech enjoyed equal respect to that of men. Commenting on the effects of society's subordination of women, Stanton said:

---

1 Anthony, <http://womenshistory.about.com/cs/quotes/a/qu_s_b_anthony.htm>.
   Stanton, <http://womenshistory.about.com/cs/quotes/a/ec_stanton.htm>.

> We have many women abundantly endowed with capabilities to understand and revise what men have thus far written. But they are all suffering from inherited ideas of their inferiority; they do not perceive it, yet such is the true explanation of their solicitude, lest they should seem to be too self-asserting [1898, p. 11].

This dual focus on the personal and the political, on encouraging individual women to find their voices and, at the same time, insisting that men and institutions change to make room for women's voices, women's equal involvement, emerged again in the 1960s with the movement that came to be known as Second Wave feminism.

Nelle Morton, US feminist and theologian, wrote of her experiences leading consciousness-raising groups in the early 1970s. Her focus was on women's personal empowerment through speech. "Women came to new speech simply because they were being heard", she said (1984, p. 17). Connecting the personal and political implications of this new speech, she went on to say: *"the new language on the lips of those experiencing liberation … both reflects and creates protests and political action"* (p. 19, emphasis in the original).

Mary Daly wrote about the silencing of women and the need for the "prisoners of patriarchy" to dis-cover a new "Spring within and among us [which] makes be-ing possible, and makes the process of integrity possible…" (1978, p. 21). Encouraging women to break free of the "deep silence" imposed on us, she said:

> Overcoming the silencing of women is an extreme act, a sequence of extreme acts. Breaking our silence means living in existential courage. It means dis-covering our deep sources, our spring. It means finding our native resiliency, springing into life, speech, action [1978, p. 21].

Adrienne Rich pointed out that generation after generation of women's dissenting voices are erased from history.

> The entire history of women's struggle for self-determination has been muffled in silence over and over. One serious cultural obstacle encountered by any feminist writer is that each feminist work has tended to be received as if it emerged from nowhere; as if each of us had lived, thought, and worked without any historical past or contextual present [1979, p. 11].

Dale Spender's *Man Made Language* devotes a whole chapter to describing the ways in which women's silence is constructed by those who own the language, namely men. Women's history and meanings are simply excluded. "There is a 'loud silence' when one searches for the meanings of women in the language." Commenting on the popular notion of women as the talkative sex, she says:

> The talkativeness of women has been gauged in comparison not with men but with silence. Women have not been judged on the grounds of whether they talk more than men, but of whether they talk more than silent women. When silence is the desired state for women ... then any talk in which a woman engages can be too much [1980, pp. 54, 42].

Audré Lorde, when diagnosed with possible breast cancer, urged all women to examine their relationship to speech. She urged them to break the silence and let their voices be heard:

> In becoming forcibly and essentially aware of my mortality, and of what I wished and wanted for my life, however short it might be ... what I most regretted were my silences ... Death ... might be coming quickly, now, without regard for whether I had ever spoken what needed to be said, or had only betrayed myself into small silences, while I planned someday to speak, or waited for someone else's words ...
>
> I was going to die, if not sooner then later, whether or not I had ever spoken myself. My silences had not protected me. Your silence will not protect you [1984, p. 41].

Julia Penelope's analysis of what she calls the Patriarchal Universe of Discourse (PUD) leads her to appeal to women to find their voices: "We must refuse to be docile PUD speakers and listeners, and choose, instead, to create an active discourse in which we are agents acting on our own behalf" (1990, pp. 229–30). Her final paragraph expresses the sentiments of all feminist theorists and activists:

> we must find new ways to perceive our world and new words and descriptions for articulating those perceptions ... If we do not learn to speak freely, imagining ourselves into an age where oppression is obsolete will remain an unaccomplished "perhaps" in the long sentence of patriarchy [1990, p. 236].

While urging women to find their voices, to break the silence about their day-to-day experiences of violence, subordination and exclusion, First and Second Wave feminists were also aware that the silencing of women was deliberate, in fact, built into the structures of societies dominated by men. Enquiries into the personal and social situation of women reveal that practices which diminish and degrade women, such as pornography and prostitution, are allowed to flourish in the name of free speech. Also, men's violence against women in the home, rape and sexual harassment, are still not designated as crimes in many countries; in those countries where they are, lawyers still find such charges almost impossible to *prove* under a legal system which gives preference to men's "evidence" over that of women. Similar enquiries into the situation of women on the global stage reveal that, while it is most often women who are the victims of war and of economic globalisation, women are almost totally excluded from discussions and decision-making about global issues.

Since the 1960s, radical feminists[2] have continuously condemned practices which diminish and degrade women. To this day, they express the view that practices which subordinate women to men entrench inequality and render women's speech inconsequential. It follows, they maintain, that the voices of women made inconsequential by violence and subordination are easy to exclude from discussions and decision-making on issues of national and international significance. Violence, subordination and exclusion work together to keep women silenced.

The central aims of this book are to focus attention on the democratic principle of freedom of speech as it relates to women; to support the feminist contention that the principle of freedom of speech, as it now stands, actually robs women of their right to free speech; to highlight violence, subordination and exclusion as practices central to the silencing of women; and to suggest that urgent attention be given to developing the ideal of fair speech, that is, free and equal speech for all.

The above discussion outlining the priority given to women's speech in First and Second Wave feminism, followed by the naming of those societal conditions identified by feminist scholars and activists as preventing women's full expression, serves as background to the more detailed attention to the principle of freedom of speech in Chapter One.

By far, the most notable feminist challenge to the concept of freedom of speech was that undertaken in the 1980s by US feminists Catharine MacKinnon and Andrea Dworkin. In 1983, they brought a civil rights anti-pornography ordinance to the Minneapolis City Council in Minnesota, claiming that pornography subordinates women to men and, in so doing, robs women of their right to equality under the Fourteenth Amendment (Dworkin 1981). Pro-pornography advocates turned the issue into a clash between the First Amendment (guaranteeing free speech) and the Fourteenth Amendment (guaranteeing equality). Eventually, men's right to free speech won out over women's right to equality and, therefore, to free speech. While the defeat of the ordinance was hugely disappointing to feminists everywhere, it proved to be the impetus for a greater feminist focus on the effects of pornography on the speech of women.

---

2 For a discussion of terms pertaining to different strands of feminist thought, see below under "Feminism today".

In the field of law, there were the writings of MacKinnon and Dworkin together (1988, 1997) and separately (MacKinnon 1979, 1987, 1989, 1993; Dworkin 1987, 1988, 2002, 2004).[3] Others writing from a legal perspective included Jocelynne Scutt (1990), Beth Gaze (1994) and Deborah Cass (1994). In the social sciences, those focusing on pornography and its effect on women's speech included Catherine Itzin (1992), Kathleen Barry (1995, 1996), Rebecca Whisnant (2004), Adriene Sere (2004) and Joan Mason-Grant (2004). Other disciplines included women's studies (Donna Hughes 1999, 2001, 2004), political science (Sheila Jeffreys 1990) and moral philosophy (Rae Langton 1994, 1997).

Feminist ethics

Since this work is undertaken from the perspective of feminist ethics, it is important to pause at this point to sketch a brief history of feminist ethics and some of its current trends, with a view to situating this work within a particular philosophical and ethical framework.

Beginning with the first stirrings of the women's liberation movement in the 1960s and early 1970s, it can be argued that all radical feminist utterances and activism have a feminist ethical base. Feminism's goal of social transformation is the same as the goal expressed in mainstream ethics. While ethics purports to be about engaging with unjust situations and societal structures with a view to changing them, similarly, feminism is about engaging with situations and societal structures which unjustly discriminate against women with a view to changing them.

Australian feminist ethicist Emma Woodley speaks of the need for feminism to be involved in ongoing action and reflection around entrenched practices oppressive to women. She describes her system of Feminist Engaged Ethics as "fundamentally political". It is concerned first and foremost with power. The *goal* is no less than the transformation of society and the *strategy* involves total engagement, appraisal, reflection, protest and action (Woodley 2005). In this sense, then, it can be said that all radical feminist activism—that is, feminist activism aimed at achieving justice for women—is a feminist ethical endeavour.

Feminism in the twentieth and twenty-first centuries has developed in the tradition of eighteenth- and nineteenth-century women who courageously spoke out against the roles and expectations which kept women "dwarfed"

---

3   Relevant publications leading up to the presentation of the ordinance included Dworkin 1976, 1979, 1981; MacKinnon 1979.

(Stanton) and "in chains" (Anthony). Using the terms "morals" or "virtues" or "moral virtues", women's morality was the subject of much attention by philosophers, educators and social commentators in the eighteenth century (Jean-Jacques Rousseau; Mary Wollstonecraft) and nineteenth century (John Stuart Mill; Harriet Taylor Mill; Catherine Beecher; Charlotte Perkins Gilman; Elizabeth Cady Stanton).

Women's morality was most often discussed in comparison with men's morality. There were those (such as Wollstonecraft and Taylor Mill) who argued that there was no difference between men's and women's virtues, that the differences were not innate but, rather, came about because of socially constructed roles. On the other hand, there were those (such as Beecher and Gillman) who highlighted the differences and even suggested that women's morality may be superior to that of men.

Twentieth-century feminist ethics is outlined and discussed most notably by Rosemarie Tong in *Feminine and Feminist Ethics* (1993).[4] Tong places feminist theories about ethics into three categories: feminine approaches to ethics; feminist approaches to ethics; and lesbian approaches to ethics. Her categories are extremely helpful, if somewhat arbitrary. My suggestion of arbitrariness relates particularly to her decision to include the work of Mary Daly and Janice Raymond in the category of lesbian ethics and exclude them from the category of feminist ethics. Such categorising could be misleading to readers who may not know the important contributions both writers have also made to feminist ethics.[5] Nevertheless, Tong's descriptions of feminine and feminist ethics and her thorough discussion of the strengths and weaknesses of each are helpful indeed.

In the category of feminine ethics, she includes Carol Gilligan's ethics of care and Nel Noddings' relational ethics, as well as the work of those writing about maternal ethics (Sara Ruddick, Virginia Held and Caroline Whitbeck). Under feminist ethics, she includes those writers whose approach to ethics is political (Alison Jaggar, Sheila Mullet, Susan Sherwin and Annette Baier). Tong argues that "a feminist approach to ethics asks questions about *power*—that is, about domination and subordination—even before it asks questions about good and evil, care and justice, or mothers and fathers" (p. 160, emphasis in the original).

---

4   See also Tong 2003.
5   Mary Daly's analysis of male power and domination and her unique way of expressing the need for women to rebel against that domination has inspired feminists, both lesbian and heterosexual, for decades. In particular, see Daly 1973, 1978 and 1984. Janice Raymond's contribution, too, encompasses a broad range of issues. As professor of medical ethics and women's studies, her research and writing focused on a feminist analysis of reproductive technologies and on the trafficking of women for prostitution; as such, it represents a huge contribution to feminist ethics. In particular, see Raymond 1986; Raymond, Klein and Dumble 1991; Raymond 1993.

Any discussion of feminist ethics today, however, must include the groundbreaking work of Carol Gilligan because, whatever label one uses to characterise her work, it is an undisputed fact (and Tong agrees) that her ethics of care represents a crucial contribution to the field of feminist ethics. In fact, she caused something of a revolution in ethics by taking the focus off the male-centred approach which had dominated the field for centuries and presenting a woman-centred ethics. Commenting on Gilligan's contribution, Alison Jaggar observed that while traditional ethics, dominated by men like Mill, Locke, Kant and Rawls, focused on "individuality, impartiality, and reason", Gilligan succeeded in expanding that focus "to include an appreciation of the moral significance of community, particularity, and emotion" (Jaggar 1990, p. 83).

In her book *In a Different Voice: Psychological Theory and Women's Development* (1982), Gilligan set about to respond to the developmental models of influential male thinkers like Freud, Piaget, Kohlberg and Erikson, all of whom either left women out of their developmental stages theories altogether or implied that women's development was inferior to that of men. Her goal, she said, was "to expand the understanding of human development by using the group left out in the construction of theory to call attention to what is missing in its account" (pp. 3–4). Throughout her book, Gilligan relies heavily on three studies conducted over several years in which a number of male and female tertiary students were asked questions "about conceptions of self and morality, about experiences of conflict and choice". Her conclusion, on analysing the results of the studies, was that a morality centred on care and a morality centred on justice were gender correlated. "In women's development [there is] the absolute of care, defined initially as not hurting others. ... For men [there are] the absolutes of truth and fairness, defined by the concepts of equality and reciprocity" (pp. 2, 166).[6]

Further describing the ethics of justice (rights) and care (responsibilities), Gilligan says:

> The morality of rights is predicated on equality and centered on the understanding of fairness, while the ethic of responsibility relies on the concept of equity, the recognition of differences in need. While the ethic of rights is a manifestation of equal respect, balancing the claims of other and self, the ethic of responsibility rests on an understanding that gives rise to compassion and care [1982, pp. 164–5].

---

6   It is on this point of gender correlation that Gilligan's work has received the most criticism from other feminists.

In her conclusion, Gilligan admits that there is a "tension between responsibilities and rights" in all of us, and that, in "the representation of maturity, both perspectives converge". She calls it a "dialogue between fairness and care [which] not only provides a better understanding of relations between the sexes but also gives rise to a more comprehensive portrayal of adult work and family relationships" (p. 174).

Clearly, Gilligan's focus is on the personal and individual and on the effect one's individual system of ethics has on one's personal and family relationships. Hence Tong's categorising of her work as a "feminine approach to ethics". Tong explains that, to qualify as feminist, "an ethicist's goal [must be] to liberate women from the social, economic, cultural, and ... biological factors that limit women's capacity for goodness..." (1993, p. 161). One ethicist who does qualify, according to Tong's classification, is Alison Jaggar.

Jaggar sets out what she calls "minimum conditions of adequacy for any approach to ethics that purports to be feminist":

1. Feminist ethics never assumes "that women and men are similarly situated..." either domestically or internationally.
2. It must be aware of issues around domination and control and "offer guides to action that will tend to subvert rather than reinforce the present systematic subordination of women...".
3. It must critically examine "the whole distinction between public and private life" and provide guidance on issues of so-called private life as well as public.
4. It "must take the moral experience of all women seriously, though not ... uncritically". It is committed to "developing approaches to ethics that will respect women's moral experience and avoid rationalizing women's subordination..." [1992, pp. 365–7].

A more recent development in feminist ethics and one which has particular relevance to the development of what I am calling fair speech, has come to be known as feminist international relations. A discussion of this trend will follow after a brief look at two of the ongoing debates in feminist academic circles.

Current debates in feminist ethics

Many of the debates seem to be a variation on the theme: liberalism versus radicalism, or the individual versus the political. Two of the better-known debates are: care versus justice and equality versus justice.

Care versus justice

Already mentioned in the previous pages, this debate was sparked in the early 1980s by Gilligan's *In a Different Voice*. It continued for close to two decades and, while the debate itself has subsided somewhat, the work of Gilligan, Ruddick, Nussbaum and others is still being discussed and critiqued by feminists today.[7]

Writing from the perspective of law, Radha Jhappan criticises Gilligan's "care orientation" for its "implicitly negative evaluation of the justice approach". She argues that "a requirement of care instead of, and to the exclusion of, justice is not a recipe for good public policy" (pp. 193, 194–5). Where proponents of the care approach do focus attention on justice, she says, it is only as it relates to the personal and individual.

> In particular, the care approach, with its emphasis on personal constructions of morality, does not seem geared towards addressing the needs of oppressed groups (such as racial/ethnic minorities, lesbians and gay men, women and people with disabilities) for recognition and respect within the polity and society of their differences, self-development, and self-determination [p. 195].

Most criticisms of Gilligan's care ethics centre on the dichotomous relationship she attributes to care and justice. While she does refer to a tension or dialogue between fairness and care, the main thrust of her argument sets them up as "dichotomous moral concepts" (Tong 1993, p. 92). Critics such as Marilyn Friedman (1987) and George Sher (1987) have no difficulty citing situations where care and justice are, in fact, complementary. Tong agrees and sums up this view by saying: "To meet with our full approval, the just person must be caring, and the caring person must be just" (p. 93).

Equality versus justice

Radha Jhappan is at the centre of another debate in feminist ethics (within the discipline of law), referred to here as the equality versus justice debate. She expresses the view that it is "quite remarkable [that] most feminists

---

[7] For one critique of Gilligan's work, see Jhappan 2002, pp. 169–216. For a discussion of Sara Ruddick's *Maternal Thinking: Towards a Politics of Peace* (1990), see Hutchings 1999, pp. 17–38. For critiques of Martha Nussbaum's work (1996, 1999, 2001), see Cannon 2005, pp. 97–110, and Schwartzman 2005, pp. 151–65.

writing about law seem to accept the inevitability of engagement [with the law]..." and that "the core discourse and objective in feminist legal strategy [continues to be] equality rights" rather than justice (2002, pp. 174, 172). Even though radical feminists such as Catharine MacKinnon "point out the impossibility of equality within patriarchy", she says, they nevertheless continue to engage with the law in an effort to achieve that which they know is impossible (p. 174).

There is no doubt that the concept of equality is fraught with difficulties for feminists working to achieve justice for women, but when equality is the only relevant claim permitted in law, the "choice" for radical feminist lawyers seems to be between arguing a case on the basis of equality or not arguing a case at all. In Canada, the Women's Legal Education and Action Fund (LEAF) have had some success arguing on the basis of "systemic sexual inequality" (Naffine 2002, p. xv) but, as Jhappan remarks, that still indicates their "fidelity to the equality/inequality discourse that has proved so ineffective so often for so many reasons" (2002, p. 215).

According to radical feminists, the concept of equality is a liberal one best suited to white middle-class feminists whose aim is equality with white middle-class men. Some of the "wins" feminists have had in Western countries in terms of changing legislation have been in relation to mainstream issues like equal employment opportunities and sexual harassment in the workplace. While such gains are important, they by no means represent a universal equality. Many feminists view the aim of equality as a step along the way to achieving greater justice for all women, but Jhappan points out that that will never happen without a total reconstitution of the "political economy and social system" (2002, p. 190).

Referring to the work of women of colour, bell hooks (1987) and Mary Ellen Turpel (1993), Jhappan argues that the "claim to equality is fundamentally contradictory ... It is impossible for subjugated groups such as women, people of Colour, lesbians, and gay men to demand and get what privileged white men have". This is because "the power and privilege enjoyed by certain white men have only been made possible by racism, imperialism, and sexism" (2002, pp. 190, 189).[8] The alternative to a goal of equality, Jhappan argues, is a goal of justice. Instead of women and other oppressed groups pursuing equality as a step toward justice, why not have justice as the primary goal? While feminist legal scholars and practitioners have been pursuing equality, she says, this has led to "the neglect of justice as a developmental discourse or as a litigation strategy" (2002, p. 191). If justice is the desired outcome for oppressed groups, then feminists must move beyond Gilligan's gender-correlated distinction and make claims on the basis of justice.

---

8   See also Jhappan 1996, p. 25.

As will be seen in Chapter One, radical feminist Catharine MacKinnon makes her legal arguments for free speech for women based on equality (1994a, pp. 49-78), but begins by describing inequality in terms of domination and subordination. In a similar vein, Iris Marion Young begins with the concepts of oppression and domination but then chooses to argue on the basis of justice rather than equality. She identifies five faces of oppression: exploitation, marginalisation, powerlessness, cultural imperialism and violence. Oppression is "the institutional constraint on self-development", and domination "the institutional constraint on self-determination" (1990, pp. 48–63, 37).

Jhappan's discussion in favour of justice over equality in the framing of legal arguments on behalf of oppressed groups is important (and necessary if the long-term goal of justice is ever to be achieved). But she concedes that, in the short-term, "the legal/constitutional system obliges groups and individuals to funnel their petitions through the narrow aperture of equality..." (2002, p. 198). When the law will only allow for petitions based on equality/inequality, it is not surprising that matters of justice for women and other disempowered groups, even when couched in terms of equality, are so often denied by the courts.

The equality versus justice debate serves as a warning to feminists concerned with the law: when fighting legal battles on the basis of equality, the ultimate goal of justice should always be kept in clear view.

Feminist ethics and international relations

Throughout this book, I assert that the silencing of women's speech occurs at all levels in their relationships with men and male institutions, from the personal to the social to the global.

In the 1980s, feminists working in the area of international relations began voicing the opinion that the absence of women from the world stage was not because they were not interested or qualified, but because they were being deliberately excluded. It was around that time that the area of study known as feminist international relations, or feminist ethics and international relations, began to emerge.

Charlotte Bunch, executive director of the Center for Women's Global Leadership at Rutgers University, highlights four areas requiring intense feminist analysis and activism in the coming decades: globalisation, fundamentalism, domestic terrorism and militarism (2002). My choice of the words violence, subordination and exclusion, which I use throughout to describe the ways by which women are silenced under patriarchy, incorporates Bunch's concerns.

- *Violence* refers to men's violence at all levels: domestic violence, rape, militarism, terrorism, war.
- *Subordination* refers to the myriad of ways women are diminished and subordinated: through fundamentalism, pornography, prostitution, trafficking, poverty caused and exacerbated by economic globalisation.
- *Exclusion*, made easy by the worldwide acceptance of women's subordination and violence against them, refers to the deliberate silencing of women's analysis and opinions and the exclusion of women from decision-making on issues of national and international significance.

Violence

In the field of international relations, a feminist analysis of how men's violence is handled by patriarchy reveals that, whether one is talking about domestic or global violence, women and women's concerns are virtually excluded from discussions and policy development. Domestically, one of the tactics used by Western governments in the 1970s and 1980s in an effort to minimise the influence of feminists and feminist theory, was to barricade women off and confine them to an area called "women's issues".[9] Government funding was made available in many countries for the establishment and day-to-day running of women's refuges, women's health centres, domestic violence support services and sexual assault counselling services. Although feminists were "grateful" for government funding, many were not prepared to keep silent in order to ensure continued funding. Feminist academics and activists kept up their focus on men's violence and demanded that politicians and community leaders give priority to its eradication.

That radical, political feminists refused to be confined to "women's issues" was apparent both domestically and globally. Their analysis of women's situation was that most of the problems faced by women and children in the private arena were caused by men's emotional and physical violence. Consequently, while continuing to support individual women, feminists had their collective eye on the broader picture. Individual men's violence against their partners and children was part of a larger agenda of violence promoted by patriarchy. Their analysis revealed that, in many Western nations, boys and men undergo constant preparation for war. Through endless commemorations of battles fought in the two world wars and more recent wars, boys and men are encouraged to see war as a noble enterprise. In men's sport (especially certain codes of football), fairness is feminised and discouraged while violence is regarded as masculine and rewarded. Men's violence against women in the home, rape of women by family members, acquaintances and strangers—

---

9   From the late 1990s to the present, governments have replaced the term "women's issues" with "gender issues" in an effort to take women out of the equation altogether and render the silencing of feminist voices complete.

indeed, all forms of male violence against women—are not discouraged in anything but a superficial way by governments which need their men to be in a perpetual state of readiness for violence and war. Bronwyn Winter, writing on this theme shortly after the start of the war on Afghanistan, expresses it forcefully:

> Violence is masculine and violence is celebrated. Be a hero. Wield power. Inflict wounds. Kick the weak when they are already down. Or, if you help them, make sure they remain beholden to you. Keep the power. That is what makes you a man [2002, p. 371].

Globally, feminist international relations focuses on the themes of war, militarism and the global arms trade (Enloe 1989/1990, 1993, 2000, 2004; Cohn 1993; Zalweski 1995; Moser and Clarke 2001; Thobani 2001; Charlesworth 2003; Rein and Sirleaf 2003; Whitworth 2004; Roy 2004; Eisenstein 2004, 2007); on masculinities (Zalewski and Parpant 1998; Enloe 2004a, 2004b); on terrorism (Morgan 2001; Cohn and Enloe 2003; Joseph and Sharma 2003); and on responses to 9/11 (*International Feminist Journal of Politics* 2002; Hawthorne and Winter 2002; Tinkner 2002; Pettman 2004).

Subordination

Violence against women takes many forms and all contribute to the subordination of women: physical, sexual and emotional violence by individual men against individual women; gang rape of women; state-sanctioned rape in times of war and conflict between men (Stiglmeyer 1994; Moon 1999; Castellanos 2007); culturally sanctioned rape of women as payback for the misdeeds of brothers and other male relatives (Mann 2005).[10]

The situation of women's subordination through violence is circular: women can be violated with apparent ease because they are seen as subordinate to men; at the same time, it is the very existence of violence against women that subordinates them and assigns to all women a subordinate status.

Feminist analysis of women's continued subordination focuses on situations around the world which demean and debase women and yet continue to enjoy cultural, religious or legal legitimacy. Among the issues identified as extremely problematic for women are:
- *fundamentalism* (Moghadam 1999, 2002; Winter 2001; Rashid 2000; Women Living Under Muslim Laws 1998, 2004; Revolutionary Association of Women of Afghanistan 2002)

---

10 The story of Mukhtar Mai, the Pakistani woman who took her fight for justice to the United States, is one example. In Washington, Seattle, "Mukhtar Mai spoke of her fight against a system back home in Pakistan that allowed a tribal council to deem it acceptable that four men could rape her to avenge their honor after her brother allegedly had sex with a woman above his class".

- ***pornography*** (Dworkin 1981; MacKinnon 1979, 1993; Itzin 1992; Dines, Jensen and Russo 1997; Stark and Whisnant 2004)
- ***prostitution*** (Jeffreys 1997, 2000; Farley et al. 1998; Farley 2004, 2007; Stark and Whisnant 2004; Sullivan 2006)
- ***trafficking*** (Coalition Against Trafficking in Women; Leidholdt 2003; Raymond 2004; Farley 2005; Wolfe 2002; Fergus 2005)
- ***poverty and displacement as effects of globalisation*** (Shiva 2000; World March of Women 2000, 2005; Marchand and Runyan 2000; Hawthorne 2002; Pettman 2004).[11]

Exclusion

Feminist International Relations asks: "Where are women's voices?" or, in Cynthia Enloe's words: "Where are the women?" (1989, p. 7). In a recent conversation between Enloe and Marysia Zalewski recorded in *The Curious Feminist: Searching for Women in a New Age of Empire* (Enloe 2004), Zalewski points out that when one asks "Where are the women?", it prompts another question: "Why haven't we noticed that they aren't there?" (p. 84). In matters of violence, war, militarism and terrorism, Enloe and others have encouraged feminists to notice that women are almost completely excluded.

In reviewing Bob Woodward's book on the US government's plans to invade Iraq (*Plan of Attack*, 2004), Enloe commented that all the books purporting to give readers an inside look at the workings of the Bush administration "are written by men, about men. With the notable exception of National Security Adviser Condoleezza Rice [who then became Secretary of State in the Bush administration], in each of these books, women remain almost invisible. Masculinities remain unexamined" (2004, p. 10). Jan Jindy Pettman of the Australian National University makes the same point about the exclusion of women in an article titled "Feminist International Relations After 9/11": "In times of national crisis and international violence, women and gender often disappear from view. Feminists, including IR feminist experts, are rarely asked to comment on large-scale organized violence" (2004, p. 85).

The exclusion of women from matters of national and international importance is not a recent phenomenon. During World War I, having noticed that women were totally left out of the discussions around war and peace, 1000 women came together at the International Women's Congress for Peace and Freedom, held in The Hague in April 1915. From that congress, the Women's International League for Peace and Freedom was born. Women were determined to have their say. To this day, feminists and other

---

11 The article by Bronwyn Winter, "Fundamental Misunderstandings: Issues in Feminist Approaches to Islam", in *Journal of Women's History*, Spring 2001, pp. 9–41, is followed by comments from Valentine Moghadam, Riffat Hassan and Margot Badran with a reply from the author, pp. 42–57.

women peace activists persist in raising their voices against war and all other forms of men's violence. But still women's voices are largely ignored in the halls of power in every country. Following the terrorist attacks on the World Trade Center on 11 September 2001, feminists again noted "the total invisibility of women": "The perpetrators were men ..., the "experts" interviewed on TV are men, most of the commentators ... are men, those making decisions about how the world should respond are men, those leading memorial services and conducting funerals are men" (McLellan 2002, p. 79).

In the field of feminist ethics and international relations, there have been two major emphases around the theme of exclusion, as discussed by Eleanor O'Gorman and Vivienne Jabri (1999, pp. 1–15). One is the attempt to "reclaim women's hidden voices":

> This first wave of feminist international relations ... has served to unravel the negation of the role of women in global politics and the exclusion of specifically feminist contributions to the analysis of such central themes as war, economic inequality, human rights, and the state [p. 1].

The other major emphasis, influenced by postmodernism, has been on "addressing the question of difference, and specifically cultural difference" among women (p. 2).

> International relations are inscribed with subjectivities of race and class as well as gender in shaping international agendas and the operation of power at the level of the international. Therefore, the question becomes how men and women—and women among themselves—are differentiated and placed in different situations of risk, powerlessness, power, and security at the international level [p. 5].

While the exclusion of women by men and male institutions is the main focus of this present critique of the principle of freedom of speech, I will also acknowledge that Indigenous women and those from culturally and linguistically diverse (CALD) backgrounds experience exclusion at the hands of men and of other women (including feminists). Feminist international relations reminds us that, as global domination by political, religious and market fundamentalism continues to promote sameness and exclude difference, all feminist analysis and activism for women's rights must give high priority to ensuring inclusiveness.

Major themes of the book

The two major themes of this book are speech and silence. An examination of the democratic principle of freedom of speech reveals that, in this neoliberal, capitalist, globalised, male-dominated, violent world, speech is free only to those who enjoy the privilege and safety of economic and political power. Men at the top of multinational corporations, media corporations and powerful political administrations have unlimited access to speech, and they have ears only for each other's speech. While they speak and respond to each other, however, their speech, their competitiveness, the power games they play with each other, dominate the lives of the rest of us. When speech belongs to the powerful, those with little or no power have little or no access to speech.

In introducing the term fair speech, this book sets up an oppositional relationship between free speech and fair speech in a deliberate attempt to mimic the better-known free trade/fair trade division and connect the speech debate to the globalisation debate. In the same way that so-called free trade is free only to those nations who are willing and able to abide by the conditions of international trade and financial institutions, so-called free speech is available only to those whose speech does not contradict the speech of the powerful. Even in ostensibly democratic countries where free speech is said to be a right of every citizen, ordinary people are actually living under strict censorship. While dissenting voices are tolerated, they are deliberately excluded from every meaningful arena, and thus silenced. For free speech to be universally free, it must be fair.

The other major theme, silence, draws attention to the patriarchal, hegemonic practice of silencing dissenting voices. In a personal sense, when silence is deliberately chosen, it can be an empowering experience. In fact, the ability to be silent when silence is appropriate, is something to be sought after because it enables one to observe, analyse, contemplate, commune with nature, connect with one's god and experience people and animals at a deeper than superficial level.

Conversely, silence that is not deliberately chosen but forced upon a person is anything but a positive experience. In a world where speech is reserved for the economically and politically powerful, anyone who would question, or disagree with, or criticise the dominant voice is silenced by exclusion. Dissenting voices may be raised but the powers of exclusion are such that dissent is blocked from reaching the ears of the masses and is most often heard only by members of one's own network, a situation commonly called preaching to the converted. Fair speech exposes the tactics of silencing and enables free speech for all.

Defining feminism

The term radical feminist is used throughout this book to refer to feminists who are engaged in deliberate dissent with a view to bringing about positive change in the status of women globally and locally. For the purposes of comparison, however, the following definitions of other categories of thought claiming the title "feminist" are important.

As a consequence of the serious divisions that have existed in feminist ranks since the mid-1970s to the present, some today speak of "feminisms" in an attempt to avoid conflict by appearing to be inclusive of all strands of feminist thought and activism. Others reject the plural, insisting that feminism is a political movement and, as such, is one force in the world rather than many. Radical feminists, in particular, are adamant that only those feminists engaged in political endeavours aimed at creating a fairer world for women, only those who refuse to be coopted by neoliberal forces, only those who keep their eye on the goal have the right to claim the title "feminist". Denise Thompson in *Radical Feminism Today* (2001) added: "The tendency to refer to 'feminisms' in the plural is an evasion of the real and important contradictions between competing assertions made in the name of feminism" (p. 17).

Early definitions

A notable attempt at defining categories of feminist thought in the early years of Second Wave feminism was that undertaken by Alison M. Jaggar and Paula Rothenberg Struhl in 1978. In *Feminist Frameworks: Alternative Theoretical Accounts of the Relations between Women and Men*, they set out five categories:[12]

- **Conservatism, or sexism as natural inequality:** The conservative view "denies that women are oppressed" and, consequently, "is not feminist" (Jaggar and Struhl 1978, p. 69) because feminism as a social movement exists only for the purpose of responding to women's lived experiences of oppression.
- **Liberalism, or sexism as legal inequality:** Liberal feminists focus on equality of opportunity and fight against discrimination in employment and education, insisting that women's legal rights should be the same as those of men. In liberalism, the roots of oppression are located in sex role stereotyping and lack of equality (p. 70).

---

12 While including the category "conservatism", the authors made the point that conservatism could not in any way be called feminist. It was, in fact, anti-feminist. The other four categories did represent attempts at responding to the oppression of women and, as such, were appropriately called feminist.

- *Traditional Marxism, or sexism as a result of the class system:* Marxists reject the liberal view that genuine equality of opportunity is possible under a capitalist and imperialist system. Women's oppression, along with that of all oppressed people, is located in a particular system of social organisation. Once the class system is overthrown and "the means of production become once again the property of society as a whole", the oppression of women will simply disappear (p. 71).
- *Radical feminism, or sexism as the fundamental inequality:* In radical feminism, men and the social institutions developed and supported by men are identified as the fundamental cause of women's oppression. While there are variations on the theme among radical feminists, all agree that "women were, historically, the first oppressed group", that "women's oppression is the most widespread" and that "women's oppression is the deepest in that it is the hardest to eradicate and cannot be removed by other social changes such as the abolition of class society" (p. 71). Jaggar and Struhl drew attention to the writing of US radical lesbian feminist Charlotte Bunch, who argued that "Since women are oppressed primarily by sexism and only secondarily by racism and class society … our struggles must be directed first of all against sexism" (p. 72).
- *Socialist feminism, or the interdependence of gender and class:* Socialist feminists agree with the Marxist analysis of the class system as fundamentally problematic but disagree that sexism is simply a product of capitalism which will be eradicated once a fairer economic system is established. They believe that "capitalism and sexism reinforce each other" and see sexism as at least as fundamental as economic oppression (p. 73).

Feminism today

Today, while three of the strands discussed by Jaggar and Struhl (1979)—liberal, socialist and radical—are still evident in Western cultures, the two which seem to have the greater prominence, perhaps because of the obvious tension between their proponents, are liberal and radical. Many socialist feminists are fighting the fight for women within anti-globalisation and anti-poverty movements and, while their voices are strong at World Social Forums and similar arenas, they are less vocal elsewhere.

Postmodern feminism

In addition to liberal and radical feminism has been the emergence of postmodern feminism, which contains within it a sharp division in terms of its commitment to political activism. On the one hand, there are those who emphasise the need to be unpolitical and undiscriminating. They encourage the use of "gender" instead of "women and men" and reject the need for a focus on oppression. According to radical feminists, this strand of postmodernism goes out of its way to depoliticise relations between women and men. When it is implied that all people are the same, any talk of oppression of one sex by the other is seen by the advocates of that philosophy to be irrelevant. It is not surprising, therefore, that the term post-feminist was coined to make the point that any need for feminist activism was in the past.

On the other hand, some postmodern feminists call for a political feminism, insisting that feminism will only be effective globally and personally if it is a feminism of dissent (see definition of political feminism below).

Transnational feminism

Influenced by that part of postmodernism's agenda which emphasises the need to address the question of cultural difference, transnational feminism has emerged. It calls for feminists to build bridges: between feminists of different philosophical persuasions; between feminists from different ethnic groups and cultures around the world; and between feminists and other women and men campaigning for human rights in a variety of ways. Mari Santiago, in her article "Building Global Solidarity through Feminist Dialogues", calls on feminists to "generate new dialogues across our differences and ... explore the possibilities of common projects and larger coalitions—both among ourselves and with other progressive movements" (2004, p. 9).

In her article "Transnational Feminisms and the World Social Forum: Encounters and Transformations in Anti-globalization Spaces", Janet Conway describes what she sees as a central question for the future of feminism, which is "how open, plural, dialogical and coalitional feminist movements will be, not just vis-a-vis each other, but in relation to movements which are recognized as broadly emancipatory but in terms other than feminist" (2007, pp. 66–7).

Another description of transnational feminism comes from the writing of Valentine M. Moghadam. In *Globalizing Women: Transnational Feminist Networks* (2005), she explains that transnational feminist networks

> ... have arisen in the context of economic, political, and cultural globalization—and they are tackling both the particularistic and the hegemonic trends of globalization. They are advancing criticisms of inequalities and forms of oppression, neoliberal economic policies, unsustainable economic growth and consumption, and patriarchal controls over women. In a word, transnational feminist networks are the organizational expression of the transnational women's movement, or global feminism [p. 104].

Political feminism
While transnational feminism seems to have come out of a combination of socialist feminism and postmodernism, another strand of postmodernism is closer to radical feminism in its emphasis on the need for dissent and political involvement, and that strand is referred to as political feminism. In her article "Feminist ethics and hegemonic global politics", Vivienne Jabri calls for a "distinctly political feminism" charged with the task of analysing present conditions and the "hegemonic practices" which generate "practices of exclusion". Feminism appears to have two options, she says: "On the one hand, there is clearly the option of complicity, a form of cooptation into the discourses of the powerful. On the other, there is the option of dissention and contestation" (2004, pp. 4, 1).

Political feminism stresses the need for an understanding of the "structures of domination" and the "relations of power" so that feminism's "disruption of the givens" will be effective in opening the way for the establishment of a more just situation for women (Jabri 2004, pp. 6, 2). Political feminism is a feminism of dissent.

Radical feminism
In many respects, political feminism and radical feminism are in agreement. Radical feminists agree with Jabri when she declares that the feminism of cooptation "lacks a discourse based on a radical critique of the present". There is agreement, also, when she insists that a far more significant feminist voice is that which "contests and through contestation enables the emergence of woman as speaking subject". Like political feminism, radical feminism is a feminism of dissent. It is "an engaged feminism" and one which is "essentially and necessarily transnational" (2004, p. 1).

The word radical implies engagement with root causes, and radical feminists are engaged in discovering and confronting the root causes of women's powerlessness and subordination. Radical feminism is political in orientation and radical feminists are committed activists.

Let us look at some notable definitions of radical feminism. In 1987, Catharine MacKinnon called it "feminism unmodified" (p. 16), a simple but apt description of the school of feminist thought which refuses to be co-opted or watered down.

Robin Morgan asserts that the strength of radical feminism lies "in the fluid energy that links unapologetic intellect with unashamed passion". She describes it as "a means, not an end; a process, not a dogma" (1996, p. 6). After a discussion of the varied situations women are confronting in their own countries around the world, Morgan says:

> What radical feminists have in common, though, includes a stubborn commitment to the people of women, the courage to dare question anything and dare redefine everything, a dedication to making the connections between issues, a sobering comprehension of the enormity of this task—freeing more than half of humanity and, by so doing, saving the other half—and perhaps most importantly of all, *radical feminists share an audacious understanding of this politics' centrality to the continuation of sentient life itself on this planet* [p. 7, emphasis in the original].

Denise Thompson's definition of radical feminism is that it is "feminism *per se*", that which "identifies and opposes male domination". Radical feminism involves itself in "a thoroughgoing critique of male domination wherever it is found and however it is manifested" (2001, pp. 2–3, 21).

Throughout this book, while the term "radical feminist" appears most often, it is used interchangeably with "political feminist", "radical political feminist" and "feminist activist".

Outline of the book

The book is divided into three parts. **Part I: Free Speech versus Fair Speech**, begins with a detailed discussion of the principle of free speech in Chapter One. The idea introduced early in the chapter, that "the existence of a *principle* of free speech does not automatically guarantee the *right* of free speech to all citizens", forms the basis for a discussion of three major arguments about free speech, including the feminist argument for equality, followed by a discussion of free speech as it relates to democracy and to power.

Chapter Two introduces and describes the concept of fair speech. Beginning with a comparison between the free speech/fair speech division and that of free trade/fair trade, the discussion of fair speech focuses on the call by feminists for equality and justice for women in relation to speech.

Part II: The Silencing of Women, illustrates the contention, developed in Part I, that women are subordinated and silenced in male-focused societies. Chapter Three discusses the various ways women are silenced worldwide, using examples of violence, subordination, fundamentalism, the privileging of culture and exclusion from power. Chapter Four uses a broader lens and invites readers to see where the silencing of women fits in the bigger picture of the silencing of dissent generally.

Chapter Five takes a hard look at the various ways women silence each other, in acknowledgement of the fact that women/feminists are sometimes the perpetrators of silencing as well as its victims. Among those silenced by other women/feminists historically and in the present are lesbians, radical feminists, Indigenous women, ethnic minorities in every country and, on the global stage, women from less powerful countries.

Part III: Speaking through the Silencing, shows that radical, political feminists will continue to speak out in spite of all attempts at silencing them. Chapter Six addresses the ethical implications of attempting to speak the unspeakable and urges activists to proceed with care. When feminist activists insist on speaking when the requirement of the power elite is that they be silent, there are implications for women in general and for feminist activists in particular. Finally, Chapter Seven looks at feminist speech in the twenty-first century with reference to non-Western as well as Western countries. While feminist speech is not expected to be welcomed or heeded into the foreseeable future, the prediction is that feminist activists will continue to speak the unspeakable in a determined effort to disrupt the status quo and bring about a new global order which has equality and justice at its centre.

Part I

FREE SPEECH
versus
FAIR SPEECH

FREE SPEECH 1

The principle of free speech is central to the political philosophy of democratic nations and the right to speak freely is taken for granted by most citizens. Where it is not simply taken for granted, freedom of speech is held up as one of the most precious of all our human rights. To be free to speak and act according to one's own motivations, it is maintained, is to have the greatest chance of satisfaction and fulfilment in life.

I happen to agree with that but, as feminist theory and other human rights theories demonstrate, the existence of a principle of free speech does not automatically guarantee the right of free speech to all citizens. Inequality and invisibility on the basis of race, for example, were written into the constitutions of many colonised nations by omission—that is, omission of any reference to the citizenship of the Indigenous inhabitants. Similarly, inequality and invisibility on the basis of sex were integral to the constitutions of most democratic nations by virtue of the fact that women were not mentioned. It must be concluded, therefore, that the freedom of speech guaranteed in statements of equal rights in countries like the United States and Australia was meant only for those belonging to the dominant group.

In the United States, proponents of the Equal Rights Amendment have lobbied over many years to have women's rights written into the constitution but have still not been successful. On a smaller scale, when the Australian government was preparing to hold a referendum in 1999 on whether or not Australia should break away from the British monarchy and become a republic, women's groups lobbied hard to have a reference to women included in the preamble to the new Australian constitution, but were unsuccessful. After a draft of the preamble was released by the then prime minister John Howard, the Women's Electoral Lobby (WEL) responded in the following terms:

> In leaving out any mention of equality of men and women, the Prime Minister has clearly not been listening to half the population.
>
> Despite raising women's expectations that there would be a specific statement of equality of men and women before the law, and having received submissions from the Women's Constitutional Convention Steering Committee calling for a clear and encompassing statement of equality of men and women, he has let us all down [WEL 1999].

When women are excluded at such a basic level, it is clear confirmation that freedom of speech as it exists in so-called democratic countries is a right only for those who enjoy the power that comes from membership in the dominant male group. The freedom of speech of women and other disempowered people exists only if and when their words are acceptable to the dominant group.

In this chapter it is my intention to identify differing arguments in support of the concept of free speech; to explore its place in democratic political theory; to analyse its relationship to issues of power and powerlessness; and to highlight the need for a rethinking of the principle of free speech so that speech becomes "free" for all citizens. At that point, it will be timely to move on to a discussion of fair speech, which is the subject of Chapter Two.

The speech of people living in democratic countries reveals that most citizens have a working knowledge of the principle of free speech, as illustrated by the following popular comments:

- You can't tell me what I can and cannot say.
- It's a free country.
- I'm free to say what I like.
- I can do whatever I like.
- I have rights.
- The government has no right to ban books/TV programmes/movies.

While those who speak out about their "rights" in these ways are in the minority, the fact that their words are understood by most who hear them is an indication that most people do have a working knowledge of the concept of free speech. Popular knowledge, however, is almost always derived from libertarian theories which do not necessarily constitute a true interpretation of the democratic principle of freedom of speech. The libertarian definition represented by the argument for self-determination (below) is, in fact, only one among many. Tom Campbell, in his essay "Rationales for Freedom of Communication", lists seven arguments in support of freedom of speech. They are:

- the sole path to truth
- the right to self-determination
- the presupposition of democracy
- the stimulus to tolerance
- the flourishing of plurality
- the efficient allocation of resources
- the intrinsic worth of the communicative experience (1994, p. 17).

Three arguments

For our purposes, attention will be given here to the first two arguments listed by Campbell (1994): the argument for truth and the argument for self-determination. A third will be added, the argument for equality, which is the major feminist argument around free speech.

The argument for truth

The most common argument for free speech in law and politics and the one which has endured the longest is the argument for truth. The statement often attributed to French philosopher Voltaire (1694–1778), "I disapprove of what you say, but I will defend to the death your right to say it",[13] is based on the argument for truth. Unrestricted speech, so the argument goes, creates the best chance for truth to emerge in any society. Individuals engaging in free and open discussion, giving their views and weighing up other people's views will lead to the most informed and advanced societies based on truth.

Clearly, the greatest weakness in the argument for truth in today's world is that it is predicated on the assumption that people actually speak the truth. We only have to listen to the speech of politicians, business leaders, media barons, advertising gurus and others to see that truth is often in short supply. In this age of spin and spin-doctors, deals and deal-makers, lies and liars, no amount of free speech will have the power to cause the truth to emerge.

The argument for truth, nevertheless, continues to be prominent in free speech discussions, most commonly highlighted in two metaphors: the marketplace of ideas and the slippery slope.

Marketplace of ideas

Using the marketplace metaphor, proponents of unrestricted free speech argue that all ideas must be permitted in the marketplace. Individuals should never be deprived of the "right" to say what they want to say and do what they want to do, nor should they be deprived of access to other people's words and actions. The metaphor of the marketplace allows proponents to compare "speech" and "ideas" with the buying and selling of goods. It implies

> a preference selection between the widest possible range of different assertions on the basis of the tastes and purposes of the "purchaser". The more opinions available, the more likely that the seeker after truth will

---

13 The closest thing to this statement Voltaire ever actually said was: "I detest what you write, but I would give my life to make it possible for you to continue to write", letter, 1770, <http://www.holysmoke.org/sdhok/voltaire.htm>.

find what she is looking for. By being able to make comparisons, the truth-hunter will get the best bargain relative to her needs [Campbell 1994, p. 24, female pronouns in the original].

John Stuart Mill, one of the best-known proponents of the individual's right to free speech, had expressed a similar view in the nineteenth century, though without the "marketplace" metaphor. In *On Liberty*, first published in 1869, he argued that

> the peculiar evil of silencing the expression of an opinion is, that it is robbing the human race; posterity as well as the existing generation; those who dissent from the opinion, still more than those who hold it. If the opinion is right, they are deprived of the opportunity of exchanging error for truth; if wrong, they lose, what is almost as great a benefit, the clearer perception and livelier impression of truth, produced by its collision with error [1999, p. 79].

The concept of the marketplace of ideas has a serious weakness: it is based on the assumptions that, in any given society, everyone enjoys equal status, everyone has an equal right to express their ideas; and that, being aware of their rights, they will, in fact, readily express their ideas. It assumes that all people possess equal confidence and ability not only to express their own ideas but also to reject other people's ideas or "products" which do not suit their "tastes". To use a different metaphor, the assumption is that there is a "level playing field"—which, in any given society, there clearly is not.

Slippery slope

Using the slippery slope metaphor, proponents of unrestricted free speech argue that, once a society introduces any restriction at all on an individual's right to free speech, it is the beginning of a downhill slide for the entire society. Something which appears to be a good decision now, they argue, can lead to a bad decision later on. The banning of any pornographic material now, for example, will inevitably lead to the banning of all kinds of valuable literature in the future.

On 12 December 2002, the editorial page of the *Boston Globe* came out against a ban on cross-burning (the signature of the racist Ku Klux Klan) in the State of Virginia, based on the slippery slope argument. As explained in *Legal Affairs Magazine*:

> *The Globe* took issue not so much with the ban itself but with the possibility that its acceptance might open the door for future bans the paper is less inclined to support. "What about the confederate flag?" the paper asked. "Or the communist hammer and sickle?" In other words, the editorial explained, the ban creates a "slippery slope" [Volokh and Newman 2003].

Another name for the slippery slope argument is the "camel's nose". The idea is that if a camel-driver allows a camel to put its nose inside the tent to protect its face in a sandstorm, soon the whole camel will be inside the tent and the camel-driver will be forced out. To allow any censorship at all can lead to censorship taking over and citizens being deprived of all their human rights.

The main weakness of the slippery slope or camel's nose argument is that it seems to be based on an unreasonable fear of setting a precedent. Such a fear, it must be said, flies in the face of generally accepted decision-making processes. To enjoy a vigorous and healthy life, or to manage a dynamic and effective business, one must have the courage to make decisions as they present themselves. To refuse to make a decision today out of fear of possible consequences some time, somewhere in the future, is to live a life which will soon become stale and stagnant or to run a business which is doomed to fail. There is no reason to believe that a society's curtailing of one aspect of speech in an effort to effect greater equality and justice will inevitably lead to the wholesale loss of human rights in that society. Each event will bring its own arguments for and against and must be decided on its own merit—at its own time.

The argument for self-determination

The libertarian argument for self-determination, self-development, self-expression and individual autonomy is the best-known argument for free speech in the general community. It asserts that self-determination—that is, the ability to speak for oneself and control one's own life—is an intrinsic individual right. "I have the right to free speech by virtue of the fact that I am a human being. Who I am gives me the right to unrestricted free speech."

It is on this point that the difference between the popular libertarian view of free speech and the view outlined in legal and political literature is most clearly seen. While libertarian arguments are based in the idea of intrinsic individual rights, political arguments are "grounded more in the idea of instrumental individual rights" (Campbell 1994, p. 34). In other words, the principle of free speech is not meant simply as an end in itself but, rather, as a means to a greater end, namely, that of enhancing relationships and developing a better society.

Frederick Schauer, in the introductory chapter of *Free Speech: A Philosophical Enquiry*, makes a distinction between self-regarding and other-regarding acts. The language of individual rights central to Libertarianism, he contends, is clearly self-regarding and based on a principle of personal liberty rather than that of freedom of speech. "Speech is plainly not a self-regarding act ... Affecting others is most often the whole point of speaking. There are words such as "deceive", "persuade", "convince", and "mislead", whose very logic presupposes that speech acts will affect others". The instrumental approach to freedom of speech emphasises "the interests of society at large rather than ... the interests of the individual" (1982, pp. 10, 47).

It must be said, as both Campbell and Schauer are careful to point out, that there can be an instrumental or other-regarding aspect to the pursuit of individual rights and personal autonomy. One can pursue one's own self-development, for example, with a view to becoming a better mother, or one can take steps to increase one's self-confidence and sense of autonomy for the purpose of developing the courage to speak out against injustices in society. The important thing is to distinguish between "two types of individual interests": those which benefit "the persons exercising the interests" and those which have instrumental value for society. The latter

> are recognized not primarily because of their ultimate value for the individual, but because the value to the person exercising them is instrumental to the value that accrues to society from the widespread exercise of individual interests ... The individual rights they generate are but a mediate step towards maximizing the goals of society at large [Schauer 1982, p. 47].

Even so, there is one major weakness in the argument for self-determination, self-expression and individual autonomy in its instrumental form. As with the argument for truth expressed in the metaphor of the marketplace of ideas, the argument for self-determination assumes an equality which does not exist. As Campbell states:

> ...freedom of expression cannot be expected to fulfil its ... function in an equitable way if there are major inequalities of capacity, education and access to communicative means. Since this is the normal situation in individualistic societies, instrumental arguments for freedom of speech seem to be particularly relevant to the defence of the interests of the articulate and powerful sections of society [1994, p. 36].

The argument for equality

The argument for equality, outlined by Catharine MacKinnon in her essay "Equality and Speech" (1994a, pp. 49–78) stands in contrast to the two arguments introduced above. While totally supporting a concept of freedom of speech, MacKinnon's argument for equality is critical of mainstream arguments and their emphasis on an absolutist notion of freedom of speech, on the grounds that they benefit the more powerful sections of society at the expense of the less powerful. With reference to the First and Fourteenth Amendments to the US constitution, MacKinnon begins her essay with the words "The law of equality and the law of freedom of speech are on a collision course" (p. 51).

For readers not familiar with the US constitution, the First Amendment guarantees freedom of speech:

> Congress shall make no law respecting an establishment of religion, or prohibiting the free exercise thereof; or abridging the freedom of speech, or of the press; or the right of the people peaceably to assemble, and to petition the government for a redress of grievances.

The Fourteenth Amendment guarantees equality:

> Section 1. All persons born or naturalized in the United States, and subject to the jurisdiction thereof, are citizens of the United States and of the state wherein they reside. No state shall make or enforce any law which shall abridge the privileges or immunities of citizens of the United States; nor shall any state deprive any person of life, liberty, or property, without due process of law; nor deny to any person within its jurisdiction the equal protection of the laws.

But, as MacKinnon points out, "the First Amendment has been interpreted, with few exceptions, as if the Fourteenth were not there" (1994a, p. 51). The right to free speech is pursued doggedly, while the right to equality is largely ignored.

As stated earlier, the most significant weakness common to the argument for truth and the argument for self-determination is the presumption of equality where equality does not exist. It is self-evident that when the issue of equality is ignored in arguments for freedom of speech, a universal principle of free speech is not possible. Rather, as Campbell points out, freedom of speech is a right enjoyed only by "the articulate and powerful sections of society" (1994, p. 36).

The argument for equality grew out of the battle against pornography waged by many feminists in the 1980s and 1990s and, in particular, the legal ordinance conceived and designed by Catharine MacKinnon and Andrea Dworkin and presented to the City of Minneapolis in 1983. The ordinance, described as "a sex equality law, a civil-rights law, a law that says that sexual subordination of women through pictures and words, this sexual traffic in women, violates women's civil rights" (MacKinnon 1990, p. 9), was "passed by the Minneapolis City Council on 30 December 1983 ... The ordinance was vetoed by the Mayor, reintroduced, passed again, and vetoed again in 1984" (MacKinnon 1989b, p. 144n).

In a speech delivered at the University of Minnesota in 1999, Dworkin repeated what she had said many times since 1983: that the Mayor's action was a blatant example of inequality. In vetoing the ordinance, she said, he "... claimed that it would violate the constitutional rights of the pornographers, which superseded in importance the speech rights of women and children who were shut up by pornography" (in Stark and Whisnant, 2004, p. 137).

This landmark law was lost on the grounds of free speech. The "absolutist" view of the First Amendment that "Congress shall make no law ... abridging the freedom of speech..." prevailed over the "balancing" view.[14] The right to free speech—that is, men's right to view women being degraded, exploited, raped, mutilated, tortured and murdered—won out over women's right to equality under the law.

The argument for equality calls on law-makers and politicians to make the principle of freedom of speech into a meaningful concept by taking the necessary steps to ensure that speech is free for all. It asserts that the prioritising of equality would have the effect of: granting free speech to all, eliminating all subordinating speech and speech acts and creating a more just society.

Granting free speech to all

If there were a determination on the part of politicians and lawyers to redress inequalities based on sexism, racism and economic status, then universal free speech could be possible. While the law continues to favour the powerful, however, social inequality remains and, as MacKinnon points out, where there is social inequality "some people get a lot more speech than others" (1994, p. 52). Until the need for equality is taken seriously, the speech of the powerful will always take precedence over and, in fact, drown out the speech of the powerless.

Eliminating all subordinating speech and speech acts

When equality is not recognised or valued in a society, the principle of free speech enables hate speech and racial vilification to go unchallenged. In such situations, one person's right to free speech is protected over the rights of the many who belong to groups other than the racially dominant group. Similarly, when equality is not valued, free speech for the powerful enables pornography, prostitution and all forms of trafficking in women to continue unchallenged. The free speech of pornographers, pimps and consumers of pornography and prostitution is protected over the rights of all women to live free of humiliation, exploitation and subordination.

Creating a more just society

Appropriating the metaphor of the marketplace of ideas, MacKinnon says: "it becomes obvious that those with the most power buy the most speech, and that the marketplace rewards the powerful, whose views then become established as truth" (1994, p. 72). Under a system of inequality, those with

---

14 For one exchange on the "absolute" versus "balancing" approaches to the First Amendment, see Mendelson 1962 and Frantz 1962.

power (multinational corporations, media corporations, sex traffickers, etc.) are the ones whose voices are heard and who, consequently, determine the standards by which the rest of us live.

The existence in many Western countries of unhealthy alliances between conservative governments and the few media corporations which now dominate the market is one example of the way in which big corporations are able to dictate how entire populations think.[15] What this means is that entire populations have their lives shaped by the issues which sell newspapers and which add to the wealth of media bosses and their shareholders. The comings and goings of sportsmen, for example, sell newspapers. News about footballers, often touted as "heroes" by the media, sells newspapers. And all the hype around football games has the effect of transforming hitherto uninterested citizens into football fanatics who "love" their "heroes".

When several members of the Bulldogs football team in Australia were accused of gang-raping a young woman in Coffs Harbour in northern New South Wales in 2004, team supporters found it difficult to believe. In fact, no one caught up in the hype around football wanted to believe it of their "heroes". When lawyers later announced that there was not enough evidence to proceed with charges (even though police had reported publicly that a rape of the nature described by the young woman did take place), that was the end of the matter for most people. While individual women and women's groups made a fuss about the favouritism shown to these alleged rapists simply because they were wealthy, high-profile men, there was no outcry, no demand for justice from the general community. After all, these men were "our heroes".

In a more equitable society, where free speech was available to all in equal proportions, the law would be required to serve the needs of the powerless as well as the powerful, the media would be required to be impartial and to give expression to a whole range of views in relation to any issue, and governments would give equal attention to the speech of all their citizens. There is no doubt that, if the principle of equality were upheld, communities would be the richer for having access to all speech, and democracy in its true form would be possible.

---

15 For an Australian example, see Chapter Seven, "Unholy Alliances", in Kingston 2004, pp. 117–41.

Free speech and democracy

The principle of freedom of speech is said to be the cornerstone of democracy. It comes as no surprise then, given the state of democracy in recent years, that freedom of speech is in trouble.

Democracy defined as rule by the people

Democracy in its pure form is "rule by the people". As such, it requires regular and open elections, universal suffrage, a principle of majority rule and a system of representative government, that is, a situation "in which the population at large has sovereignty in theory and practice" (Schauer 1982, p. 37). It is

> ...a system that acknowledges that ultimate political power resides in the population at large, that the people as a body are sovereign, and that they, either directly or through their elected representatives, in a significant sense actually control the operation of government [p. 36].

Democracy in this true sense would incorporate the principles of equality and freedom of speech and require that governments acknowledge the primacy of certain basic rights.

- *The right to know:* In order for people to be able to exercise their sovereign power and enter into informed and meaningful debate with a view to forming opinions and making decisions, politicians and other community leaders have an obligation to keep citizens informed—and citizens need to be able to trust that their leaders are not lying.
- *The right to speak and be heard:* Representative government is a system designed to give all citizens access to government. In such a system, any person exercising his or her democratic right to freedom of speech is assured of a hearing and a response.
- *The right to be represented:* The success of representative government depends on two things: the willingness of citizens to convey their opinions to their local politicians; and the willingness of those politicians to put aside their own opinions in order to give voice to the opinions of the people they represent.
- *The right to criticise:* The right to criticise enables citizens to hold politicians and government officials accountable for their decisions and actions. While politicians and bureaucrats have been entrusted with the task of carrying out the affairs of government, all of them are, in fact, "public servants" and are accountable to the people.

- **The right to protest:** While majority rule,[16] which is a necessary though imperfect feature of democracy, is seen as the fairest way to accommodate differing views, it inevitably leads to frustration and anger on the part of those in the minority. The right to protest through carefully targeted letters, marches, rallies, vigils and other peaceful demonstrations provides an avenue for the expression of opinions and the venting of feelings which, in turn, helps reduce the potential for anarchy.
- **The right to influence decision-making:** When democracy is working well and freedom of speech is for all, the above rights—to know, speak, be heard, be represented, criticise, protest—will result in ordinary citizens having the opportunity to influence decision-making at the highest levels of government.

Democracy defined as rule for the people

Sadly, the definition of democracy in any given country is usually decided by the government of the day and the majority of citizens, busy dealing with day-to-day events and pressures in their own lives, offer little resistance. Not surprisingly, the definition favoured particularly by conservative governments[17] is that which places maximum power in their hands, namely, "rule for the people". In this form of democracy, the only independent role the people have is that of casting their vote. Once votes have been cast and the political party with the majority of seats comes to power (under the Westminster system), the government takes it upon itself to rule on the people's behalf.

In an attempt to legitimise the grasping for power inherent in the dictum "rule for the people", governments are heard to repeat certain mantras.

The national interest
When a government wants to keep important information from its citizens, the secrecy is said to be "in the national interest". The impression is created that there could be dire consequences for the nation if politicians broke their silence when, more often than not, the purpose of the secrecy is simply to

---

16   The principle of majority rule, where no effort is made to incorporate the opinions and desires of minority groups, is one of the serious weaknesses of democracy. Under conservative governments, it becomes "rule by and for the mainstream", where voices of dissent are ignored and equality non-existent.

17   The word conservative is used here to denote conservative forces in all political parties. Prime Minister Tony Blair's Labour government, for example, was a conservative version of Britain's traditionally left-wing party. In Australia, the federal Labor government as well as most state Labor governments have also moved to the right in an effort to gain and retain power. In the United States the Democratic Party is barely distinguishable from the Republican Party on many issues.

circumvent protests. Politicians are well aware that, when people are presented with a done deal at the end of secret negotiations with foreign governments or with business corporations, protests are usually far less effective. "In the national interest" is a theme used to rob citizens of their democratic right to know, to criticise and to mount effective protests.

Noam Chomsky saw this term as a euphemism for "in the interests of a small group of dominant elites". He said that the term "national interest"

> ...is commonly used as if it's something good for us, and people are supposed to understand that. So if a political leader says that "I'm doing this in the national interest," you're supposed to feel good because that's for you. However, if you look closely, it turns out that the national interest is not defined as what's in the interest of the entire population; it's what's in the interests of a small group of dominant elites who happen to be able to command the resources that enable them to control the state—basically, corporate-based elites [1992, p. 47].

National security

Since the terrorist attacks of 11 September 2001 on the United States, governments of Western countries seem to believe they have a ready-made excuse for curtailing freedom of speech whenever they choose. The issue of national security is used to manipulate people into believing that they need to be protected and that the greater restrictions on their civil liberties are for their own good. Laws are passed, police powers are increased, civil liberties are encroached upon, all "in the interest of national security". People assembling for whatever reason can be moved on. Marches and demonstrations are monitored by police. During the anti-war protests in the lead-up to the Iraq War in 2003, there were media reports of people being detained in the United States for refusing to remove T-shirts with anti-war messages on them. "In the interest of national security" is a theme used to rob citizens of basic civil liberties.

Mandate

Political parties who see their election to government as an opportunity to maximise their own power are fond of the word "mandate". They interpret their election as a *carte blanche*. They believe that they have been elected to rule on behalf of the people, and anyone who speaks out against any one of their policies can be accused of being unsupportive or disrespectful of their mandate. Those who make a habit of criticising their government are in danger of, at worst, being arrested or, at best, being treated as *persona non grata*, being ignored.

In Australia, there are numerous examples (at both federal and state levels) of non-government organisations which have lost government funding and been forced to close because their agenda was seen to be not fully supportive of the government's mandate. The notion of "mandate" is used to rob citizens of their democratic right to speak, be heard, criticise, protest and influence decision-making.

Party solidarity

The requirement by major political parties that all politicians toe the party line has turned the notion of representative government into a farce. Democracy requires that local politicians represent their constituents in parliament. Their main task is to ensure that the views of their constituents are heard in the halls of power. The requirement of "party solidarity", however, has worked to turn that democratic responsibility on its head. It has created a situation where, rather than local politicians representing the views of their constituents to government, they now represent the views of government to their constituents.

As in an autocracy, governments who choose to define democracy as rule for the people, make decisions about what is best for the people and, then, judge the "success" of local politicians on whether or not they have been able to convince their constituents to support the government's decisions. In such situations, the only speech seen to have legitimacy (and, therefore, the only speech that is heard) is that of the ruling political party. Again people are robbed of the right to have their speech heard.

An example of "rule *for* the people"

In Australia, in the state of Queensland, the conservative Labor government under Premier Peter Beattie developed elaborate and expensive systems designed to give the impression of a government listening to the people when, in reality, their attitude was that "father knows best".

Soon after Beattie and his government came to power in 1998, a system of regular ministerial regional community forums was instigated in which regional representatives were to have the opportunity to present concerns brought to them by the people. The idea was that all concerns brought by regional representatives would be heard by two government ministers who would be in attendance at every forum. Their task was to respond to the concerns on the spot or, failing that, to take the concerns to the relevant government minister for attention. On the surface, it looked like a commendable democratic system until one dug deeper and found that all regional representatives were appointed by the government. Certainly, all citizens were free to apply for the available regional representative positions but it was the government that approved or rejected those applications. Not surprisingly, anyone who had the potential to raise controversial matters or to be critical of the government was screened out.

Another innovation of the Queensland Labor government was that of having parliament sit periodically in regional centres so that citizens outside the capital city could have access to ministers and other politicians and also have the opportunity of sitting in the gallery and observing their parliamentarians at work. Again, the idea is to be applauded but the reality was less than satisfactory. The undemocratic nature of "rule for the people" became obvious to a particular group of women who decided to demonstrate outside one of those regional parliamentary sittings to highlight the need for the state government to provide more realistic funding for domestic violence services. The group was very small, twenty women in all, but they stood with banners and balloons courageously enacting their democratic right to protest.

As one woman tells the story, the aggressively negative response which followed could never have been anticipated by the protesters. Government politicians let it be known that they were deeply hurt and affronted by the "audacity", the "criticism", the "lack of support" for all that the government was trying to do for women. According to the protesters, the overwhelmingly negative response seemed out of proportion to the size and intent of the protest.

This example raises important questions about the democratic right to free speech under a government which chooses to define democracy as rule for the people. Is free speech to be allowed only when one's speech is acceptable to the government of the day? How will dissenting voices be heard if demonstrations and protests are discouraged or, even, quashed? Is free speech really free when citizens are only free to agree?

In concluding this discussion of free speech and democracy, it must be said that there is a dilemma in this for radical feminists and other radical social justice advocates. While "rule by the people" is far more palatable than "rule for the people", it remains that the democratic principles of "equal participation" and "majority rule" present problems which cannot be ignored. The problem with the notion of equal participation is that it inevitably moves a society in the direction of focusing on the individual. Thus it creates a situation where democracy is interpreted as "respect for individual dignity, individual choice, and equal treatment of all individuals..." (Schauer 1982, p. 41), rather than a focus on what is best for society as a whole.

Equal participation, as defined by liberalism, takes on an intrinsic, personal focus rather than the instrumental focus intended by democratic theory and leads to a situation where some individuals see themselves as "more equal than others". Those who are more successful, more wealthy, more articulate have a tendency to see themselves, also, as more worthy. Similarly, the notion of majority rule is taken by conservative governments as permission to listen only to the mainstream and govern for them to the exclusion of others. The challenge for radical thinkers is to maintain the focus on the instrumental nature of free speech as a democratic principle so that the emphasis is kept on society as a whole. Any emphasis on the individual is to be seen in the context of creating the best possible society for all.

Free speech and power

One of the significant contributions of the feminist argument for equality in speech, expressed by Catharine MacKinnon as "...those with the most power buy the most speech..." (1994a, p. 72), requires further attention.

The relationship between power and speech is a cyclical one: power (derived usually from wealth or position) gives one access to speech which, in turn, gives one access to more power. The power enjoyed by governments, media barons and business corporations gives them easy access to speech, and the fact that they often speak in unison only serves to consolidate their power. Through speech, the power of the powerful increases while the power of the disempowered, who have little or no access to speech, is diminished even further.

To gain a clearer understanding of the relationship between power and speech, it is necessary to take a look at the various forms of power operating at the beginning of this twenty-first century.

Collusion between governments and corporations
Collusion between governments and business leaders with the aim of keeping power in the hands of the wealthy is not new, but some of their methods are. It is those new methods which students and critics of globalisation have worked hard to expose. Thanks to scholars like Tony Clarke and Maude Barlow in Canada, Vandana Shiva in India and Susan Hawthorne in Australia,[18] the shroud of mystery deliberately constructed by those with a vested interest in keeping the masses ignorant is slowly being lifted.

The most far-reaching and influential new method has been the establishment of global institutions for economics, trade and intellectual property rights, and the development of rules to regulate the trading and other behaviour of nation states around the world. Such institutions together with their rules and regulations have been established by wealthy players in wealthy countries (in particular, the United States) with a view to maximising their own wealth and influence globally. As Hawthorne puts it: "The multilateralisation of the world economy has developed in tandem with

---

18 See, for example, Clarke and Barlow 1997; Shiva 2000; Hawthorne 2002.

globalising institutions, which have sewn up the rules that govern behaviour of states and corporations in such a way as to benefit those who hold power" (2002, pp. 322–3).

One of the results of the "multilateralisation of the world economy" is the establishment of a global monoculture through the "homogenising of diversity" (Hawthorne 2002, p. 25). Wherever one travels in the world, one is sure to find a McDonald's or a Pizza Hut or to have the opportunity of staying at a Western-style resort just like all the rest. Hawthorne speaks of Westerners travelling to other countries and experiencing the local culture "as nothing more than an exotic backdrop to a homogenised and sanitised Western lifestyle in resorts which accept US dollars and sell the same resort labels and commodified experience throughout the world" (p. 194).

At the end of World War II, the General Agreement on Tariffs and Trade (GATT) was signed in Geneva by twenty-three countries. The World Bank and the International Monetary Fund were also established around that time. Another global institution, Trade Related Intellectual Property Rights (TRIPs), began as an instrument of GATT, but when the World Trade Organization (WTO) came into being in 1995, TRIPs was included as an integral part of that institution. "TRIPs means that US patent laws are internationalised so that the laws apply worldwide" (Hawthorne 2002, p. 333). The WTO was founded for the purpose of regulating trade throughout the world or, as some critics say, for the purpose of spreading Western systems of law throughout the world to satisfy the "needs of industrialized countries" (Pretnar 1990, p. 249). "The regulation of trade does not focus on the people who produce goods; rather, it focuses on those who benefit most from globalisation, namely, transnational corporations, international banks and national elites" (Hawthorne 2002, p. 331).

Collusion between Western governments, multinational corporations and global institutions works to ensure that powerful countries grow more powerful and that the speech of the powerful is heard throughout the world.

Increasing the stress on individuals and families

Features of the collusion between governments and business leaders for the purpose of maximising profits for the business sector include: industrial relations legislation in favour of employers; the outsourcing of work; the shifting of operations off-shore; staff cut-backs; more work for fewer staff; the casualisation of staff, which makes them ineligible for workplace benefits; greater profits for businesses; huge salaries for those at the top; and a scraping to make ends meet for those at the bottom.

The resulting increase in stress on individuals and families renders people powerless and voiceless. Living in a state of continual stress, needing to pay continual attention to one's own survival, precludes the ability to speak out in one's own defence. As a ploy to keep power and speech in the hands of the powerful, the tactic of deliberately increasing stress in the lives of workers and their families has been very successful.

Dumbing-down of society

Another of the modern-day forms of power exercised by governments with the help of the media is the deliberate dumbing-down of populations. One of the ways this occurs is by taking steps to reduce the influence of universities and other academic bodies.

When governments have the power to dictate numbers of places to be made available in government-funded universities, and also to reduce funding so that universities are forced to increase fees to students, university education and access to the professions are available only to the privileged few who can afford it. One strategy Australian universities have used in recent years to address the funding shortfall is that of encouraging full fee paying international students to enrol in their programmes. While the increasing multicultural nature of universities has the potential to enrich the experience of tertiary education for all concerned, there is anecdotal evidence of international students being exploited by universities under financial stress.

Another area which suffered from government cut-backs to universities during Prime Minister John Howard's time in office was that of research. Funding for independent research and other independent intellectual pursuits was cut drastically, while funding for research in areas that support the government's agenda was freely available. It was impossible, for example, to obtain funding for any research project pertaining to the education of girls, while there was what seemed like unlimited funding available for educational research into the situation of boys. This is one example of the backlash against the feminist research of the 1980s and 1990s that highlighted the ways in which girls were disadvantaged by the education system and a clear indication of the lengths conservative governments will go to to make sure no fundamental change takes place.

Along with their efforts to reduce emphasis on general university pursuits, the Howard government focused people's attention on more practical, technical courses. Potential students were encouraged to seek the kinds of technical education which would get them quickly into the workforce so that they could become part of the chain which services the businesses of the wealthy and, as a consequence, increases their power.[19]

Another way governments work to dumb down society is by colluding with the media to stir up a spirit of mindless nationalism among the people. Let me be quick to say that there is nothing wrong with national pride. Indeed, national pride is a positive thing until it turns to mindless hysteria. Mass hysteria whipped up by the media and supported by governments is nothing short of mind-manipulation with the aim of keeping citizens on side and under control.

The growing hysteria in Australia around (men's) sport is a case in point. Leading up to a football match, for example, the media report it from every angle. A footballer with a "groin injury" or a "hamstring strain" becomes headline news and can stay in the headlines for days. The conversation of many people before and after a match is limited to plans to watch the game or, having watched it, to rehashing every aspect of it. The endless media coverage surrounding the World Cup in 2006, for example, was designed to have everyone focus on and become a devotee of football.

Support for the defence force is another area in which governments try to whip up a degree of hysteria when it suits them. Those citizens who marched in early 2003 to demonstrate against the United States, the United Kingdom, Poland and Australia waging war against Iraq were accused by government politicians of "not supporting our troops". The purpose of such accusations—given that the demonstrations were clearly not against defence force personnel but against the pre-emptive nature of the war—was to stir up sentiment about the troops themselves in the hope that it would have a flow-on effect as support for the government's decision to go to war.

Another example of mindless nationalism is the spectacle of mass outpourings of grief. Again, there is nothing wrong with citizens of a nation joining together and expressing their grief in the wake of a national tragedy. In fact, it can be a healthy thing to do and a bonding experience for a nation trying to deal with a tragedy. When Princess Diana died suddenly on 31 August 1997 as a result of an automobile accident, for example, many

---

19 This is not to say that Western countries should discourage people from pursuing technical education, because there is an ongoing need for tradespeople in every field. The point I am making is that those students who do opt for technical training ought to be supported for their own sake, as students preparing for their chosen fields of work, not for what their labour will be able to do to service the increasing wealth and power of big business.

Britons felt the need to express their grief together. They took flowers and cards and messages to several central points as an outward sign of the grief they were sharing. In the United States, immediately after the tragedy of 11 September 2001, when thousands of people were killed as a result of terrorist attacks on the World Trade Center and the Pentagon, US citizens had an overwhelming need to grieve together. Again, after the Bali bombings on 12 October 2002, when terrorists targeted two nightclubs usually frequented by westerners and 88 Australians were among the 202 people who died, Australia as a nation felt the need to express its grief.

The concern is not that such mass outpourings of grief occur but that, when they do occur, the media and the government seize on them as occasions to encourage hysteria and increase an irrational sense of nationalism. Who can forget, in relation to each of these tragedies, the images of television reporters willing big burly men and others to squeeze out a little tear—for the cameras? Genuine grief is private and personal (even when it is similar to the way millions of others might be feeling after a national tragedy) and needs to be expressed in a private and personal way. Being put on the spot and encouraged to act out one's "grief" for the cameras makes a mockery of an individual's and a nation's grief.

This externalising of people's private grief is reminiscent of Janice Raymond's criticism of therapy for therapy's sake. Raymond, a US feminist ethicist, spoke of the potential for therapy to "thingify" one's true self "by externalizing and wrenching the inner life out of its depths". That is precisely the danger faced when the media intrudes on people's genuine grief experiences in the hope of getting a "good story". People are being encouraged to demonstrate their emotions rather than feel them deep inside themselves. When the "telling of emotions" becomes more important for reality than the emotions themselves, a person (and a nation) is in danger of becoming an empty shell (1986, p. 157).

The dumbing-down of society in such ways creates a situation where the speech of the people becomes harmless in relation to those who hold the power. Irrational mob fervour pumped up by the media and supported by governments around sport, support for the defence force or following a national tragedy interferes with people's ability or desire to think through situations and form their own opinions. In that dumbed-down state, they offer no threat at all to those who hold the reins of power firmly in their hands. If and when they speak, their words are always in line with those of their masters. Their speech is harmless.

Lies and deceit

Governments, multinational corporations and global trade institutions have all moved, in recent years, in the direction of employing spin-doctors (media liaisons, psychologists, public relations experts) whose task it is to figure out the kinds of "spin" their employers need to put on information in order to make it more palatable to the masses. If given in its raw form—that is, if the truth were told—people might be outraged and speak out against it. But if it is tarted up with lies and deception, one of three responses can be expected: either people will be kept guessing about the facts and, therefore, unable to speak out; or they will be completely fooled into believing the lies; or, being fully aware of the lies and their own powerlessness to make a difference, simply give up caring. Whatever the response, the fallout is minimal and the power of the powerful is protected.

The lead-up to the war on Iraq in 2003 presented a clear example of the way governments, supported by some of the world's most influential media corporations, are prepared to lie to achieve their own ends. The president of the United States and the prime ministers of the United Kingdom and Australia, supported by senior members of their administrations, joined together to fabricate the story that they had proof of the existence in Iraq of weapons of mass destruction with which Saddam Hussein was planning to wreak havoc on Israel and other unnamed nations. Even in the face of reliable information to the contrary from United Nations personnel and foreign affairs intelligence in each country, the leaders persisted with their lies and kept finding new "evidence" to support their decision to wage war on Iraq.

Needless to say, even though opinion polls showed the majority of citizens did not support the idea of going to war without UN approval, they did it anyway. Even the spectre of millions of people across the world demonstrating for peace did not deter them from their destructive goal. In an address to the nation on 20 March 2003, the then prime minister of Australia, John Howard, stated:

> The Government has decided to commit Australian forces to action to disarm Iraq because we believe it is right, it is lawful and it's in Australia's national interest. We are determined to join other countries to deprive Iraq of its weapons of mass destruction, its chemical and biological weapons, which even in minute quantities are capable of causing death and destruction on a mammoth scale.[20]

Subsequently, the extent of the lies and deceit of the coalition of leaders became clearer but, as is the way with all unrepentent liars, they simply invented more lies to justify the initial ones.

---

20 <http://www.alp.org.au/features/lies.php>.

Some Australian citizens became so concerned about the increasing propensity of Howard to lie and deceive that they created a website devoted entirely to highlighting his lies and the lies of his government. The website gave actual quotes from the prime minister in each of twenty-one "categories of lies", together with evidence revealing the lie in each case.[21]

Even as recently as ten years ago in Australia there was an expectation that elected politicians would govern with some degree of ethical commitment and that truth-telling would be high on their list of ethical standards. Then, after more than a decade of Howard's conservative government, whose agenda was to move the population's focus away from social justice issues and on to economics, greed, competition and individual monetary gain, the expectation of truth-telling had diminished. While people in vast numbers were still fond of saying "you can't trust a politician", the repeated re-election of the government responsible for such a loss of trust made one wonder if the majority of citizens were not really bothered by the lies and deception which masqueraded as good, strong government. The demise of the Howard government and the election, by a landslide, of the Labor government led by Kevin Rudd in 2007 gave some hope to those who campaigned for truth and human rights.

Deception has become the trade of most large media corporations, too. While operating under the guise of impartial reporting of events, they deliberately and systematically support conservative governments whose agenda enhances their own ability to increase their wealth. Arundhati Roy, in her City of Sydney Peace Prize Lecture (3 November 2004) referred to the "embedded, corporate media in which the doctrine of Free Speech has been substituted by the doctrine of Free If You Agree Speech" (2004b, p. 3). The media's power to give voice to the powerful and deny a voice to anyone with a different view is immeasurable.

Also involved in deception on a big scale are the global institutions formed to assist powerful nations achieve their economic and trade ambitions. Using the language of equality and human rights, the WTO, the International Monetary Fund and the World Bank work to convince poorer nations that poverty will be eliminated once they allow multinational corporations to come in and replace the subsistence farming of the peasant families. The reality is, however, that once multilateral trade agreements have been signed and large multinational corporations steal the birthright of millions of peasant families, displacement, poverty and homelessness on a massive scale are usually the result. The kind of equality and human rights promised by global trade institutions is only possible among equals.

---

21   Originally at <www.johnhowardlies.com>, it has now been incorporated in the website of the Australian Labor Party, <http://www.alp.org.au/features/lies.php>.

As Hawthorne reminds her readers, "two parties starting from unequal positions require unequal treatment in order to achieve a just outcome" (2002, pp. 345–6). If these global institutions really were aiming for equality, they would be giving serious attention to positive discrimination measures to enable poorer nations and individuals to come up to a standard where they could actually compete with wealthier nations and individuals in a fair and equitable way while keeping their own unique national identity. Failing that, it must be concluded that their language of equality and human rights is manipulative and calculated to deceive.

Ignoring the speech of the powerless

Another tactic of the powerful in their determination to implement their agenda without interruption is that of ignoring the speech of those who do not (or might not) agree with them. Between them, governments and the media have the power to prevent contrary voices ever being heard, and they have no hesitation in using that power. Roy reminds her audience that "there's really no such thing as the 'voiceless'. There are only the deliberately silenced, or the preferably unheard" (2004b, p. 1).

Feminists all around the world are among the "deliberately silenced" and "preferably unheard" at the beginning of the twenty-first century. In the West, they have been ignored and excluded since the first flush of feminist activism in the 1960s and 1970s. At first, their determination to have their voices heard took the establishment by surprise but, once the men in power figured out how to compete with women's new-found strength and win, they did not hesitate.

One of their tactics was, and continues to be, that of co-opting liberal women to speak on their behalf for the purpose of setting up a situation of conflict between women—the well-worn tactic of divide and conquer. The role played by the media in this game is that of choosing their own "feminist voices" to speak on behalf of all feminists. By deciding which women's voices will be heard, they are effectively able to ignore and silence the voices of all feminists who are critical of the dominant male culture and who persist in calling for radical change.

Even when issues such as domestic violence, rape, child sexual abuse, pornography, prostitution or abortion come to the attention of governments or the media, an incomprehensible situation occurs. One would assume that, if they were serious about wanting to confront such issues honestly and accurately, the first place they would go for analysis and comment would be to feminist organisations or individual feminists who are intimately involved with the whole body of research in these areas, but feminists are deliberately passed by. Actually asking feminists for their analyses and opinions on these issues might mean that society has to confront the truth about a system which condones men's violence against women and children—a system which is unquestionably supported by the powerful. So, they look for other "experts" and deprive society of the benefits which would come from hearing and engaging with the facts.

Feminists are not the only ones who are ignored and deprived of a voice in conservative times. All who are members of disempowered groups, and all who commit themselves to fighting for justice for the disempowered, are seen as "dangerous" and, therefore, ignored. To be deprived of the power to be heard is to be denied the right of free speech.

My conclusion is that Catharine MacKinnon's assertion that "those with the most power buy the most speech" is correct. In this examination of the relationship between free speech and power, it is evident that the power of the powerful is bolstered by their collusion with one another and their attention to one another's speech, and that the speech of the powerless is rarely heard.

The discussion above of the tactics used by the powerful to deprive the powerless of access to free speech can be summarised as:
- increasing the stress on individuals and families so that they are effectively too stressed to speak out
- engineering the dumbing-down of society so that the speech of the people is most often of no consequence and, therefore, harmless
- lying to citizens so that the speech of those who are confused is hesitant and the speech of those who are lulled into a false sense of security is non-existent
- ignoring the speech of anyone who dares to disagree so that their speech is never heard or, if heard, immediately trivialised and ridiculed.

Free speech for all

If the principle of free speech is to have any credibility as one of the important principles underpinning democracy, free speech must be for all. This is not to say that such a principle would be easy to implement. As mentioned earlier, free speech historically was never intended to be for all. It was meant for the elite, for men, men of the dominant race, men who were educated, men who enjoyed some standing in the community. But it is not inconceivable that free speech could be for all, if only the powerful who have access to most of the speech could be motivated to share their power.

Advances in social justice during the nineteenth and twentieth centuries saw the abolition of slavery in the United Kingdom and the United States, votes for women throughout the Western world, the abolition of the

White Australia Policy and the consequent inclusion of Aboriginal citizens in Australia's national census, affirmative action legislation in Western countries, and international covenants against discrimination on the basis of race and gender. Admittedly, those nations which took such remarkable steps in the name of equality and social justice have witnessed a huge backlash by conservative forces intent on restoring power and influence to middle-class men of the dominant race but, even so, having caught a glimpse of equality, I continue to believe that free speech for all is a real possibility—a contention which will be explored further in the next chapter.

FAIR SPEECH 2

In the free speech debate, the feminist argument for equality outlined in Chapter One calls for universal freedom of speech. If speech is available to some citizens more than to others, if there is not equality in speech, then the democratic principle of free speech cannot be said to be free for all. This chapter introduces the concept of fair speech to support my belief that, for free speech to be truly free, it must be fair. As will be obvious to readers, the oppositional relationship set up in this book between free speech and fair speech is a deliberate attempt to mimic the better-known free trade/fair trade division. The principles are similar. Both free trade and free speech favour the powerful over the powerless and, in so doing, entrench inequality, while fair trade and fair speech call for greater attention to equality and justice.

The context for fair speech

Before embarking on the real business of this chapter, which is to introduce and discuss the concept of fair speech, it will be helpful first to see it in context. How does free speech compare with free trade? And how does fair speech compare with fair trade?

The major criticisms of free speech discussed in Chapter One were that it delivers more power to the powerful; it fosters and entrenches inequality; and it focuses on the individual. In so doing, it ignores quality of life for those groups of people who are silenced and subordinated by the inequalities inherent in a principle that gives absolute freedom of speech to the few.

For evidence that quality of life is diminished for those who are victims of the free speech of others, one only has to look at the effects of such victimisation and subordination in everyday life. Inequality on the basis of race, for example, is exacerbated by the existence of hate speech or racial vilification; inequality on the basis of sex is exacerbated by the existence of those activities which allow men to use and abuse women—pornography, prostitution and trafficking; and inequality on the basis of sexual orientation is exacerbated by hate speech.

What follows is that members of racial minorities as well as lesbians and gay men are subject to violence and abuse usually by strangers, while women are subject to physical, sexual and emotional violence by intimates as well as by strangers. The quality of life of such subordinated groups is diminished also by low self-esteem, low confidence, depression and anxiety, all of which can be traced directly to their subordinated social status.

Free trade

The major criticisms of free trade are very similar to the criticisms of free speech. The centrepiece of neoliberalism, free trade is based on the principle that the market rules. The "free" in free trade has two meanings: that individual corporations and individual nations are free to trade anywhere in the world; and that the global market is free of government interference in terms of tariffs and regulations.

In her discussion of a definition of free trade, Susan Hawthorne points out that, although the rhetoric of free trade implies that global institutions and transnational corporations will be responsible in their use of freedom, the opposite is actually true. She maintains that

> the language of "free trade" and "free choice" [in global economic talk] misrepresents the idea of "freedom" as one that is closely inter-twined with responsibility. Within the realm of neo-classical economics, globalisation and the free-trade mantras of transnational companies, freedom has no association with responsibility at all. In the world of international trade, transnational companies, the US government and institutions such as the World Trade Organization [WTO] are playing a free and irresponsible game. As the more powerful players they get to make the rules, tip the playing field so that it is not level, and score the game as well [2003, p. 29].

Critics of free trade around the world (and there are many) speak as if in unison about the weaknesses of globalisation and so-called free trade. They maintain that international trade laws: favour the rich and powerful at the expense of the poor and powerless; foster and entrench inequality; focus on the individual to the detriment of the public good; and ignore quality of life issues.

Free trade favours the powerful

It is no secret that the World Trade Organization (WTO) and other global institutions supporting and aggressively pushing free trade principles are heavily influenced by the most powerful nation on earth, the United States. In fact, the Washington Consensus, "a group of powerful CEOs, government bureaucrats, media and academics, has been pushing the ideology of free-market economies since the 1970s" (Hawthorne 2002, p. 133).[22] George Soros,

---

22 See also <http://www.globalissues.org/TradeRelated/FreeTrade/Criticisms.asp#Growingcriticisms>.

writing for a South African business journal, expresses the view that it is the rich and powerful nations which control international trade. "In practice", he says, "international financial markets never have been left to their own devices. Rich countries, led by the US, are in charge. Their primary task is protecting their own interests" (2002).[23] In an article in *Le Monde diplomatique*, Noelle Burgi and Philip Golub speak of "a new balance of power between the states that hardens the sovereignty of some while reducing the autonomy of the others ... The players with knowledge and power lay down the rules; the others fall into line" (2000).[24]

Recounting the experience of farmers in India, Vandana Shiva suggests that "Forced Trade" may be a more appropriate term than "Free Trade" (2000, p. 9). In *Stolen Harvest: The Hijacking of the Global Food Supply*, she tells the story "of how corporate control of food and globalization of agriculture are robbing millions of their livelihoods and their right to food". She continues:

> this phenomenon of the stolen harvest ... is being experienced in every society, as small farms and small farmers are pushed to extinction, as monocultures replace biodiverse crops, as farming is transformed from the production of nourishing and diverse foods into the creation of markets for genetically engineered seeds, herbicides, and pesticides. As farmers are transformed from producers into consumers of corporate-patented agricultural products, as markets are destroyed locally and nationally but expanded globally, the myth of "free trade" and the global economy becomes a means for the rich to rob the poor of their right to food and even their right to life [p. 7].

Nelson Mandela, too, during a lecture at the British Museum on 16 November 2000, raised the issue of the potential for globalisation and free trade to favour the powerful. After expressing the view that the process of globalisation should be welcomed, he then went on to warn against powerful countries using globalisation to "dominate and submerge" weaker countries:

> if globalisation is to create real peace and stability across the world, it must be a process benefiting all. It must not allow the most economically and politically powerful countries to dominate and submerge the countries of the weaker and peripheral regions. It should not be allowed to drain the wealth of smaller countries towards the larger ones, or to increase inequality between richer and poorer regions [2000].

By January 2003, Mandela was not so welcoming of globalisation. In a memorable address before the International Women's Forum in Johannesburg on

---

23 See also <http://allafrica.com/stories/200210040454.html >.
24 See also <http://mondediplo.com/2000/04>.

30 January 2003, in which he was highly critical of President George W. Bush and his plans to wage war on Iraq, he made a connection between war and globalisation. In the *Independent* (Cape Town), he was reported as saying:

> A war on Iraq is something we must condemn without reservation ... We must fight globalisation which is for the high and mighty ... All Bush wants is Iraqi oil, because Iraq produces 64 percent of oil and he wants to get hold of it [2003].

Or, in the more colourful language of Arundhati Roy: "Iraq has been 'liberated'. Its people have been subjugated and its markets have been 'freed'. That's the anthem of neoliberalism: Free the markets. Screw the people" (2004b).

Such are the views of all who believe that globalisation, global financial agreements and free trade favour the rich and powerful at the expense of the poor and powerless.

Free trade fosters and entrenches inequality

Closely linked to the contention that free trade favours the powerful is the criticism of free trade as fostering and entrenching inequality. The Global Issues website expresses concern about increasing global inequalities:

> Growth and development for some have been immense. Unfortunately, for most people in the world there has been an increase in poverty and the innovation and growth has not been designed to meet immediate needs for many of the world's people. Global inequalities on various indicators are sharp. For example:
> - Some 3 billion people—or half of humanity—live on under 2 dollars a day.
> - 86 percent of the world's resources are consumed by the world's wealthiest 20 percent.[25]

The issue of inequality has also been highlighted in the writings of the World March of Women, a movement of women mobilising throughout the world against poverty and violence against women. In the lead-up to World March activities in the year 2000, the Fédération des femmes du Quebec, who coordinated the project, released a book which they called a "mosaic in tribute to women's struggles world-wide". One major theme of the book is the inequality caused by globalisation.

> The outcome [of globalisation] is that power and wealth are increasingly concentrated in the hands of a minority. The majority, meanwhile, becomes poorer at a faster pace. Women and children in particular watch as their living conditions worsen and their human, social and economic rights crumble.

---

25 <http://www.globalissues.org/TradeRelated/FreeTrade/Neoliberalism.asp#Neoliberalismis>.

Labour laws are eliminated to promote competition and profit making. Many governments no longer control trade and financial transactions in their own countries [2000, p. 8].

To foster inequality is to ignore any need for equity and justice. Arundhati Roy, in her address at the opening of the World Social Forum in Mumbai in January 2004, stated categorically that the whole purpose of free trade laws is to "institutionalise inequity".

> International instruments of trade and finance oversee a complex system of multilateral trade laws and financial agreements that keep the poor in their Bantustans anyway. Its whole purpose is to institutionalise inequity ... Why else would it be that rich countries that spend over a billion dollars a day on subsidies to farmers demand that poor countries like India withdraw all agricultural subsidies, including subsidised electricity? Why else would it be that after having been plundered by colonising regimes for more than half a century, former colonies are steeped in debt to those same regimes, and repay them some $382 billion a year? [2004a].

Free trade focuses on the individual

The concept of free trade, which favours the powerful and entrenches inequality, is criticised also for its strongly individual focus. The theory is that individual greed and ambition encourage competition and that competition is good for the market. Therefore, a focus on the individual is to be encouraged and any concern for "community" or "the public good" is to be discouraged. Cooperation among diverse groups for the collective good is unacceptable because it reduces the opportunity for individual competition.

Critics contend that, although neoliberalism's strong focus on the individual may be good for those individuals who have the capacity to compete and win, for those who have little or no access to the success structures of their society because they belong to one of that society's disempowered groups (women, Indigenous people, the unemployed, the working poor, etc.), it has nothing to offer except blame. In a neoliberal society, individuals who are not successful are forced to wear the blame for their own inability to succeed. While the focus is kept on the individual, there is no room for analysis of the system that causes the misery of so many individual people and families, nor of the effects of that system on different categories or groups of people.

When governments, large corporations and smaller companies combine to encourage this kind of individual focus, societies as well as individual citizens are in real danger of becoming stagnant through constant self-obsession and lack of concern for others.

In the aftermath of the devastating tsunami on 26 December 2004, for example, when an estimated 225,000 people lost their lives and millions of others lost their homes and all their possessions, a representative of the Australian Shareholders' Association (ASA) demonstrated the kind of meanness and lack of compassion which can result from a strict neoliberal, free trade focus. While the world was witnessing a great outpouring of generosity toward the worst-affected countries; while governments of some of the world's wealthier nations were almost competing with each other to see who could offer the most help; while NGOs, business corporations and individual citizens opened their hearts and their purses to give and give and give, Stephen Matthews of the ASA "expressed disapproval at companies pledging money ... saying they have no approval [from shareholders] for their philanthropy". He said on ABC Radio and was reported in Yahoo! News, that companies "should not generally give without expecting something in return ... donations should only be made in situations that are likely to benefit the company through greater market exposure".[26]

After Australian entrepreneur Dick Smith (who personally donated $1 million) spoke out about the stand taken by some Australian companies, calling it "a cop-out", the ASA attempted to distance itself from Matthews' comments,[27] but the damage had already been done. In stressing that the top priority of companies is to ensure maximum profits for their shareholders, Matthews had inadvertently revealed one of the "rules" of free trade: profit for the individual takes precedence over compassion and the collective good.

Free trade ignores quality of life

When the market reigns supreme and "the survival of the fittest" philosophy is firmly in place, when profit for individuals takes precedence over the collective good, it goes without saying that quality of life is no longer seen as the responsibility of society or government. Individual people and families are on their own, left to grapple with the harsh realities of their lives after economic globalisation has stripped them of their livelihood and dignity.

At the Mumbai World Social Forum, Roy reminded her audience of the "massive programme of privatisation and structural adjustment" forced on Nelson Mandela's South African government in 1994 by global market forces, which, she says, "has left millions of people homeless, jobless and without water and electricity". In India, also, there are those who have been

> displaced and dispossessed and sentenced to a lifetime of starvation and deprivation ... Millions of people have been dispossessed by "development" projects. In the past 55 years, Big Dams alone have displaced between 33 million and 55 million people in India. They have no recourse to justice [2004a].

---

26 7 January 2005; see <http://au.news.yahoo.com/050106/21/p/sh8f.html>.
27 "Boards Can Donate, ASA says", *Herald Sun*, 8 January 2005.

The World March of Women, too, spoke of some of the "disastrous effects" of globalisation: "the standard of living is deteriorating along with health care, human rights are trampled, natural resources are wasted and the environment degraded" (2000, p. 7). In its updated charter (adopted on 10 December 2004), the World March of Women presents a list of injustices it firmly denounces and discusses the role international financial organisations, such as the World Bank and the International Monetary Fund, play in the diminishing quality of life of many:

> [We denounce] International financial organizations' imposition on poor countries of structural adjustment programs and other measures that result in cuts to public services, spiralling debt and relentless impoverishment [2004, p. 3].

As the poverty of developing nations deepens and they become more and more dependent on aid from richer countries and loans from international monetary organisations, their debt increases exponentially. Structural adjustment policies are then imposed on them "to ensure debt repayment and economic restructuring". The result is:

> poor countries [are required] to reduce spending on things like health, education and development, while debt repayment and other economic policies have been made the priority. *In effect, the IMF and World Bank have demanded that poor nations lower the standard of living of their people* [Shah 2008, emphasis in the original].

Far from reducing poverty and improving the quality of people's lives, as claimed by international trade-related organisations, free trade increases poverty for the majority and causes untold hardship and deprivation for all but the few rich and powerful individuals for whose benefit the system was invented.

Free speech

To reiterate the criticisms of free speech outlined in Chapter One for the purposes of comparison:
- ***Free speech favours the powerful:*** Catharine MacKinnon's contention that "those with the most power buy the most speech…" (p. 72) is a theme running throughout Chapter One. Free speech gives voice to the powerful and silences the powerless. In an ever-increasing spiral, the powerful have access to speech which, in turn, gives them more power which, in turn, gives them more access to speech, and so on.
- ***Free speech fosters and entrenches inequality:*** The feminist argument for equality in speech is based on the fact that hate speech,

racial vilification, pornography and all forms of trafficking in women go unchallenged in a society based on inequality. For as long as the oppressive speech of the powerful is protected, inequality will be entrenched and the speech of women and other disempowered groups will continue to be silenced.

- *Free speech focuses on the individual:* In most democracies free speech is viewed as an individual right. The argument for self-determination, in particular, presents freedom of speech as the absolute right to speak and act as one pleases, regardless of the harm one's speech may do to others. A principle of free speech that fails to take into account the rights of diverse groups of citizens, automatically operates to consolidate the rights of those individuals with the most power.
- *Free speech ignores quality of life:* Quality of life is diminished for those who are silenced and subordinated by the inequalities inherent in a principle of absolute freedom of speech. Those who are victims of the free speech of others are forced to live every day with the effects of subordination and oppression which, as mentioned earlier, include hate speech, racial vilification, physical, sexual and emotional violence.

Fair trade and fair speech compared

The discussion of the similarities between free trade and free speech has shown that both "freedoms" favour the powerful and entrench inequality, inequity and injustice. Turning now to a discussion of fair trade and fair speech it will be seen, once again, that there are similarities. Both are based on the demand for equality and justice. After a brief look at the aims and objectives of the movement for fair trade together with calls from activists for a fairer, more equal distribution of the world's goods, the remainder of this chapter will discuss the concept of fair speech.

Fair trade

Those who see little cause for optimism in free trade and globalisation are committed to finding a new and fairer approach to world trade. At a seminar on world trade and poverty in 2002, Kevin Watkins, senior policy advisor for Oxfam, presented a paper titled "Trade, Globalisation and Poverty Reduction: Why the Rules of the Game Matter". After a detailed and thoughtful discussion of globalisation's contribution to "a world scarred by mass poverty and extreme inequality", he concluded:

> We urgently need a new approach to the management of world trade. That approach needs to extend the distribution of benefits from globalisation beyond the few to the many—and it needs to underpin the multilateral system with values based on social justice and a shared commitment to poverty reduction. In short, we need to abandon the legacy of the old order and create a multilateralism capable of meeting the challenges of a new millennium [Watkins 2002, p. 13].

This "new approach", in the opinion of many, is fair trade. It is not only a concept, but also the name given to an actual trading partnership formed to work toward "greater equity in international trade". This network of fair trade organisations defines fair trade as:

> a trading partnership, based on dialogue, transparency and respect, that seeks greater equity in international trade. It contributes to sustainable development by offering better trading conditions to, and securing the rights of, marginalised producers and workers—especially in the South. Fair Trade organisations (backed by consumers) are engaged actively in supporting producers, awareness raising, and in campaigning for changes in the rules and practice of conventional international trade.[28]

All the critics of free trade, quoted earlier, make an urgent plea for justice and equality. Vandana Shiva, for example, calls on the world to "make trade subservient to the higher values of the protection of the earth and people's livelihoods" (2000, p. 127). She speaks of the need to reclaim food democracy:

> The central concern of citizens' movements, North and South, is creating democratic control over the food system to ensure sustainable and safe production and equitable distribution and access to food. Democratic control over food requires the reining in of the unaccountable power of corporations. It involves replacing the "free trade" order of corporate totalitarianism with an ecological and just system of food production and distribution, in which the earth is protected, farmers are protected, and consumers are protected [p. 117].

Nelson Mandela, at a rally in London's Trafalgar Square in February 2005 organised by the Make Poverty History coalition, demanded that the wealthy nations of the world provide debt relief to poorer nations and, in so doing, free the "poverty slaves":

---

28 <http://www.maketradefair.com/en/index.php?file=21052002111743.htm&cat=4&subcat=1&select=5>.

> Overcoming poverty is not a gesture of charity. It is an act of justice. It is the protection of a fundamental human right—the right to dignity and a decent life. While poverty persists, there is no freedom ... In this century, millions of people in the world's poorest countries remain imprisoned, enslaved and in chains. They are trapped in the prison of poverty. It is time to set them free [2005, p. 13].

Arundhati Roy reminded her listeners at the World Social Forum about the urgency of resisting US imperialism:

> For the first time in history, a single Empire with an arsenal of weapons that could obliterate the world in an afternoon has complete, unipolar, economic and military hegemony. It uses different weapons to break open different markets. There isn't a country on God's earth that is not caught in the cross hairs of the American cruise missile and the IMF chequebook [2004a].

Later in her speech, she urged her listeners "to become the global resistance ..." and demand "justice and survival".

The World March of Women advocated "substantial changes in global political and economic structures" and emphasised the need for "equity, sharing and democracy" as well as solidarity among women (2000, pp. 8, 19). In their charter, after stating their rejection of the oppressive systems of patriarchy and capitalism, they declare: "We propose to build another world where exploitation, oppression, intolerance and exclusion no longer exist, and where integrity, diversity and the rights and freedoms of all are respected" (2004, p. 1).

Oxfam's Kevin Watkins also calls for "a new approach ... based on social justice and a shared commitment to poverty reduction" (2002, p. 13).

There is a constant movement of people around the world determined to replace free trade with fair trade. The theme of the 2004 World Social Forum declared "Another World is Possible", and all who flock to those forums every year in their tens of thousands are committed to bringing about a new and more just world.

In addition to global actions and events, there are grassroots organisations, NGOs, feminist groups, trade unions, environmentalists and consumer groups all working to bring about a world which prioritises justice and equality. Oxfam "considers that partnerships and collaboration ... [between] networks and groups, which share the same core objective of sustainable and equitable development, are absolutely essential".[29]

---

29 See <http://www.maketradefair.com/en/index.php?file=18072002163823.htm>.

The concept of fair speech

Having looked at the context in which the need for fair speech has arisen, the rest of this chapter will focus on the theory and practice of fair speech. Although no one in any democratic country anywhere in the world would advocate abolishing the principle of free speech, many are calling for limitations on the freedom of those whose speech effectively denies others their democratic right to speech. They contend that, for free speech to have and maintain credibility, every effort must be made to ensure that access to speech is freely available to all. "Fair speech" is a term coined here to draw attention to the fact that, for any nation to ensure access to speech for all its citizens, attention must be given to issues of equality and justice. The feminist argument for equality in speech (see Chapter One) is an argument for justice and equity for women and for all other categories of people who are subordinated by the speech of others.

The following discussion of fair speech focuses primarily on the situation of women and considers first some of the important theoretical and philosophical arguments advanced by feminist scholars in law, the social sciences and moral philosophy. Then the focus moves from theory to social reality. The theoretical arguments that women are subordinated and silenced by those forms of speech that exist primarily for the benefit of men, is tested by taking a brief look at the actual social situation of women in the early years of the twenty-first century.

Feminist theory

The ordinance brought by Catharine MacKinnon and Andrea Dworkin in 1983 was opposed in court by a group calling themselves the Feminist Anti-Censorship Task Force (FACT), whose intervention MacKinnon later described as "an act of extraordinary horizontal hostility" (1990, p. 9). Their argument that "Pornography … is sex equality" was incomprehensible to many feminists who had agitated long and hard to make "acts against women actionable—acts like coercion, force, assault, trafficking in our flesh" (p. 10).

This one example demonstrates the disparity which existed and still exists between groups of women calling themselves feminist when it comes to issues of free speech. On the one hand, there are those who hold the liberal view that women and men are equal and that, if only women would claim their power and act on it as men do, there would be no need to legislate for equality. On the other hand, there are those who believe that society is constructed in such a way as to ensure sex inequality. Men, particularly mainstream men, have ready access to forms of speech and speech acts that subordinate and silence women, and their "right" to such speech is protected by law.

Before outlining the thoughts of feminists Catharine MacKinnon, Rae Langton and others on free speech, it will be helpful to look first at some of the attitudes to equality which emerged for discussion in the latter part of the twentieth century. The Australian Law Reform Commission (ALRC), in *Equality before the Law: Women's Equality* (1994), sets out three contemporary approaches to equality. Part 1 of the report "documented the unequal position of women in Australian society" with focus on "women's unequal treatment before the law". Part 2 "discusses the need for a comprehensive legal response to women's inequality" in law and society.[30]

Approaches to equality

The three contemporary approaches to the notion of equality and inequality highlighted in the ALRC report are:
- the formal equality or gender-neutral approach
- the differences approach
- the subordination or dominance approach.

Formal equality or gender-neutral approach

This first approach, influenced by a liberal, mainstream view of the world, has been used as the basis for anti-discrimination and equal opportunity legislation and is based on the belief that there is no difference between the sexes. It "requires simply that women and men be treated exactly the same in all circumstances ... [and] assumes that the creation of a level playing field, of itself, will achieve equality" (ALRC 1994, Part 2, p. 45). Critics of this approach point out that "laws and policies [based on this model] ignore gender as a relevant characteristic". The notion of formal equality "ignores the social, historical and economic context in which women and men live ... wrongly assumes that women and men start from the same position ... [and never questions the] male view of reality" (p. 46).

The formal equality or gender-neutral approach takes the experience of men as the benchmark and expects women to live up to the standard set by men for men in a comprehensively male world.

Differences approach

While the formal approach is based on the belief that women and men are the same, the differences approach starts from the position that women and men are quite different and, therefore, ought not be treated the same. There

---

30 See Australian Law Reform Commission 1994, Part 1, Chapter Two; Part 2, p. 43.

have been some benefits for women in relation to identifying differences—for example, the introduction of maternity leave, which acknowledges that pregnancy and childbirth are areas of obvious difference between the sexes in the workplace and that positive discrimination on that basis should be encouraged.[31]

The potential benefits accruing to women from the differences approach, however, are outweighed by its tendency to entrench inequality. When difference is assumed, men and men's abilities will always be used as the standard to measure what it means to be human, and women will always be seen as not measuring up. When women are seen as different, discrimination against them can always be justified.

The differences approach, while appearing to be the opposite of the formal or gender-neutral approach is, in fact, similar. Both "use men as the benchmark. One requires women to be the same as men while the other stresses women's differences from men. Neither challenges male experience or characteristics as the standard from which women are measured". A worrying effect of using men as the benchmark is that of "distracting attention from the major issue of systemic inequality between women and men" (ALRC 1994, Part 2, p. 47). It is this "systemic inequality" which is the focus of the third approach.

Subordination or dominance approach

This approach analyses inequality as "the consequence of the relative distribution of power between women and men". Beginning with the premise that "the sexes are not equal", the subordination or dominance approach "looks at laws, policies and practices to determine whether they operate to maintain women in a subordinate position" (ALRC 1994, Part 2, p. 47). It asks "whether a practice or rule has harmed women or has been detrimental to them by obstructing the achievement of equality in a particular context" (p. 48). The concern is not with equal opportunities as such, but with systemic power imbalances between the sexes.

The ALRC report states that most submissions to the commission on the question of how equality should be defined endorsed the "subordination approach". One example is the submission from the Women's Electoral Lobby:

> If gender and equality are approached as issues of power rather than merely of difference then the legal response to issues affecting women would be substantially different. The legal response would focus on the subordinating effects of laws and practices, and ask, what do women experience as

---

31 Following the introduction of maternity leave in some countries, proponents of the formal approach soon argued successfully that, in the name of "sameness", paternity leave ought to be available also for fathers on the birth of a baby.

the effects of these practices and laws. If differences are identified as the justification for the laws and practices then those differences would be examined to ascertain their meaning within a culture that has historically oppressed women. The focus then would be one of striving to redress the power imbalance between women and men [ALRC 1994, Part 2, p. 48].

Fair speech and the subordination approach to equality

The feminist concept of fair speech is based on the belief that equality in speech is not possible in a society where women are subordinated and silenced by speech and speech acts which exploit and degrade them and which are protected by law. It seeks to respond to the overwhelming emphasis in law and society, most noticeably in democracies like the United States, the United Kingdom and Australia, on theories justifying the protection of the individual's right to freedom of speech while, in comparison, very little support has emerged for theories justifying the need to place limitations on the protection of speech in the name of equality.[32]

Arguments for equality are well developed in relation to two groups in particular: women (Dworkin 1979, 1987; MacKinnon 1987, 1994: Itzin 1992; Langton 1994, 1997; Gaze 1994) and racial minorities (Matsuda 1989, 1993; Sadurski 1994, 1999; Gelber and Stone 2007). In the same way that racial vilification subordinates racial minorities, the feminist argument for equality takes the position that the objectification of women for the sexual pleasure of men (as in pornography and prostitution), subordinates all women and deprives all women of effective access to free speech.

Most of the work done by feminists in the area of free speech has focused on pornography as the issue that most clearly epitomises the subordination of women through speech. Other areas of feminist enquiry into the systematic silencing of women include: rape, domestic violence, prostitution, armed conflict, fundamentalism and exclusion from national and international decision-making, all of which will be discussed in Chapter Three. Here, the focus is on pornography with particular reference to the work of Catharine MacKinnon and Rae Langton, both of whom identify subordination and silencing of women as the two major effects of the harms caused by pornography. Feminists argue that the harm done to women through the existence of pornography ought to be enough to convince governments and

---

32 Interestingly, this absolute priority given to freedom of speech has been shaken by the rise of international human rights law which attributes to "equality" the status of a fundamental value, while freedom of speech is not mentioned until Article 19 of the International Covenant on Civil and Political Rights (ICCPR). See <http://www.ohchr.org/english/law/ccpr.htm>.

lawyers of the need for limitations on the kinds of speech which exploit and degrade women but, to date, the men who hold the reins of power have not been moved.

The discussion of the harms of pornography will lead to an analysis of the argument that pornography subordinates and silences women.

The question of harm

Integral to the free speech debate is the question of whether or not an individual's right to free speech should include the right to cause harm to others. On the one side, there are those who agree with John Stuart Mill; he considered it important to include in his otherwise very liberal argument for free speech the comment that it does not and should not extend to the right to harm others. In *On Liberty*, while asserting that an individual has absolute sovereignty "Over himself, over his own body and mind", Mill added, "the only purpose for which power can be rightfully exercised over any member of a civilised community, against his will, is to prevent harm to others". He suggests that, in such situations, state intervention, legal penalties or "the moral coercion of public opinion" are appropriate (1999, pp. 73, 72).

On the other side of the debate about harm, there are those who insist that the principle of freedom of speech would be diminished by censorship of any kind. Freedom of speech is so central to democratic theory, they assert, that harm in itself is not a reason for state intervention or censorship. Speech must be protected at any cost. Frederick Schauer echoes this position by first admitting that "speech clearly can and frequently does cause harm" and then stating that "it takes more than the identification of harm to provide a sufficient reason for regulation" (1982, pp. 10, 12). Radical feminists disagree. Contrary to the views expressed by liberal, pro-pornography "feminists", radical feminists maintain that there is ample evidence that women are harmed by the speech of others: by pornography and the law's protection of pornography; by rape and the willingness of the law often to excuse rape and blame it on the victim; by prostitution and its legalisation; by violence and the condoning of men's violence against them. Consequently, radical feminist activists have no hesitation in calling for the regulation of such speech in the name of equality and justice.

Pornography as harmful practice

With particular reference to pornography, Catharine MacKinnon explains in the preface to *Only Words*, that her book "attempts to move people to face the reality of harm done through what is called speech…" The point of her book, she says, is "to stop the harm and open a space for subordinated voices, those shut down and shut out through the expressive forms inequality takes" (1994b, p. x). Women are subordinated and silenced by those who produce pornography, those who promote it and those who use it. Pornography makes violence against women acceptable by arguing that it is not really real.

MacKinnon discusses three common denials. One is that pornography is "fantasy", regardless of the fact that it is happening to real women. The second is that the sex is "simulated". The rapes are not really rapes because the actors are simply acting, regardless of the fact that it is happening to those women on the screen. The third denial is that it is "representational", not the real world, even though it is happening to real women in the real world and the effects of it will be felt by real women in the real world who are subordinated and abused as a result of their partner's or other men's involvement with pornography.

The harms to women were clearly spelled out by Dworkin and MacKinnon in the definition of pornography at the beginning of their *Model Ordinance* which sought to make pornography "actionable as a civil rights violation" (MacKinnon 1994b, p. 87, n32). Pornography, they said, depicts women

> dehumanized as sexual objects, things or commodities; enjoying pain or humiliation or rape; being tied up, cut up, mutilated, bruised, or physically hurt; in postures of sexual submission or servility or display; reduced to body parts, penetrated by objects or animals, or presented in scenarios of degradation, injury, torture; shown as filthy or inferior; bleeding, bruised or hurt in a context which makes these conditions sexual [MacKinnon 1987, p. 176].

Beth Gaze, in her article "Theories of Free Speech, Pornography and Sexual Equality", also discusses the harms of pornography.

> The types of harms range from offence to insult, defamation, discrimination, and physical injuries, as well as more subtle effects legitimating domination and subordination on the attitudes of both men and women. The effects are to degrade women, and depict and lead to violence against and coercion of women [1994, pp. 141–2].

She speaks of various categories of women potentially or actually harmed by pornography: women involved in the production of pornography when "actions portrayed may actually be painful to them, although depicted as pleasure"; women attacked by men imitating the criminal acts they have seen depicted in pornography; women and children who come across it in newsagents or other stores where they learn that "devaluation and dehumanization of women are acceptable in society"; and women in general who are affected by "the subordinating impact of pornography" on them. It acts "as a reminder to women of our subordinate status, the fact that we can be treated as objects for another person's use, and reminds us of our lack of physical safety in society..." (p. 142).

Gaze sums up her section on "Feminism and Pornography" by saying that there are three elements of harm identified in feminist theory:

> These are direct harm, for example through copycat attacks on women; defamation in what pornography says about women and their appropriate roles; and discriminatory harm to women's equality rights which flows from pornography as a pervasive, even dominant form of representing women [1994, p. 146].

Pornography's representation of women, Gaze continues, "encourages their treatment as object not subject, and both subtly and overtly reinforces a social climate in which women's roles and opportunities are extensively limited on the basis of their sex" (p. 146).

Dworkin, in her 1999 address at the University of Minnesota, commented on the lack of concern about the harms of pornography and other oppressive speech:

> in the United States, every time one brings up the hurt of people, an organized hurt, an organized way of injuring a particular group of people, one is told ... that the rights of those doing the hurting are more important than the rights of those who are being hurt [in Stark & Whisnant 2004, p. 139].

The harms of pornography, expressed by MacKinnon, Gaze and Dworkin, are reiterated by Catherine Itzin: it "subordinates women"; portrays women as "seeking and enjoying sexual violence and humiliation"; "sexualizes violence ... legitimates violence against women"; "stimulates some men to commit specific acts of sexual violence against some women" (1992, pp. 66–7). Itzin concludes that pornography is "propaganda against women. It is a practice which perpetuates sexism, sex discrimination and sexual violence" (p. 70).[33]

Writing more recently, Rebecca Whisnant calls pornography "hate propaganda". She speaks of "violence and contempt openly expressed". Describing her own and other feminists' experience when researching pornography, she says "the depths of its hatred and erasure of women must be experienced to be believed" (in Stark and Whisnant 2004, p. 18).

Having discovered and confronted the immense amount of harm done to women through the existence and use of pornography, it is not surprising that radical feminist scholars conclude that pornography subordinates and pornography silences.

---

33 For more of the wide range of harms, see Itzin 1992, Part Three, which contains ten articles by various authors under the heading, "Pornography and Evidence of Harm", pp. 201–397.

Pornography subordinates

In defining pornography as "graphic sexually explicit materials that subordinate women through pictures and words", Dworkin and MacKinnon sought to highlight the fact that pornography harms women by what it says—that is, "its function as defamation or hate speech"; and, more particularly, by what it does—that is, "its role as subordination, as sex discrimination, including what it does through what it says" (MacKinnon 1994b, pp. 15, 16).

Feminist moral philosopher Rae Langton, engaging with these ideas, discusses the possibility that pornography is a "speech act" which depicts subordination, causes subordination and, in fact, *is* subordination (1994, pp. 95–6). She accepts the feminist view that pornography *depicts* subordination by presenting women in dehumanised and humiliating situations "enjoying" being violated, raped, degraded, tortured and mutilated. That it *causes* subordination is supported by Judge Frank Easterbrook writing at the time of the antipornography legislation. In his words, such depictions of subordination "tend to perpetuate subordination. The subordinate status of women in turn leads to affront and lower pay at work, insult and injury at home, battery and rape on the streets" (in Langton 1994, p. 95). On this view, says Langton, pornography depicts and causes subordination. She goes on to point out that Dworkin and MacKinnon took it a step further. With the words "We define pornography as the graphic sexually explicit subordination of women..." they were saying, not only that it depicts and causes subordination, but that "pornography *is*, in and of itself, a form of subordination" (pp. 95, 96, emphasis in the original).

Langton's comparison of the speech acts of pornography with the speech acts of apartheid is very helpful. She invites readers to consider the words "Blacks are not permitted to vote" or the words: "Whites only". Then she explains that the speech acts of apartheid subordinate because of

> at least the following three features ... They *rank* blacks as having inferior worth. They *legitimate* discriminatory behaviour on the part of whites. And finally, they *deprive* blacks of some important powers: for example, the power to go to certain areas and the power to vote [1994, p. 102; emphasis in the original].

Feminists make these same claims about pornography, Langton continues. The first two claims are clearly demonstrated: pornography *ranks* women as sex objects and *legitimates* sexual violence against them. The third claim, that it subordinates women and *deprives* them of certain rights and powers, is concluded from the first two. The fact that pornography "celebrates, promotes, authorizes and legitimates" behaviour such as "rape, battery, sexual harassment..." (MacKinnon 1987, p. 171) is interpreted by feminists as a clear demonstration that it is an act of subordination (Langton 1994, pp. 105–06).

Supporting MacKinnon's contention that it is what pornography *does* that is important, Langton draws on the work of J. L. Austin, "a philosopher who took as his starting point the slogan: 'to say something is to *do* something'". She explains that, in *How to Do Things with Words* (1962), Austin complained that philosophy had a tendency "to overlook something of great importance: a tendency to consider the content of a linguistic utterance, and its effect on its hearers, but to overlook the action constituted by it" (Langton 1994, p. 96).[34] MacKinnon supplies a "description of the actions constituted by pornographic utterances" when she says that "pornography is an act of subordination" (Langton 1994, p. 97).[35]

Wojciech Sadurski critiques Langton's work on speech and speech acts in his important volume for the Law and Philosophy Library, titled *Freedom of Speech and Its Limits* (1999). In it, he looks at some of the arguments in favour of restrictions on hate speech and pornography with the aim of placing them "in a framework that facilitates legal reasoning about rights" (1999, p. 2). While he is not convinced by Langton's argument that "pornography silences women" (see below), he does find substance in her argument that "pornography subordinates women". On the subject of subordination, he sees a parallel between Langton's work and that of Mari Matsuda who, in her article "Public Response to Racist Speech: Considering the Victim's Story", called racist speech "a mechanism of subordination" (1989, p. 2358). It is "the structural subordination of a group based on an idea of racial inferiority", she said (Matsuda, in Sadurski 1999, p. 119).

Like Langton, Sadurski finds J. L. Austin's philosophy of language helpful in providing a framework for discussing pornography as subordination. He agrees that words are not simply their locutionary meanings or their effects on hearers. Words, he says, "can do a variety of things, including subordinating others" (Sadurski 1999, p. 122). It is the belief that pornography ranks women as sexual objects and legitimates discriminatory behaviour against them that leads Langton to the conclusion that "pornography is an illocutionary act of subordination".

Pornography silences

Proponents of free speech who oppose any kind of censorship, any kind of limitation on the free speech principle, argue that women are quite capable of fighting pornographic speech with more speech. Langton suggests that "if pornography not only subordinates but silences women, it is not easy to see

---

34 Langton makes good use of Austin's categories of speech acts: locutionary (the speaking of words which have a particular, generally accepted meaning); perlocutionary (the effect one's speech has on others, to influence, persuade, legitimate); and illocutionary (the actions constituted by the speech itself). Pornography, Langton claims, is "an *illocutionary* act of subordination" (1994, p. 106).

35 Mason-Grant 2004 has more recent work on this important point, especially Chapter Three, "The Subordination of Pornography as Illocutionary Force", pp. 69–92.

how there can be any such fight ... Whether women can fight speech with more speech depends on whether, and to what extent, women can speak" (1994, p. 111).

In response to the feminist demand for equality in speech, Sadurski chooses to focus on "equality of opportunity" as "the most plausible type of equality that one can demand in the realm of communicative acts", and interprets that as "the equality of opportunity to speak and be heard". Based on his "equality of opportunity" focus, he maintains that the feminist argument that pornography silences women fails "because banning hate speech and pornography does not improve communicative opportunities for vilified racial minorities or women" (1999, pp. 74, 119).

When Langton examined the feminist contention that pornography silences women, her focus was not on equal opportunity *per se* but on the kind of silencing which "prevents women from doing things with their words" (1994, p. 111). She identified three kinds of silencing apparent in society which, for our purposes, will be named: powerlessness, being ignored and disablement.

Silenced by powerlessness

A classic example of the silencing effect of powerlessness comes from women who are victims of domestic violence. Knowing that anything they say could be the cause of their partner's next violent explosion, they learn not to speak. This is one example of Langton's "first and most basic level" of silencing. Members of powerless groups, she explains "may be silent because they are intimidated, or because they believe no one will listen. They do not protest at all, because they think that protest is futile ... In such cases no words are uttered at all" (1994, p. 112) or, in Austin's terms, no *locutionary* act is performed.

Silenced by being ignored

Women who do find the courage to speak often find that their words fail to have the effect they were hoping for. Such perlocutionary frustration is common, Langton comments: "one argues but no one is persuaded; one invites, but nobody attends the party; one votes, hoping to oust the government, but one is outnumbered" (1994, p. 112). A recent example of the failure of an intended perlocutionary act is that of the millions of women and men around the world who demonstrated in the early months of 2003 against the threatened pre-emptive strike by the United States, the United Kingdom and Australia on the nation of Iraq. Their speech was ignored. The aggressors went to war regardless of the powerful speech of the protesters. Millions spoke but their words had no effect.

Silenced by disablement

In this kind of silencing, one is disabled from achieving the action intended. Speech is turned around and used against the speaker and has the opposite effect from the one intended or, in Langton's words, "speech misfires", it is "made unspeakable" (1994, pp. 112, 113). Referring again to Austin, Langton says: "although the appropriate words are uttered, with the appropriate intention, the speaker fails to perform the intended illocutionary act" (1994, p. 112). This is illocutionary disablement.

Addressing MacKinnon's claim that "pornographic speech ... silences the speech of women", Langton draws attention to two examples of the silencing of women's speech through disablement. The first she calls "refusal" and the second "protest".

Refusal is most commonly communicated by use of the word no. While no seems to be a reasonably easy word to understand, in the sexual context it is often taken to mean its opposite. Statistics on the prevalence of date rape reveal that for an alarming number of women, their no is disabled. When a woman says no, Langton explains,

> She performs the appropriate locutionary act. She means what she says. She intends to refuse. She tries to refuse. But what she says misfires. Something about her, something about the role she occupies, prevents her from voicing refusal. Refusal—in that context—has become unspeakable for her. In this case refusal is not simply frustrated but disabled [1994, p. 117].

Langton's second example of disablement applies to protest. There are many examples of women's protests being disabled, but the one Langton chooses to highlight illustrates very clearly how disablement occurs. In 1980, Linda Marchiano wrote a book (with Mike McGrady) called *Ordeal* to protest the way she, as Linda Lovelace, was forced into making the pornographic movie *Deep Throat*. In her book, Marchiano describes "how she was beaten, hypnotized, and tortured in order to perform her starring role". As a protest, the book clearly denounces the pornography industry. "It does not invite fantasy and arousal. It invites indignation. It does not 'endorse the degradation'; it does not 'celebrate, promote, authorize and legitimate' the sexual violence" (Langton 1994, pp. 117–18). Regardless of the author's intention, however, Linda Marchiano's book has been taken over by the pornography industry who list it in their mail-order catalog of "adult reading", as follows:

> ORDEAL: an autobiography by Linda Lovelace. With M. McGrady. The star of Deep Throat tells the shocking story of her enslavement in the pornographic underworld, a nightmarish ordeal of savage violence and unspeakable perversion, of thrill seeking celebrities and sadistic criminals. For Sale to Adults Over 21 Only [Langton 1994, p. 117].

Her protest has been effectively disabled, turned around and used for the opposite purpose from the one Marchiano intended. How could this happen?

> Marchiano says the words appropriate for an act of protest. She uses the right locutions, words that graphically depict her own subordination. She intends to protest. But her speech misfires. Something about who she is, something about the role she occupies, prevents her from [protesting] ... What she tries to say comes out as pornography. Her protest has been disabled [Langton 1994, p. 118].

A report in the *Guardian* on 9 February 2005 reveals the continuing disablement of Linda Marchiano's protest. It was reported that Las Vegas-based Arrow Productions, the company which owns the rights to the film *Deep Throat*, was in the process of striking prints of the film to be re-released for distribution around the United States and, Arrow hopes, around the United Kingdom. Raymond Pistol from Arrow Productions reported that, in one version, he was having some of the explicit material cut out in an effort to obtain the kind of rating which would enable the film to be seen by children under seventeen if accompanied by an adult. Another version which, as he put it, would be "*au naturelle*", currently holds a XXX rating.

The move to re-release *Deep Throat* came at the same time as the release of a documentary "which charts the unhappy tale of Linda Lovelace's humiliations at the hands of her pimp boyfriend, Chuck Traynor, who forced her, she said, to perform her sexual feats at gun- or knifepoint". The documentary, called *Inside Deep Throat*, was set to be shown alongside *Deep Throat* in some cinemas as they "plan to show the two in a double bill".[36] It seems that the illocutionary disablement of Linda Marchiano's protest will continue for as long as pornographers are permitted to subordinate and silence women.

In analysing the misfires which occur in relation to women's speech, when "attempted refusal is not even recognized as a refusal; ... [when] attempted protest is not recognized as protest", Langton concludes: "These misfires betray the presence of structural constraints on women's speech ... Something is robbing the speech of its intended force" (1994, p. 119).

One need look no further than structural inequality to understand what it is that robs women's speech of its intended force. When the right of pornographers to present women as sex objects to be exploited and humiliated for the sexual pleasure of men is protected by law; when the right of consumers of pornography to seek sexual arousal through such images is protected; when prostitution is legalised and men's right to buy women for sex is protected, then clearly governments and the law are supporting the subordination of women, and they do it in the name of protecting "free

---

36 *Guardian*, 9 February 2005.

speech". The role women occupy in societies which condone such inequality renders women speechless. What is ironic is that it is in the name of free speech that women are robbed of their right to speak.

Having examined radical feminist theory around the subordination approach to equality and looked at the role pornography plays in subordinating and silencing women, it will be helpful now to take a closer look at the social situation of women. What is the reality of women's lives? Is there evidence that women are subordinated and their speech silenced?

Evidence of the ongoing subordination and silencing of women is not difficult to find. Judge Frank Easterbrook's judgement that depictions of subordination found in pornography "tend to perpetuate subordination" in everyday life is borne out by reliable research into domestic violence, sexual assault, fundamentalism, and the deliberate exclusion of women from decision-making on matters of national and international significance.

Violence against women

Statistics showing a consistently high level of domestic violence, sexual assault and sexual harassment of women are a concern for those who have pushed for the total elimination of violence against women. Over many years feminist researchers, NGOs and activists have made strenuous efforts to "break the silence" and expose the high levels of violence perpetrated by men against women, with a view to bringing about change; despite them, the incidence of physical and sexual abuse of women remains constant.

Feminists have identified the public/private distinction in law and society as problematic in their quest to obtain equality and justice for women. While it is acknowledged that the distinction was made by lawyers in an attempt to protect the individual's right to privacy, the problem for women has been that "individual" has historically been interpreted as "man".

> Until very recently men could claim their houses to be their castles — their private sphere — such that it was legitimate for them to beat their children ... or to rape their wives ....
> Feminist scholarship has led to critiques of the public/private distinction in law (see for example O'Donovan [1985]) from which it emerges that the main sufferers have been women [Gaze and Jones 1990, p. 345].

In her later article, "Theories of Free Speech, Pornography and Sexual Equality", Beth Gaze commented that the public/private distinction in law "conveniently enables many of the most important sources of women's oppression, such as domestic violence and subordination within the family, to remain outside the true concerns of politics and law" (1994, p. 136).

Human rights theory, too, has traditionally focused on the public arena. According to Lara Fergus, this has enabled human rights activists to overlook injustices occurring in the private sphere. In her article "Making Rights a Reality: The Human Rights Approach to Stopping Violence against Women", Fergus traces the development in awareness of one human rights group, Amnesty International, and discusses Amnesty's decision to expand their work to include a more comprehensive treatment of the human rights of women. The new direction taken by Amnesty to include the private as well as the public, Fergus explains, is an acknowledgment of "the sites of greatest danger for women" (2004).

Expressing the concern of the World Health Organization about the public/private distinction, Gro Harlem Brundtland, its former director-general, said in her preface to the organisation's *World Report on Violence and Health*, "To many people, staying out of harm's way is a matter of locking doors and windows and avoiding dangerous places. To others, escape is not possible. The threat of violence is behind those doors—well hidden from public view" (WHO 2002).

The following statistics, which many researchers suspect are just the tip of the iceberg, reflect something of the violence against women tolerated by societies around the world.

Physical violence by an intimate partner

The WHO reported that the proportion of female victims of intimate violence in different countries varied between 10 and 34 per cent, as indicated in the following selection:
- Paraguay, 10 per cent
- Philippines, 10 per cent
- United States, 22.1 per cent
- Canada, 29 per cent
- Egypt, 34.4 per cent (2002, p. 11)

A survey called *Women's Safety Australia* conducted by the Australian Bureau of Statistics found that, of the 6,300 Australian women surveyed:
- 42 per cent of women who had been in a previous relationship had experienced an incident of physical and/or sexual violence by a previous partner.
- 23 per cent of women who had ever been married or in a defacto relationship had experienced violence in that relationship.
- 8 per cent of women who were in a current relationship had experienced violence in that relationship.

- Half of the women who had experienced violence by their partner reported that more than one incident had occurred, with 7.4 per cent saying that it occurred often (ABS 1996).

Other figures from the same survey included:
- 42 per cent of women who experienced violence from a former partner reported that they had been pregnant at the time, and 11 per cent of those incidents resulted in miscarriage.[37]
- 25 per cent of Australian children have witnessed violence against their mother or stepmother (WESNET 2004b).

The Women's Services Network (WESNET) in Australia reports that, in the year 2002/03, there were 56,100 women, accompanied by 53,700 children, accommodated in women's refuges.[38]

Sexual assault

The WHO reported that the proportion of women who are victims of sexual assault in countries around the world varied between 15 and 25 per cent, as indicated in the following selected cities and provinces:
- Toronto, Canada, 15.3 per cent
- Leon, Nicaragua, 21.7 per cent
- London, England, 23 per cent
- One province in Zimbabwe, 25 per cent (2002, p. 11).

The *Crime and Safety Survey* (ABS 2002) reported that, in the twelve months prior to the national survey:
- Approximately 62,700 incidents of sexual assault were experienced by female victims (this includes incidences of both reported and unreported crimes to the police).
- 80 per cent of all sexual assault victims were female.
- In 93 per cent of cases the offender was male.
- In 58 per cent of cases the offender was known to the victim.
- 77 per cent of female victims indicated there was a single offender.
- The most frequently recorded locations for sexual assault were the victim's or another's home (40 per cent) and a public venue (37 per cent) such as a place of entertainment or car park.
- 93 per cent of female victims reported that no weapon was used.
- 72 per cent of female victims were not injured.

---

37 For more on this, see Taft 2002.
38 See also the Australian Domestic and Family Violence Clearinghouse website at <http://www.austdvclearinghouse.unsw.edu.au/>.

- While 77 per cent of female victims considered their sexual assault a crime, 80 per cent of victims did not tell the police about the incident.
- 49 per cent of cases reported to the police did not proceed to trial.
- In the higher courts, there is a 51 per cent acquittal rate for sexual assault and related offences.[39]

Emotional and verbal abuse

While the incidence of emotional violence is difficult to quantify, anecdotal evidence leads researchers to believe that emotional violence against women by their male partners exists in epidemic proportions. According to Jane Mulroney of the Australian Domestic and Family Violence Clearinghouse, data reported in *Women's Safety Australia* (ABS 1996) "does not reflect the entire picture of women's experiences of domestic and family violence as it does not record other forms of abuse (emotional, social, financial etc.) that occur in tandem with acts of violence" (Mulroney 2003, p. 1).

Research conducted in South Australia in the form of a phone-in (funded by the federal government's programme Partnerships Against Domestic Violence) revealed that "89 per cent of callers had experienced verbal abuse" and "Emotional abuse was reported by 84 per cent of callers" (Partnerships Against Domestic Violence 2000, p. 22). Appendix 3 of the data analysis explains:

> Many of the women's stories commenced with the "verbal" and "emotional" aspects of abuse which to them were more insidious and oppressive than even the sometimes quite life-threatening physical incidents … Psychological and emotional abuse was so often built into the relationship, occurring around the "little things" of daily life [2000, p. 31].

A report on research in Tasmania in 2003, titled "Pathways: How Women Leave Violent Men", describes the findings from in-depth interviews with 53 women victims of domestic violence. Commenting on the extent of psychological and emotional abuse reported by participants, the report said:

> Almost every woman in the current study described psychological abuse including demeaning behaviour from the man, being controlled, embarrassed in front of the children, shamed publicly and living in fear. Women also spoke of "mind games" they felt their partner played which left them doubting their own reasoning or even, their sanity [Government of Tasmania 2003, p. 33].

---

39 <http://ffasa.org/hpages.asp?PageID=29>. See also reports from the Australian Centre for the Study of Sexual Assault on the Australian Institute of Family Studies website, <http://www.aifs.gov.au/acssa/pubs/>.

Sexual harassment

A 2003 survey into sexual harassment in Australian workplaces conducted by Patricia Hayes for Working Against Sexual Harassment (WASH) reports that:

- 75 per cent of respondents experienced/witnessed sexual comment, jokes or innuendo and 57 per cent experienced/witnessed uninvited physical contact or gestures.
- 50 per cent of respondents reported suffering emotionally as a result of the sexual harassment experience.
- 37 per cent of respondents reported, at some level, instances of sexual harassment that they had themselves witnessed or experienced.
- 31 per cent left their jobs as a result of the sexual harassment while clear consequences for the harasser were infrequent.
- 5 per cent of respondents reported using the Equal Opportunity Commission or the Human Rights and Equal Opportunity Commission.[40]

Kate Gilmore, executive deputy secretary-general of Amnesty International, expressed the view that violence against women "is a human rights scandal of unparalleled dimension ... whose eradication must be sought without reservation, without equivocation and without delay" (quoted in Fergus 2004, p. 1). Gilmore's words echo the sentiments of feminists Catharine MacKinnon and Andrea Dworkin, who insist that pornography must be eradicated if women are to have equal status to men in any society. Pornography subordinates women and legitimates all forms of violence against them. Similarly, Amnesty's report "It's in Our Hands: Stop Violence against Women", declares that "violence [against women] is both rooted in discrimination and serves to reinforce discrimination, preventing women from exercising their rights and freedoms on a basis of equality with men" (Amnesty 2004, p. 5).

Fundamentalism

The dominant forces in the world today are political fundamentalism, religious fundamentalism and market fundamentalism, all of which not only exclude women but actually pursue an agenda which is anti-woman.

Women Against Fundamentalism state clearly and unequivocally their belief that "at the heart of all fundamentalist agendas is the control of women's minds and bodies". Susan Hawthorne expressed a similar view on a feminist email discussion list when she commented that "fascism and fundamentalism are anti-women. The only thing that fundamentalists all agree on (Christian,

---

40 Hayes 2003. See also Jennie Child's review of the report, <http://www.aifs.gov.au/acssa/pubs/newsletter/n4.html#sexharass>.

Muslim, market fundamentalisms) is that women should stay in their place and women's sexuality should be controlled by men".[41]

Women Living Under Muslim Laws prepared a statement to be presented at the World Social Forum in Porto Alegre in January 2005, titled "Appeal against Fundamentalisms". It began: "The rise of fundamentalisms is part and parcel of the rise of the extreme right movements and of the expansion of liberal neo-capitalist politics in the world today". They identified "the warning signs of fundamentalisms to be anti-women policies", which include "the attacks on contraception and abortion in the USA and in Europe, or the imposition of dress codes and forced veiling and the attacks on freedom of movement and on the rights to education and work under Taliban-like regimes". To further demonstrate anti-woman policies, they referred to "Afghan women starving under their burqa" and "Nigerian women sentenced to death by stoning for sex outside marriage" (WLUML 2005).

Courageous Iraqi women, too, are speaking out against the oppression of women under fundamentalist rule. In an appeal issued on International Women's Day 2008, the Organization of Women's Freedom in Iraq (OWFI) stated:

> Make it a day to say No! To Islamic Sharia law in Iraq!
>
> For secularism, equality and freedom!
>
> The US-UK occupation has pushed Iraqi society back into a medieval world in which "honour killings", beheadings, forced veiling and seclusion and sexual servitude are now a part of everyday life ...
>
> For the last three years Iraqi women have stood up against not only the occupation but against political Islamist groups who are fighting to establish an Iranian or Saudi Arabian-type regime of gender apartheid, with all marital and family matters regulated by Islamic Sharia law ...
>
> We call upon you to join with us this International Women's Day (8 March) to say No to religious law in Iraq and yes to equality and freedom.
>
> No to Islamic Sharia Law in Iraq!
>
> Long Live International Women's Day! Long live freedom, equality, and secularism! (OWFI 2008).

A serious concern raised by WLUML is that of the loss of support for women by "progressive forces in the West" in their attempt to "denounce racism". To demonstrate their anti-racism credentials, some anti-globalisation activists, human rights activists, liberal feminists and others "often choose to sacrifice

---

41 <http://waf.gn.apc.org/body.htm>; f-agenda email discussion list, 4 February 2005, quoted with permission.

both women and our own internal ... opposition forces to fundamentalist theocratic dictatorship". They forge alliances with Muslim fundamentalists and, in so doing, abandon those in Muslim countries who resist fundamentalism.

> We have already witnessed prominent Left intellectuals and activists publicly share the view that they could not care less if fundamentalist theocratic regimes come to power in Palestine or Iraq, provided that the USA and Israel get booted out. We have witnessed representatives of fundamentalist organizations and their ideologists be invited and cheered in Social Fora. We have witnessed prominent feminists defend the "right to veil" — and this sadly reminds us of the defense of the "cultural right" to female genital mutilation, some decades ago.

Concluding their statement, they called on all at the World Social Forum in Porto Alegre and, more specifically, on the women's movement, "to give international visibility and recognition to progressive forces and to the women's movement within it, that oppose the fundamentalist theocratic project". Their total refusal to accept fundamentalism's silencing was expressed in the powerful declaration: "We dare dissent. We dissent as women, i.e. the most visible victims of fundamentalist policies, and we dissent as progressive democratic anti-theocratic people's movement" (WLUML 2005).

Exclusion from power

Whether under fundamentalism, conservatism or liberalism, the social reality for women around the world is that they are excluded from any kind of effective power nationally and internationally. When searching for clues as to why such discrimination exists, one need look no further than Catharine MacKinnon's description of pornography as "actively subordinating, treating unequally, as less than human, on the basis of sex" (1995, p. 16), or Judge Easterbrook's opinion that pornography's depictions of subordination "tend to perpetuate subordination", or Amnesty International's opinion that violence against women "serves to reinforce discrimination ... and denies women equality with men..." (Amnesty 2004, p. 5).

Fundamentalists and other political and religious conservatives seem to have a high tolerance for behaviour which excludes women. Terrorists, almost always men, pursue a male agenda of violence and destruction. The United States, the United Kingdom, Poland and Australia, named the "Coalition of the Willing" by President George W. Bush just prior to the start of the 2003 war on Iraq, all pursue a male agenda of power and domination.

The Australian government under Prime Minister John Howard, at the behest of the US administration, expanded its agenda of power and domination by appointing itself "leader" (or, as President Bush put it, "deputy sheriff") in South-East Asia and the South Pacific.

Domestically, major political parties in many Western nations are fond of bragging about their gender-equity credentials by pointing to the number of women who are now elected members of their party. The fact that is never acknowledged is that women politicians generally, including those token members who become ministers in their government, are still excluded from any real access to power.[42] It would be interesting to know, for example, how many women were consulted in any serious way by George W. Bush, Tony Blair or John Howard before the final decision was made to visit war on Iraq. More than likely the answer would be "none". Women in powerful positions like Condaleezza Rice, who took up the position of US secretary of state at the beginning of 2005, or Hillary Clinton who took over from her in 2009, still take their orders from, and are accountable to, the men in more senior positions.

Despite all the rhetoric one hears in Western nations about equality, the reality is that women are still excluded from access to all forms of power that might open the door for women's views and women's agenda to have a significant impact on world affairs.

Part II discusses the social reality for women in greater detail under the title "The Silencing of Women".

For genuine sex-equality to become a reality, there needs to be a focus on justice and equity for all women. Throughout the 1980s and 1990s, the feminist call for equality was taken over by liberal forces within the movement, whose agenda was to focus attention on the kinds of inequalities which they judged would be more acceptable to men and to the mainstream population. Consequently, the emphasis came to be on issues like equal employment opportunities, maternity leave for women in employment, equal pay, equal opportunity in higher education and easier access to abortion. While these are important issues and much progress has been made on behalf of women, genuine equality still eludes women. A new focus on equality, from the perspective of justice and equity, is needed if women and men alike are to enjoy the benefits of equal relationships socially and personally.

---

42 While it must be acknowledged that some women elevated to positions of power are happy in the role of willing accomplice in the pursuit of patriarchy's agenda, many are not.

Part II

THE SILENCING OF WOMEN

SILENCING WOMEN'S VOICES   3

In light of the ongoing social reality for women discussed in the previous chapter, it would be easy for women activists to become depressed at what seems like a hopeless situation and give up the fight for equality and justice. For feminists, however, disengagement is not an option. No matter how difficult or hopeless a situation may appear, radical feminists are determined to stay engaged. Their task, as they express it, is to: analyse what is happening globally, nationally and in individual women's lives; keep up to date in a rapidly changing world; develop a thorough understanding of current social and political attitudes and their impact on women; interpret their findings in light of the power dynamics that exist between women and men; and then, as always, act to transform every situation of inequality and injustice into one of equality and justice. The deliberate systematic silencing of women at every level is one practice receiving feminism's urgent attention at the beginning of the twenty-first century.

Although the silencing of women through violence, subordination and exclusion is not a new phenomenon, the ways in which such silencing occurs can be different with every generation. In this chapter I discuss both old and new tactics of silencing. The old, persistent tactics men use to keep women in a secondary position are revisited and updated under the heading "tactics of silencing". Then some of the latest tactics, exacerbated by the demands of globalisation, are presented and discussed. Far from the belief of Second Wave feminists that equality and justice would eventuate between the sexes once men understood the effect their dominance had on women, it is clear that the divide, instead of narrowing, has become wider. When men and male-dominated governments chose to interpret the women's liberation movement and feminism as a challenge to their authority, their resolve to retain control deepened. Instead of engaging with feminists in a genuine effort to understand the concerns of women and effect a greater degree of equality they, in the main, chose to see it as an all-out war which they were determined to win.

From as early as the 1970s, Western governments have made a show of listening to women but, instead of seeking to address the unequal status of women at its root and force a greater equality, successive governments have been happy to trim around the edges. They displayed a willingness to respond to liberal feminist demands for equal employment and educational opportunities for women, funded services to address "women's issues" and recruited selected women into politics. All of these initiatives gave the appearance of men attempting to address inequality but, in fact, little actual power changed hands. If male-dominated political parties were serious about their expressed commitment to equality, they would follow up their rhetoric with initiatives aimed at getting to the root of inequality based on sex and force change. The word "force" is used deliberately here because requesting, cajoling, encouraging men to share power with women has never worked. Governments have it in their power to legislate against practices which keep women subordinated and silenced but, to date, most have chosen not to do so. A good place for governments to begin, feminists believe, would be to set an example by changing their own practices of ignoring and excluding women, and insisting that the media do the same.

Tactics of silencing

With every generation in every society and culture, new tactics for silencing women emerge. While some of the old, core tactics are replaced by the new and disappear, others persist like an incurable disease, keeping half of humanity in a state of incapacity.

As spelled out in the previous chapter, the silencing of women occurs through violence, through religious and cultural fundamentalism, through the use and abuse of women's bodies, and through exclusion by male hegemonic hierarchies. Such methods of silencing have been around for a long time and have proved remarkably effective in keeping women sidelined and their opinions unheard. Rather than repeat the facts and statistics set out in Chapter Two, this section illustrates the findings of the research with examples from selected countries.

Violence and threats of violence

Violence against heterosexual women is most often perpetrated by their male partners, a situation referred to as "intimate partner violence". Lesbians, on the other hand, are more likely to be victims of persecution, torture and murder at the hands of governments, religious and community leaders, and members of their own families.

Violence against heterosexual women

In Australia where there are laws against domestic and family violence, women still suffer violence, torture and murder at the hands of intimate partners. In February 2006, Gennaro Migliore was found guilty of the 2004 murder of his wife of fifteen years, Patricia Markwell. After several years struggling with a dysfunctional marriage, Markwell wanted a separation and announced she was taking a job in another city. Migliore made threats against Markwell to friends, saying "nobody messes with Gennaro". He then confronted his wife and attacked her with a knife. Forensic evidence revealed that Markwell had "33 stab wounds to her body, with three fatal blows made to her throat and neck". He was sentenced to life in prison for her murder.[43]

Donna Carson, a school teacher for fifteen years, had her world turned upside down when, during an argument, she was doused in petrol and set alight by her partner. After five and a half months in hospital, fifteen months in rehabilitation and nineteen operations, still scarred and disfigured, she began working to help others in similar situations to her own. In 2004, she received an Australian of the Year award for her courage and compassion for others.[44]

Amy Norman wrote of her ordeal in *Dancing with the Devil* (2005) which her publishers call "The shocking true story of how a woman escaped the daily terror of a violent partner to build a new life". After four years of extreme violence and unspeakable torment and after leaving him and returning many times, Amy finally "packed up the children and spent three years travelling around Australia—changing her identity time after time to avoid him".[45]

Patricia Hughes tells of her experiences of terror and torment at the hands of her violent partner in *Enough* (2004). Every day, she lived in fear but found herself so low in self-esteem, so demoralised, so weakened by his violence and constant threats, that she was literally unable to leave him. One day, in the depths of despair, she finally found the courage to say "enough". Recalling that moment, she says:

> ...he lifted his half-finished can and threw it at my face. When I turned away, he grabbed my hair and yanked me back. ... It's amazing how fear had become a habit I was learning to live with. I had my eyes closed but I could sense him, smell him, standing over me. Then I opened my eyes. As if in slow motion, I saw his fist rise, then I felt the usual pain as it connected with my face, splitting my lips yet again ...
>
> As I slumped to the floor quietly sobbing, I felt the usual sinking inevitability but, this time, something had changed. I thought of all the times he'd done this to me and all the times I'd excused him and forgiven him. I remembered all the vile names he'd called me and almost had me believe. But not anymore. The straw had finally broken the camel's back [pp. 102–3].

---

43   *Townsville Bulletin*, 8 February 2006, p. 5.
44   <<http://www.australianoftheyear.gov.au/recipient.asp?pID=94>.
45   <http://www.randomhouse.com.au/WEB_ASP/ttle_detail.asp?isbn=1863254684>.
     The book was published in the United Kingdom as *Living with the Devil* (2006).

In the mid-1990s, Patricia Easteal from the Australian Institute of Criminology brought together the responses of women to a national survey about rape and sexual abuse in *Voices of the Survivors* (1994). Almost 3000 women responded to the survey, telling their stories of rape and sexual abuse in childhood and in adulthood, by boyfriends, acquaintances, husbands, fathers, bosses, doctors, priests and strangers.[46]

In Saudi Arabia, Rania al-Baz "enjoyed the distinction of being the only young, attractive, female television presenter in a country where women cannot vote, drive a car, leave home without a chaperone or admit themselves to hospital without the permission of a male relative". Her breakfast programme, *The Kingdom this Morning*, was very popular with women viewers. Suddenly, one morning in April 2004, her involvement in the show ceased.

> Her husband had beaten her to a pulp in a fit of rage, smashing her head repeatedly against the marble floor of their home. Although she had defied doctors' expectations by living to tell her tale, her days as a presenter on Saudi Arabian breakfast television were over [Campbell 2005].

In Pakistan, Dr Shazia Khalid courageously tells her story, which one *New York Times* journalist referred to as "a window into the debasement that is the lot of women in much of the world" (Kristof 2005). At the age of thirty-two, Shazia took a job as a doctor at a Pakistan Petroleum plant in Baluchistan. One night, a man broke into her quarters and raped her repeatedly throughout the night. At first she thought she was having a nightmare:

> this person was really pulling hard on my hair, and then he started pressing on my throat so I couldn't breathe ... He tied the telephone cord around my throat. I resisted and struggled, and he beat me on the head with the telephone receiver. When I tried to scream, he said, "Shut up—there's a man standing outside named Amjad, and he's got kerosene. If you scream, I'll take it and burn you alive." ... Then he took my prayer scarf and he blindfolded me with it, and he took the telephone cord and tied my wrists, and he laid me down on the bed. I tried hard to fight but he raped me [Kristof 2005].

In the morning, when the rapist finally left, Dr Shazia dragged herself into the nurses' quarters, semiconscious and bleeding from her nose and ear. Officials from Pakistan Petroleum warned her not to tell anyone because she could be arrested for adultery. She begged them to allow her to contact her husband and members of her family but, instead, she was drugged and confined to a psychiatric hospital.

---

46 For more current studies on sexual abuse in Australia, see the Australian Centre for the Study of Sexual Assault, <http://www.aifs.gov.au/acssa/>.

When news of her brutal attack finally reached her husband, who was working as an engineer in Libya, he rushed back to comfort his wife and insisted that they report the crime to the police. Her rapist, allegedly an army officer, was never caught. The government of Pakistan forced Shazia to leave Pakistan, and left her and her husband stranded in the United Kingdom, where they are currently seeking asylum.

The story of Mukhtar Mai mentioned in the Introduction is another example of the brutality of the Pakistani system against women. Determined to speak out about the injustice of the system, Mukhtar Mai (also known as Mukhtaran Bibi) travelled to the United States to tell her story. In 2002, her rape was ordered "by a council of elders in Meerwala, her home village in eastern Punjab province, as punishment for her 13-year-old brother's alleged affair with a woman from a higher-caste family". It was deemed acceptable that four men could rape her "to avenge their honor...". Mai's decision to speak out brought international attention to her case and, subsequently, not four but fourteen men were arrested and charged with rape (Mann 2005).

Violence against lesbians

Amnesty International's 2001 report, *Crimes of Hate, Conspiracy of Silence: Torture and Ill-Treatment Based on Sexual Identity*, includes documented evidence of violence against and torture of lesbians in many countries around the world. Susan Hawthorne, who has written several articles and spoken at various conferences on the topic of lesbian torture, asks why lesbians are virtually left out of campaigns on violence against women. The horrendous violence occurring against lesbians is allowed to continue, she says, because no one wants to make it the focus of attention.

> Because lesbians are "disappeared" in the mainstream terminology and because no one wants to make lesbians the centre of any campaign, lesbians continue to be tortured around the world. The torture of lesbians occurs under every kind of political regime, and the so-called developed world is not immune [Hawthorne 2005b, p. 2].[47]

The Amnesty report documents examples of lesbians being confined in psychiatric institutions and being sent to prisons and detention centres, where they are often raped by guards and other detainees. The torture of lesbians in institutions commonly takes the form of sexual harassment, sexual assault, rape and gang rape. In Amnesty's *Crimes of Hate*, a Ugandan lesbian activist arrested and sent to a detention centre reports being beaten and threatened with rape by the soldiers and then actually raped by three male detainees:

---

47 See other articles on the same topic by Susan Hawthorne: 2004a, 2004b, 2005a. See also Reinfelder 1996, pp. 11–29.

"Coming midnight, they said 'we want to show you something'. They took my clothes off and raped me. I remember being raped by two of them, then I passed out" (Amnesty 2001, p. 4). In the United States, where there are no legal sanctions against lesbian sexual practice, lesbians in institutions are still not safe. Robin Lucas was jailed for credit card fraud in California in 1995. *Crimes of Hate* reports: "One evening in September 1995, three male inmates unlocked the door of her cell, handcuffed her and raped her. Robin Lucas suffered severe injuries to her neck, arms, back and vaginal and anal areas" (p. 18).

Hawthorne tells of the violence against Consuelo Rivera-Fuentes, a political activist in Chile in the 1970s:

> She was arrested and tortured. As a political prisoner, she was marked because she was a lesbian and the torture meted out to her was directed at her sexuality. So again, a double jeopardy, arrested for resistance against the government, punished as a lesbian [2005b, p. 7].

Fanny Ann Eddy, a lesbian from Sierra Leone, gave testimony before the United Nations Commission on Human Rights in Geneva. The final paragraph of her statement reads:

> Silence creates vulnerability. You, members of the Commission on Human Rights, can break the silence. You can acknowledge that we exist, throughout Africa and on every continent, and that human rights violations based on sexual orientation or gender identity are committed every day. You can help us combat those violations and achieve our full rights and freedoms, in every society, including my beloved Sierra Leone [Eddy 2004].

On 29 September 2004, Fanny Ann Eddy, aged thirty, was found dead at the offices of the Sierra Leone Lesbian and Gay Association. She had been "raped repeatedly, stabbed and her neck was broken".[48]

Other women report torture at the hands of family members. A Zimbabwean lesbian living in Harare reported: "They locked me in a room and brought him every day to rape me so I would fall pregnant and be forced to marry him. They did this to me until I was pregnant" (Machida 1996, p. 123).

Human Rights Watch reported on the brutal murder of a lesbian in South Africa, which occurred on 4 February 2006. Under the headline "South Africa: Murder Highlights Violence Against Lesbians", they say:

> The vicious murder of Zoliswa Nkonyana, a lesbian killed by a mob in a Cape Flats township, points to the brutal reality that despite constitutional protections, lesbians in South Africa continue to experience egregious assaults on their human rights ...

---

48 See <http://hrw.org/english/docs/2004/10/04/sierra9440.htm>.

> Nkonyana, a 19-year old lesbian from the Khayelitsha township near Cape Town, was walking near her home February 4 with a lesbian friend. The friend said they were confronted by a schoolgirl who taunted them for being "tomboys" who "wanted to be raped." A mob of young men gathered around them. Nkonyana's friend ran away, but the mob caught Nkonyana. They beat her with golf clubs, threw bricks at her, and stabbed her. She died in the hospital shortly thereafter [Human Rights Watch 2006].

Violence against heterosexual women in order to silence them includes physical, sexual and emotional violence by intimate partners, rape, sexual abuse in childhood, and murder. Violence against lesbians in order to render them invisible includes sexual violence and torture, psychiatric incarceration, forced heterosexual marriage, and murder.

Fundamentalism

Another of the ways women are silenced around the world is through fundamentalism: religious and cultural as well as market fundamentalism.

Religious and cultural fundamentalism

A central feature of religious and cultural fundamentalism has always been its focus on curtailing the freedoms of women. Members of the Revolutionary Association of the Women of Afghanistan (RAWA) have been successful in drawing global attention to the silencing of women by successive fundamentalist regimes in Afghanistan. Inspired by the example of their founding leader, Meena Kishwar, who was assassinated in 1987 (Chavis 2004, pp. 197–221), they continue courageously to agitate against fundamentalism and insist on democracy. Their statement issued in Peshawar, Pakistan, on International Women's Day 2002, titled "Let Us Struggle Against War and Fundamentalism and for Peace and Democracy!", said:

> The women of the world celebrate International Women's Day with spirit and enthusiasm; in Afghanistan women still don't feel safe enough to throw away their wretched burqa shrouds, let alone raise their voices in the thousands in support of freedom and democracy. There is still a wide chasm between us and the glorious future we have fixed our eyes, hearts and minds upon. It is as if Fate has decreed that this most pauperised nation on earth should not be able to throw the chains and shackles of despots and vampire fundamentalists away so easily [RAWA, in Hawthorne and Winter 2002, p. 232].[49]

---

49 See also <http://www.rawa.us/mar8-02en.htm>.

Valentine Moghadam outlines the history of fundamentalist politics in Afghanistan with particular reference to the targeting of women. She explains that, before the mujahideen came to power in 1992, they

> ...issued a fatwa (a holy writ) stating that women were not to wear perfume, noisy bangles, or Western clothes. Veils had to cover the body at all times and clothes were not to be made of material which was soft or which rustled. Women were not to walk in the middle of the street or swing their hips; they were not to talk, laugh or joke with strangers or foreigners [2002, p. 272].

Once they came to power, Moghadam states, the mujahideen factions began to fight among themselves but, she says, the one thing the men did agree on was the question of women. "Thus the very first order of the new government was that all women should wear the burqa" (p. 272).

Within a few years the Taliban, who "adhered to a particularly orthodox brand of Islam", were proving a threat to the ruling mujahideen. By 1996, they had seized power in many parts of Afghanistan and again women were targeted.

> [The Taliban] decreed that women would be forbidden to work outside their homes ... girls had been expelled from schools and young women from colleges ... Women were also told that if they went shopping in the bazaars, they had to be accompanied by male kinfolk and wear the traditional burqa [Moghadam 2002, pp. 273–4].

Following the terrorist attacks of 11 September 2001, the United States, in preparation for an all-out war on Afghanistan, entered into negotiations with various factions of the mujahideen which they chose to re-name the Northern Alliance. After a period of merciless bombing and the retreat of the Taliban government, the United States declared that Afghanistan had been liberated. RAWA stated emphatically:

> One fundamentalist band cannot be fought by siding with and supporting another. In its war on the Taliban and the al-Qaeda, the US has taken the "Northern Alliance" into service through wooing and arming certain infamous warlords. By so doing, the US is in fact abetting the worst enemies of our people ...
>
> The existence of one or two showpiece women in the transitional administration ... is more an insult to Afghan women than a symbol of the restoration of their status and legal rights. The women of Afghanistan have not been liberated [Moghadam 2002, pp. 234–5].

The same is true in Iraq. In fact, when the constitutional committee began drafting Iraq's new constitution in 2005, it was reported that "Iraqi women who enjoyed basic human rights under one of the world's most repressive regimes headed by former President Saddam Hussein are now on the verge of losing their hard-won freedoms under a U.S.-blessed administration..." (Deen 2005). In an appeal to the United Nations, the Iraqi Women's Movement stated:

> The Iraqi women's movement expresses its deepest concern and worry towards the drafts lately released by the Constitutional Committee, specifically in the Chapter of Duties & Rights, in which the Shari'a law was clearly stated as the main source for legislation in the new Iraq Constitution [Iraqi Women's Movement 2005].

In a classic example of doublespeak, the transitional government in Iraq acknowledged the importance of equal rights of men and women—"as long as it doesn't contradict ... sharia law" (Deen 2005).

Christian fundamentalist regimes, such as that led by President George W. Bush in the United States, Prime Minister Tony Blair in the United Kingdom and Prime Minister John Howard in Australia in the early years of this century, are as committed to rendering women invisible in their determination to favour the input of mainstream men as are Islamic fundamentalist regimes. While Western leaders may have learned to be more subtle in the ways they silence women, the result is the same. Women are subordinated and ignored.

Market fundamentalism
While the effects of religious and cultural fundamentalism on women are dire, so too are the effects of market fundamentalism, especially on women in poorer countries of the world. Poverty and homelessness escalate in the face of "corporate control of food and globalization of agriculture" (Shiva 2000, p. 7). Describing how millions in India are being robbed of their livelihoods by the demands of international trade organisatioins, Vandana Shiva compared the current situation with the Bengal famine of 1943, when India was used "as a supply base for the British military". Britain "forcefully appropriated" food grains from the peasants "under a colonial system of rent collection". In addition to the millions who died of starvation, many more millions were dispossessed of their homes and farms. "Dispossessed peasants moved to Calcutta. Thousands of female destitutes were turned into prostitutes. Parents started to sell their children" (pp. 5, 6).

Huge dispossession is occurring today in India due to genetic engineering practices by multinational corporations, and the claiming of patents on seeds and other natural life-forms. Millions of subsistence farmers, the majority of whom are women, are being forced off their land and are moving to cities in search of work and sustenance. In Mumbai, as in other major centres, millions of homeless women, men and children now live on the streets desperately trying to find ways to survive. Once proud women are sending their children out to beg and are themselves turning to prostitution. Preoccupation with survival renders these women harmless to their oppressors and ensures their silence. Poverty, homelessness, despair and loss of dignity, all in the name of profit-making for large Western companies and their shareholders, are ever-present reminders of the silencing of women through market fundamentalism.

The use and abuse of women's bodies

In the early years of Second Wave feminism, many women spoke out against the portrayal and use of women as "sex objects". There were campaigns to expose the subtle and not-so-subtle use of women's bodies in the media, both for the advertising of products and for entertainment. Half-naked women draped over cars on television is a classic example of the way women were used in television advertising while "page three girls" were seen to be mandatory for men's entertainment in many mainstream newspapers. Feminist calls for fairness and a more equal treatment of women had some effect for a brief period in the 1970s and 1980s, but economic rationalism and the concept of a global market brought with them an "anything goes" attitude, and women's sexuality, women's bodies are once more being used in the service of the market and for men's entertainment. Today, radical feminists speak of the "objectification" and "commodification" of women's bodies and continue to agitate against the use and abuse of women in these ways.

In addition to media advertising, women are used as "topless waitresses" in hotels and restaurants, as pole dancers and lap dancers in nightclubs and as escorts for business executives. There are burgeoning multimillion-dollar industries around pornography, prostitution and trafficking. Also, there is the long-held acceptance of the use of prostitutes by military personnel and by men involved in sport either as players or spectators.

Abuse of women by military personnel

By their silence, governments condone the use of women in the sexual service of military personnel. The most notorious example of the keeping of military sex slaves is that of the so-called comfort women used by the Japanese military during World War II. The Historical Museum of Japanese Military Sexual Slavery, established near Seoul, South Korea, in 1998,

> ...documents the Japanese military's abduction and sexual enslavement of over 200,000 women during World War II. Most of the slaves, whom the Japanese military called "comfort women," were young, poor Koreans.

The young women were kidnapped or tricked into entering the military brothels by men who made false promises of legitimate employment. There, the women were raped by as many as 20 or 30 Japanese soldiers each day.[50]

In November 1990, spurred on by the Japanese government's continued denial of its involvement in the recruitment of "comfort women", Korean women formed the Korean Council for the Women Drafted for Military Sexual Slavery by Japan. Their first action was to send an open letter to the then Japanese prime minister, setting out six demands:

1. That the Japanese government admit the forced draft of Korean women as comfort women;
2. That a public apology be made for this;
3. That all barbarities be fully disclosed;
4. That a memorial be raised for the victims;
5. That the survivors or their bereaved families be compensated;
6. That these facts be continuously related in historical education so that such misdeeds are not repeated.

The response from the Japanese government was simply to claim that "there was no evidence of the forced draft of Korean women, and hence no public apology, disclosure, nor memorial were forthcoming".[51]

The Special Rapporteur on Violence against Women for the UN's Commission on Human Rights, Radhika Coomaraswamy, was invited by the governments of the Republic of Korea and Japan to conduct a study on "the issue of military sexual slavery in wartime". Her report outlines the "evidence" the Japanese government had hitherto claimed did not exist. On the question of the term "comfort women", the report states:

> ...the Special Rapporteur concurs entirely with the view held by members of the Working Group on Contemporary Forms of Slavery, as well as by representatives of non-governmental organizations and some academics, that the phrase "comfort women" does not in the least reflect the suffering, such as multiple rapes on an everyday basis and severe physical abuse, that women victims had to endure during their forced prostitution and sexual subjugation and abuse in wartime. The Special Rapporteur, therefore, considers with conviction that the phrase "military sexual slaves" represents a much more accurate and appropriate terminology.[52]

---

50 See <http://www.feminist.org/news/newsbyte/uswirestory.asp?id=1672>.
51 See <http://online.sfsu.edu/~soh/comfortwomen.html>.
52 See <http://www.unhchr.ch/Huridocda/Huridoca.nsf/TestFrame/b6ad5f3990967f3e802566d600575fcb?Opendocument>.

Regardless of the continuing, unrelenting demands by Japanese, Korean and other feminists, however, the Japanese government still refuses to accept responsibility for its actions and the effect such extreme abuse has had on the lives of those, mainly Korean, women.

Abuse of women as integral to men's sport

Similarly governments condone, in some cases by their silence and in others by their active support, the sexual use of women at sporting events. Prior to the World Cup Games in Germany in June–July 2006, when 3 million football fans, mostly men, were expected to pour into the twelve cities hosting the games, it was estimated that 40,000 women would be imported into Germany to "sexually service" the men. Women from all parts of the world raised their voices in protest against such overt abuse of women. The Coalition Against Trafficking in Women (CATW) issued a statement calling for a worldwide protest against Germany's promotion of prostitution. Included in their statement was a call to "The German government and its chancellor Angela Merkel, the German football federation and its president, Gerhard Mayer-Vorfelder, to stop this traffic in women for prostitution and to discourage the male demand that fosters prostitution." The points raised in CATW's statement included:

- Buying sex is not a sport. It is sexual exploitation in which women are physically and psychologically harmed, and women's bodies are treated as commodities to be bought and sold.
- Treating women's bodies as sexual commodities violates international standards of sport that promote equality, mutual respect and non-discrimination.
- Honorable men do not buy sex because they respect the dignity and integrity of all human beings.
- No to the organization of prostitution for the World Cup Games.[53]

Taking refuge in the fact that Germany legalised the sex industry in 2002, both the German government and the Fédération Internationale de Football Association (FIFA) chose to focus on the legal aspects of the situation, claiming that they had no power to take legal action. FIFA issued a statement condemning "any human rights violations, particularly in terms of human trafficking and forced prostitution" but pointing out that, as world football's governing body, it has no power to intervene and "cannot be held responsible for such matters".[54]

---

53 See <http://www.catwepetition.ouvaton.org/telechar/WorldCupStatement-en.pdf>.
54 See <http://www.fifa.com/en/media/index/0,1369,116822,00.html>.

In Australia, there are regular reports of sexual abuse of women by rugby league players and also, to a lesser extent, by Australian Football League players. The Canterbury Bulldogs rugby league team have had several complaints made against them over the years by women claiming to have been sexually assaulted by team members. In 2003 "a 42-year-old woman claimed she had consensual sex with one player, but woke up having sex with another player, while a third looked on". In 2004 a 20-year-old woman "accused as many as six Bulldogs ... players of sexually assaulting her at a resort" in Coffs Harbour.[55]

Three members of the Brisbane Broncos rugby league team were questioned by police in 2008 over complaints by a young woman that they had sexually assaulted her in the men's toilet at an inner-city hotel. A report in the *Daily Telegraph* said:

> the three engaged in oral sex with a woman in the men's toilets of the Alhambra Lounge after a day of drinking at the Story Bridge Hotel. Two of the players are then alleged to have had sexual intercourse with the woman while the third recorded the acts on a mobile phone camera.[56]

After a damning report on ABC television's *Four Corners* program in May 2009, which focused on the sexual assault of a 19-year-old woman in Christchurch, New Zealand, in 2002, officials of the National Rugby League responded by apologising and assuring the Australian community that they were determined to stamp out such behaviour by members of the rugby league code. *Four Corners* journalist Sarah Ferguson revealed details of the assault on the teenager by twelve players and staff in a report titled "Code of Silence".[57]

Those details were outlined in newspapers throughout the country, ensuring that the code of silence on this particular event was broken. One journalist, Michael Pelly, reported in an article in *The Weekend Australian*:

> During dinner at the Racecourse Hotel, the players were served by a woman (called Clare on the ABC) who later agreed to accompany the team's scrum-base duo—five-eighth [Matthew] Johns and halfback Brett Firman—to their room ... It appears that while Johns was having sex with Clare, other players entered the room ... At one point the door must have been closed because Clare says some climbed through the bathroom window [2009, p. 19].

---

55 <http://www.smh.com.au/articles/2004/02/23/1077497518522.html>.
56 <http://www.news.com.au/story/0,23599,24345350-1248,00.html>.
57 <http://www.abc.net.au/4corners/content/2009/s2565007.htm>.

A rugby league analyst, Phil Gould, expressed his frustration at the players on a panel following the *Four Corners* report: "For so long we've been sitting on panels like this discussing incidents, whether it was drugs or alcohol or abuse of women, and we all walk away saying: 'Well, that was a wake-up call', but no one wakes up" (Pelly 2009, p. 19).

Commenting on players' complaints that they faced constant harassment from young women, journalist David Penberthy wrote: "This is the most repellent aspect of the debate: that in this day and age, people still think that a 19-year-old girl, confronted by a group of men more than a decade older than her, can somehow be the instigator or predator in the equation" (2009, p. 26). Picking up the theme of the *Four Corners* program "Code of Silence", Penberthy said: "This story ... is in essence a story about silence: male silence, where a group of men ... have conspired to suppress or ignore terrible events" (p. 26).

It is interesting to note that many reports about alleged gang rape by Australian football players end with the same refrain: "The case was dropped for lack of evidence". Football players who use the sexual assault of women as an exercise in team bonding, do so with impunity.

Pornography and prostitution

With the exception of trafficking in women, which is seen as forced prostitution and therefore not acceptable, many on the left of the political spectrum, including many feminists, rationalise their acceptance of pornography and prostitution on the basis of choice. Women are not forced into pornography and prostitution, they argue. It is a choice women make, and no one has the right to deny them that choice. One of the most convincing of the radical feminist arguments against "choice" is that pornography, prostitution, lap dancing, pole dancing, etc. have the effect of presenting all women as commodities or potential commodities capable of being bought and sold by men. As such, womankind is diminished, subordinated and shut out of any possibility of equality with men.

Susan Griffin, writing in 1981, spoke powerfully about the silencing of women through pornography. We are encouraged, she said, to think of pornography "as part of a larger movement toward sexual liberation ... a revolution against silence", but it is, in fact, the opposite. A distinction must be made "between the libertine's idea of liberty 'to do as one likes', and a vision of human 'liberation'" (1981, p. 1). Pornography deprives women of the possibility of liberation by deepening and expanding their silencing.

After listing the ways in which women have been silenced throughout history—from the creation of a God in the image of man right through to the invisibility of today's mothers "unimagined and unrecognized", to the suspicion with which women's testimony is held in court—Griffin declares that it is this

> silence of women [which is] the very surface on which pornography is played ... Over and over, pornography depicts acts of terrible violence to women's bodies. Yet even as part of these images of women beaten and dying and always as a ghost image behind these sufferings, a more silent and invisible death takes place. For pornography is violent to a women's soul. In the wake of pornographic images, a woman ceases to know herself [1981, pp. 201, 202].

The pornification of Western societies means that little girls are socialised into a pornographic image of woman. From an early age, a girl begins to mould herself to fit that image and, because it is not the truth about herself but, in fact, a false image, she "ceases to know herself". Griffin speaks of the self-deception that is required of girls and women:

> When we speak of deception, we must speak of a self destroyed. For the deceiver has two selves. One is a false self, manufactured for appearance' sake and set before an audience. This self is allowed to speak, to act, to express, to live. But the other self, who is the real self, is consigned to silence. She is hidden, denied, eventually forgotten, and even, in some cases, unnamed. Thus the deceiver is in danger of never remembering that she has a real self. The real self continues to experience, to feel, to move through life. But in our minds, we destroy her experience, and thus we lose ourselves [1981, p. 202].

Who is this false self? Griffin asks. "She is the pornographic idea of the female. We have learned to impersonate her" while our real selves are "cast back into silence" (p. 202).

The silencing of women through pornography, prostitution and cosmetic surgery has been reiterated in recent times, most notably by Sheila Jeffreys (1990, 1997, 2005, 2009). Jeffreys highlights the fact that, with the support of powerful politicians like President Bill Clinton and Prime Minister Tony Blair, the international sex industry has succeeded in normalising both prostitution and pornography (2005, pp. 67–8). Prostitution is renamed "sex work", prostitutes are "sex workers", and the work they do is "a job like any other" (1997, pp. 161–95). Prostitution has been "industrialized and globalized", she says (2009, p. 3). In Australia, prostitution has been legalised in four states. The Labor government in Queensland, ostensibly to take greater control of the sex industry, passed the Prostitution Act of 1999 legalising prostitution in brothels.[58] It was declared that approval would be given to the establishment of a certain number of brothels in various regional and urban centres and that protests by local government councils, by individual people or by community and church groups would not be entertained. Brothels then began appearing all around the state. As soon as prostitution was normalised in this way, reports which appeared from time to time in local newspapers of brothels having to "put on extra girls" because a US naval ship was in port or because there was a major football game in town, confirmed that men using women as prostitutes was now "normal behaviour".

So "normal" is prostitution in Victoria, legalised since 1984, that the Labor government has set up occupational health and safety (OHS) guidelines for "sex workers" on the assumption that it is work that any girl or woman could aspire to and, therefore, it must be treated the same as any other job.[59] After a careful examination of Victoria's OHS strategies for the state's sex industry, Mary Sullivan came to the conclusion that

> ...normalising the violence of prostitution as just another work-place safety issue ignores that this population of "workers" is vulnerable to very specific and unique kinds of harm due to the nature of the "work" they are doing. In practice, the application of OHS to the sex industry makes acceptable the violence of prostitution [2004, p. 253].[60]

Pornography, too, has been normalised globally. Although most countries have laws against child pornography, there are no such laws against the pornographic use and abuse of women. The growing emphasis on competition and free trade has enabled the pornography industry to expand exponentially, the effects of which can be seen in what Jeffreys calls "the pornographization of culture": "The values of pornography, and its practices, extended outwards from magazines and movies to become the dominating values of fashion and beauty advertising, and the advertising of many other products and services" (2005, p. 67).

Little girls are being socialised into what Griffin called "the pornographic idea of the female" (1981, p. 202). The "slut" look is everywhere. T-shirts for young girls proudly announce "Porn Star". The bunny logo on clothes, shoes, notebooks, diaries is all the rage. The anorexic Barbie doll now has to compete with various ranges of sexed-up dolls. The "Bratz doll", described on the About.com website as "the super cool funky fashion Bratz dolls", has been described by one young mother as looking "like a miniature porn star".[61]

---

58 <http://www.legislation.qld.gov.au/LEGISLTN/CURRENT/P/ProstitutA99.pdf>.
59 See <http://www.sexworker.org.au/safetyinfo/>.
60 See also Sullivan 2006.
61 Email to f-agenda discussion list 12 April 2006, quoted with permission.

Another mother wrote to a blog:

> ...my daughter was given a "bratz baby" doll for christmas—they are ridiculously pornographic (possibly even more so than the adult bratz) with tiny skirts, short enough that the white knickers are clearly visible, with lipsticked pouts, and milk bottle necklace accessories. you should see the porno poses on the cardboard boxes the female dolls come in! [62]

The increasing sexualisation of children, particularly girls, is a serious concern to many parents. Emma Rush and Andrea La Nauze undertook a comprehensive study of this phenomenon in Australia looking at advertising, girls' magazines and television programs. They reported their findings in a discussion paper titled "Corporate Paedophilia: Sexualisation of Children in Australia":

> ...it is apparent that young children today, particularly girls, face sexualising pressure unlike that faced by any of today's adults in their childhood. Such sexualising pressure has the potential to harm children in a variety of ways, and the paper draws on research from a range of disciplines to illustrate the risks to children of premature sexualisation [Rush and La Nauze 2006a, p. 4].[63]

The normalising of prostitution and pornography, as illustrated by the growing number of governments supporting such practices, by the increased acceptance of the use and abuse of women by military and sports personnel and by the sex industry's growing influence over fashion and beauty practices, entrenches inequality between the sexes and thus is a powerful force in the silencing of women.[64]

---

62 See <http://aradfem.blogspot.com/>.
63 They followed it with another paper, "Letting Children be Children. Stopping the Sexualisation of Children in Australia": Rush and La Nauze 2006b. For significant commentary on the sexualisation of girls and women, see Tankard Reist 2009.
64 For more on the sexualisation of women and girls, see Chapter Six.

Exclusion

The exclusion of women and women's voices from national and international arenas is no mere oversight. In every generation, the exclusion is deliberate. In today's neoliberal capitalist world, power is kept in the hands of the few: women, especially dissenting feminists, are not included. Some who claim to be feminists are included, but they are usually the ones whose agenda is to speak the words the patriarchal elite want to hear and are chosen for their value as token women (discussed further below).

Even in the United Nations, which purports to support the notion of "gender equality", there are precious few women in senior positions. Stephen Lewis, Canadian ambassador to the United Nations from 1984 to 1988, began the fourth of his 2005 Massey lectures, "Women: Half the World, Barely Represented", by describing a photograph on the wall of his study at home. "It's a stunning photograph of the entire leadership of the United Nations secretariat in 1985", he said. "The Secretary-General ... all of his Under-Secretaries-General and all of his Assistant Secretaries-General ... thirty-two of them in all." And then he added: "Not one woman". Critiquing that disturbing situation, he commented: "That just about says everything there is to say about multilateralism and gender" (Lewis 2005, p. 109).[65]

Feminists in the twenty-first century are encouraging a fresh look at the structures of power or, as Vivienne Jabri names it, "the structures of domination" impinging on women's lives (2004, p 2). Questions are being raised in a new way around issues such as men's exclusive hold on power; men's use of token women; the exclusion of women in the name of war; the exclusion of women in the name of peace; and the psychological and sociological effects of exclusion.

Men's exclusive hold on power

When Cynthia Enloe asked "Where are the women?", her intention was not only to point to the exclusion of women but also to get people thinking about who actually *was* there. Men. And to ask "the important next questions, which are: why are they there, who got them there, and what happens to your understanding ... once you see them there?" (2004, p. 84).

In her earlier work, *Bananas, Beaches and Bases: Making Feminist Sense of International Politics*, Enloe urged readers to question the generally accepted belief that men's exclusive hold on power is natural and inevitable.

---

[65] Today, the situation for women in the United Nations Organisation has improved slightly with several women in senior positions. In fact, the deputy secretary-general, the second-highest-ranking official in the United Nations after the secretary-general, is Asha-Rose Mtengeti Migiro, a lawyer and politician from Tanzania. Also, several women occupy positions in the secretary-general's Senior Management Group, whose task is to ensure strategic coherence and direction in the work of the United Nations.

> As one learns to look at this world through feminist eyes, one learns to ask whether anything that passes for inevitable, inherent, "traditional" or biological has in fact been *made*. One begins to ask how all sorts of things have been *made* — a treeless landscape, a rifle-wielding police force, the "Irishman joke", an all-women typing pool. Asking how something has been made implies that it has been made by someone. Suddenly there are clues to trace... [2000, p. 3].

Far from being natural and inevitable, masculinity's exclusive hold on power has taken some effort: "it has required the daily exercise of power—domestic power, national power, and ... international power" (p. 3). Enloe admits that, to this point,

> feminist analysis has had little impact on international politics. Foreign-policy commentators and decision-makers seem particularly confident in dismissing feminist ideas ... Consequently, how the conduct of international politics has *depended* on men's control of women has been left unexamined. This has meant that those wielding influence over foreign policy have escaped responsibility for how women have been affected by international politics [pp. 3–4, emphasis in the original].

Vivienne Jabri, in her article "Feminist Ethics and Hegemonic Global Politics", stresses the absolute necessity for contemporary feminists to understand the "structures of domination" which permeate global politics and produce particularly compliant individuals. Posing the question "How in the present does power operate?", she explains that "neoliberal capitalism of the late-modern form makes possible the integration of forms of power traditionally conceived as separate, an integration that results from the intersection of economic and political power, in a sense producing a single power". The union between powerful multinational corporations and powerful political administrations has enabled "the government (surveillance, confinement, pacification) of groups and populations at the transnational/global level". It "recognizes no boundary," and "sees the entire global population within its remit of control" (2004, p. 2).

Such absolute control of the many by the few has depended on the acquiescence of the masses, that is, populations believing the lies and accepting that what was presented to them was the only way to proceed.

> The ultimate force of a hegemonic discourse is when its self-legitimization is based on an assertion that it is the only story available, a narrative constructed as the outcome of dialogue with its subjects, even as the latter remain somehow absent, empty, and hence open to occupation [Jabri 2004, p. 6].

Jabri argues for a "feminism of dissent", a concept which will be raised again in the final chapters of this book.

Men's use of token women

When token women are included, as in the transitional government in Afghanistan, it would be wrong to suppose that those women will automatically turn their backs on women and women's issues. Often, however, it does happen because they are chosen for their allegiance to the agenda of the men in power. Anticipating the make-up of Afghanistan's transitional government, Fariba Nawa, writing on 14 November 2001, said:

> If women are given a role in a transitional government, one of the likeliest candidates is Fatana Gailani, director of the moderate Afghanistan Women's Council. A member of a politically powerful Afghan family ... Fatana Gailani says she does not expect deeper issues of women's rights and social change to be addressed until after a stable government is in place.
> "Let the men get along first, then we will get involved," she says. "Until our country has been rescued, the women's issue is a non-issue" [2002, p. 177].

In the United States one woman, Condoleezza Rice, was elevated to powerful positions in the administration of President George W. Bush, first as security adviser to the president and then secretary of state. While no one could dispute Rice's competence and fitness for the task, she was nevertheless one lone token woman.

In Australia, Prime Minister Kevin Rudd was careful to be seen to be choosing competent women for top ministries in his government, but four women out of a total of twenty leaves him open to a charge of tokenism. (Even when the opportunity for a cabinet reshuffle presented itself to the Prime Minister in 2009, he chose not to add any more women to the inner cabinet). While there is no question about the competence of the four women, the fact that they are so few in number means that they will never have the power to challenge the maleness of the system. For as long as they cooperate with the system created by and for men, they will be allowed to retain their positions. Other instances of tokenism can be found in the media's use of token feminists. In every Western country, the media has its favourite "feminists" and uses them to the exclusion of all others.

The exclusion of women in the name of war

Nowhere is the invisibility and exclusion of women more evident than in matters relating to war. When politicians of any nation contemplate going to war, women are rarely, if ever, consulted because war is "men's business". How such a war will affect a nation's women and children is never considered.

Questions by feminists about the use of pornography and prostitution in preparation of men for war are ignored. Issues such as the rape of women, the keeping of military sexual slaves, the rape of female military personnel are simply denied or reframed. Protests against the targeting of civilians, mainly women and children, are of no consequence to men intent on humiliating and defeating the enemy by whatever means.

The exclusion of women in the name of peace

In addition to the exclusion of women in the name of war, there is also the exclusion of women in the name of peace. In the lead-up to Australia's involvement in the war on Iraq, when millions of Australians marched and rallied to demonstrate their objections to the war, women commented on the anti-women attitudes of some of the male peace activists. One woman spoke of "the inability of male organisers to recognise that women should get a space to speak". Some women who wanted to speak, she said, were "more or less ignored or brushed off".[66]

While men who are leaders in dissenting, activist groups are always happy to see women involved to swell the numbers, they are often reluctant to share any real power with those women. Enloe made a similar observation in relation to foreign policy and international relations:

> ...activists (from either the right or the left) who are trying to persuade women to "get involved" are not inviting women to reinterpret international politics by drawing on their own experiences as women ... [Women] are asked to join an international campaign—for peace, against communism, for refugees, against apartheid, for religious evangelism, against hunger—but are not allowed to define the problem [2000, p. 15].

The devastating effects of exclusion

Men's deliberate exclusion of women is no insignificant matter in terms of its psychological and sociological effects. Psychologically, the effects on individual women can be described in terms of alienation, defined as "estrangement from society; feelings of being an outsider, foreigner or outcast" (Miller and Keane 1987).

In a survey undertaken in Australia at the beginning of the war on Iraq (2003), women were asked to respond to questions about how they felt in the lead-up to the war and again after the war began. They responded with words like powerlessness, helplessness, hopelessness, depression, sadness, fear, anxiety, all of which point to an experience of alienation. One respondent commented on the exclusion of women from the decision-making processes

---

66 Email to f-agenda discussion list 18 April 2003, quoted with permission.

in the lead-up to the war: "I have been reminded just how fragile my position is … being a woman in a society where we had hoped women had come a long way towards making joint decisions for a better world". Another said:

> As a woman, I don't feel at home anymore. All the images of war are foreign to me—the propaganda, the lies, the threats, the violence, the ease with which people are murdered, the sanitised language, the obvious delight in the humiliation of the enemy. Where do I belong? [McLellan 2003].

Sociologically, the effects of the deliberate exclusion of women are obvious. Put simply, the world is deprived of the ideas, opinions, energy, enthusiasm and wise counsel of 50 per cent of the population on matters of national and international importance.

Constant silencing and exclusion creates a situation where women are so far out of sight that they, literally, cannot be found. Second Wave feminists writing in the 1970s described how difficult it was to find and empower women who had been shut out for so long.

In his 2005 Massey Lectures, Stephen Lewis recounted a bizarre experience he had when he was Canada's ambassador to the United Nations. As a result of his pursuing "a very tough line on discrimination against women within the UN system" with the blessing of the Canadian Ministry of Foreign Affairs, the then secretary-general, Perez de Cuellar, finally decided to appoint a woman to a vacant undersecretary-general's position in the Department of Public Information, and asked Canada to recommend someone. When Lewis excitedly phoned the Ministry of Foreign Affairs to discuss who they might nominate, "they had not a single candidate in reserve". He continued:

> …here we were, advancing the cause of female appointments within the secretariat, and given the opportunity, we couldn't come up with a name! It was a perfect commentary on the indelible pattern of male privilege … What was nuts, of course, is that there were numbers upon numbers of talented women to do the job, but they were invisible, living in the refracted shadows of the glass ceiling [Lewis 2005, p. 111].

Thanks to the feminist movement and to the work of women and men committed to justice and equality, women did emerge ready to take their place in the world alongside men, but the wave of conservatism currently washing over the globe has seen a backlash against the advancement of women and, once again, women are involuntarily retreating into obscurity.

The exclusion of women by men in the twenty-first century is commonplace, so much so that the absence of women and women's voices seems, once again, to be normal and inevitable. Women are excluded by men's determination to keep power in their own hands, aided by their use of token women as a sop to more radical women who demand to be heard. Excluded by men on the left as well as by those on the right, women who believe it to be their right to have equal input with men into national and international affairs are forced into a situation of psychological and sociological alienation. Societies all over the world are the poorer because of the exclusion of women.

Twenty-first-century tactics

While the above tactics employed to silence women are referred to here as "core" and "old", they actually never have a chance to grow old because they are renewed with every generation. Similarly, it can be argued that the "twenty-first-century" or "new" tactics discussed in this present section are not entirely new because each has its roots in previous generations, but the division is convenient and, I hope, helpful.

New tactics include silencing of women by international economic imperatives, by the language of corporate governance, by the perceived need for community and cultural solidarity, and by calls from the left for anti-racism and cultural inclusiveness.

International economic imperatives

It is argued convincingly by feminists and other human rights advocates that international trade and finance organisations are responsible for increased poverty in some of the poorest nations on earth, and that the majority of poverty's victims are women and children. Just as convincingly, it is argued that the mobilising of women from poorer countries to richer countries to take up work as nannies and maids for wealthy families, as well as in sweatshops, rationalised by international trade and finance bodies as providing legitimate work options in an era of global competition, are exploitative in the extreme.

The globalising of trade, purported to be in the best interests of poorer nations because of its potential to facilitate development has, in fact, resulted in the resources of poorer nations being transferred to the coffers of richer nations. Similarly, the globalising of job opportunities for individuals desperate for work, purported to be in the best interests of the unemployed or under-employed, in fact, results in increased profits for multinational companies and a seriously overworked and underpaid workforce.

Poverty

Structural Adjustment Programmes imposed by international financial institutions—the International Monetary Fund and the World Bank—have, in Arundhati Roy's words, left millions of people "displaced and dispossessed and sentenced to a lifetime of starvation and deprivation..." (2004). The website Globalissues agrees and adds that, even though there was a change of name from Structural Adjustment to Poverty Reduction Growth Facility in 1999, the requirements of the programme remained the same.[67] Both programmes were driven by "conditionality"—that is, when loans were offered, strict conditions were imposed on recipient countries: "The conditions ranged from the sale of public sector corporations, to the imposition of 'cost sharing' (the euphemism for user fees imposed on health and education), to savage cut-backs in employment levels in the public service" (Lewis 2005, p. 5). Consequently, many African and other developing nations have suffered wholesale neglect of basic infrastructure, the decimation of the social sector and a drastic lowering of the numbers of public sector workers. Billions of people are now unable to afford much-needed medical treatment for their families and education for their children.

Time and again those who find the present situation obscene have pointed out, particularly in relation to African countries, that millions of lives could be saved in Africa every year if money going to debt repayment could be diverted to improving the treatment of serious health conditions such as HIV/AIDS, malaria, acute respiratory infections, measles, diarrhoea and malnutrition. Human rights activists in wealthy nations work tirelessly to convince their governments of the need to redress the imbalances, to work with governments of developing nations with a view to reducing extreme poverty and increasing their capacity to respond to the health, education and welfare needs of their people.

Worldwide campaigns such as "Make Poverty History" had some success in convincing governments at the G8 Summit held in Gleneagles, Scotland, in July 2005, of the need to cancel the debt owed to them by some of the most impoverished nations on earth. G8 nations signed the Multilateral Debt Relief Initiative, committing themselves to cancelling the debt of eighteen of the most heavily indebted countries.[68]

---

[67] <http://www.globalissues.org/TradeRelated/SAP.asp>. See also World Development Movement press release, "New Report shows IMF Poverty Reduction Plans are 'Barrier to pro-poor policies'", 26 June 2000, <http://www.wdm.org.uk/news/presrel/current/PRSP_critique.htm>.

[68] The G8, or Group of Eight, consists of seven of the world's leading industrialised democratic nations (Canada, France, Germany, Italy, Japan, the United Kingdom and the United States), plus Russia.

On World Debt Day, 16 May 2006, Jubilee Australia called for "debt relief to be extended to 66 countries and made a strong case for cancelling the debts of Indonesia, the Philippines and Bangladesh" (Bhandari 2006). The Inter Press Service News Agency reported:

> Almost 80 million Filipinos, Indonesians and Bangladeshis are living on less than one dollar a day. These countries have massive debts, mostly incurred by former "corrupt" regimes, and lack sufficient funds to address the health and educational requirements of their large populations.
>
> Indonesia and the Philippines spend three times more on debt repayments than on health and education [Bhandari 2006].

While Australia agreed to cancel 80 per cent of Iraq's debt by 2008 and to participate in the debt deal forged at the G8 Summit, it does not accept that the debts incurred by corrupt regimes are worthy of cancellation (Bhandari 2006).

Much of the debt owed by African nations, also, is the result of past corrupt regimes and, as Stephen Lewis explains, it is the requirement to keep on paying off those debts that keeps current governments in extreme poverty.

> It may seem hard to believe, but between 1970 and 2002, Africa acquired $294 billion of debt. Much of the debt was assumed by military dictators who profited beyond the dreams of avarice, and left for the people of their countries, the crushing burden of payment.
>
> Over the same period, it paid back $260 billion mostly in interest. At the end of it all, Africa continued to owe upwards of $230 billion in debt. Surely that is the definition of international economic obscenity. Here you have the poorest continent in the world paying off its debt, again and again, and forever being grotesquely in hock [2005, p. 22].

Dorothy Makasa, a Zambian woman now living in Australia, tells of the difference debt relief has made already to countries like Zambia and Tanzania. On a visit to Zambia, she saw with her own eyes how "pro-active" governments were "using debt relief funds for lifting people from poverty". She goes on to say that this "raises hope, but developed nations must do more and cancel all debt" (Bhandari 2006).[69]

While anti-poverty campaigners were heartened to see, in 2005, that G8 nations were serious about their desire to "make poverty history" by continuing to work toward the millennium goals set in 2000, the global financial crisis which began in July 2007 placed question marks over the

---

69 See also "A Case for Debt Relief", Research Paper, Jubilee Australia, May 2006, <http://www.jubileeaustralia.org/files/_730_reports/A%20Case%20for%20Debt%20Relief.pdf>.

future of the campaign. They noted that the bail-out of Wall Street by the US government represented an amount far greater than the combined budgets of many of the poorer nations of the world. In an interview with *Age* journalist Doug Conway, anti-poverty campaigners Simon Moss and Hugh Evans said:

> The Bush plan to underwrite $US700 billion worth of bad loans has a price tag that surpasses the combined gross national products of the 26 countries that make up middle and western Africa.
>
> Great gains have been made ... But at the rate we're going, we will fail to meet the UN millennium development goals that we set in 2000 in order to halve extreme poverty by 2015 [Conway 2009].

They expressed alarm that G8 countries were lagging far behind the targets they set for themselves.

> At last year's landmark UN meeting on poverty, Prime Minister Kevin Rudd and other world leaders were told that, at the half way point to the target date of 2015, the richest G8 countries had delivered only 14 per cent of their promised aid increase [Conway 2009].

It is not difficult to see how whole nations as well as individual citizens are silenced by poverty. Any nation forced to focus on repaying the interest on its debt over and over is forever in a state of powerlessness and inferiority in relation to other nations—and therefore silenced. Individual citizens living in poverty with little or no access to basic health and education are silenced by the need to focus day after day on their own family's survival. Such poverty affects women in far greater numbers than men because men in poverty-stricken countries fall into one of two categories: those who have given up hope and those who continue to hope.

Men who succumb to their oppressed and demoralised situation and simply give up hope will either stay at home drinking (if they have access to alcohol) or spend their days socialising with other men. The expectation is that their wives and children will go to the village or nearby town every day to beg and search for food. In desperation, some of those women turn to prostitution. A fact which intensifies the feelings of desperation in women is that, in such situations, the incidence of men's violence against them in the home is often high. Not only do women have to endure the indignity of begging or prostitution but also the abuse and violence of their frustrated husbands.

Men who maintain hope in circumstances of extreme poverty often have to leave home in search of work. The intention is to send money home regularly to sustain their families, but the reality often is that wages are low and men who give priority to their own needs for food, alcohol and gambling find that they have little or nothing left to send home. Again, women are forced into begging or prostitution in order to be able to feed their children.

Overwhelmingly, the victims of poverty are women and children. While many women would like to rail against the injustice of it all, the daily desperate quest for survival is a very effective silencer.

Migrant domestic workers

Today's international trade and economic imperatives have opened up another type of "job opportunity" for women from developing countries attempting to escape poverty for themselves and their families—that of migrant domestic workers. The phenomenon of couples from wealthy countries employing women from countries like the Philippines and Indonesia as domestic workers, maids and nannies is fraught with danger for women taking up those positions.

Although it is almost impossible to get a true picture of the situation of migrant workers around the world, Human Rights Watch reported in 2005 that the situation of women migrant workers was of particular concern. In a report on women from poor Asian countries who migrate to Singapore for work, they highlight many and varied abuses, including death, forced confinement, restricted communication, low wages, unpaid wages, physical abuse, sexual abuse and harassment, verbal abuse and threats, food deprivation, and restrictions on religious freedom (Human Rights Watch 2005). In addition to Singapore, Human Rights Watch also names Malaysia and Saudi Arabia as countries where women migrant workers are "especially vulnerable to abuse, including trafficking and forced labor".[70]

In a letter to the governments of Malaysia and Indonesia, dated 15 April 2006, Human Rights Watch urged the two governments to negotiate a memorandum of understanding aimed at protecting the approximately 300,000 Indonesian domestic workers employed in Malaysia. After acknowledging the mutual benefit of such an arrangement for both countries, the letter goes on to say:

> Despite the critical role these women play to support families in both Malaysia and Indonesia, they often encounter grave abuses during recruitment, training, transit, employment, and return.
>
> Indonesian domestic workers are excluded from key provisions in Malaysia's Employment Act of 1955, denying them protections enjoyed by all other workers. These include a weekly day off, a limit on working hours per week, and annual leave. In addition, many domestic workers

---

70 <http://www.hrw.org/women/labor.html>.

experience flagrant abuses such as unpaid wages, restrictions on freedom of movement, physical abuse, and abuses committed by recruitment and employment agencies.[71]

A report presented in 2003 by the Fédération Internationale des Ligues des Droits de l'Homme and the Egyptian Organisation for Human Rights to the International Committee on the Elimination of Racial Discrimination points to the particular vulnerability of migrant women working in Saudi Arabia.

> In Saudi Arabia, migrant women are often subject to forced confinement, in violation of the right to freedom of movement (article 5.d.i). Female domestic workers are often forbidden to ever leave the house in which they work for the entire duration of their stay in Saudi Arabia, thus living in near total isolation ...
>
> In addition to being overworked, underpaid, and often held in complete isolation inside the household, female domestic workers are sometimes physically abused and raped by their employers.[72]

There is concern in the Philippines, too, about the treatment of Filipina migrant domestic workers. In October 2005, a Filipina who had been studying in Australia wrote to the f-agenda discussion list:

> Since I arrived [back home] on the last week of July, there were three Filipina domestic helpers in other countries, who were reported dead. One was in Hong Kong who fall down from a high building whose employer alleged as a case of suicide. The other is in Spain whose throat was cut. The last one was in Singapore where her body was cut into many parts. One of them was a school teacher. It is too painful for the family to receive this news that their daughters who strive hard to help the family were killed in those ways.
>
> Yesterday, our local community and school were shocked to hear that our former student who went to Lebanon to work as a domestic helper was imprisoned by the Lebanese airport personnel because she was found to have gold jewelleries in her luggage. She wrote to her parents that her employer maltreated her and tried raping her. She was able to escape from her employer but was held in the airport in coming back.

Analysing the situation poor families in the Philippines find themselves in, she went on to say:

> What else can Filipinas do in this sick and poor country? The poverty is being pushed to women to bear and find ways how to survive. Yet when they find alternatives like going to other countries to work as maids, rather

---

71 <http://hrw.org/english/docs/2006/04/14/malays13184.htm>.
72 <http://www.fidh.org/intgouv/onu/rapport/2003/sa0103a.pdf>.

than in prostitution, it is still no escape from the reality that women from poor countries are considered as animals by the prevailing patriarchal and rich countries.[73]

Responding to this, another member from the Philippines remarked that this only reflects "the reported cases which get media attention. This means that we do not know the real number of Filipina workers who may have died, more so those which were murdered or disappeared". She went on:

> Domestic workers could be raped and prostituted. There is of course a very thin line between these two; though what is publicized in the news especially our local media is when the woman resists rape and gets killed, or kills the perpetrator in self-defence. I wonder at how many other women are just forced to keep quiet to maintain their jobs, or in fear for their lives.
>
> This does not happen to Filipina workers only. Workers from Indonesia, Pakistan, Bangladesh, India, and other countries in the wrong side of the globalized economy do experience the abuses from the so-called rich countries.[74]

The Centre for Women's Research in Colombo, Sri Lanka, works to raise awareness of the treatment of Sri Lankan women who migrate, particularly to Middle Eastern countries, for work. The following are just two of the many examples of abuse suffered at the hands of employers. In Saudi Arabia:

> The case of H. B. Kusumawathie, the Sri Lankan housemaid who was brought back from Saudi Arabia after acid was forced down her throat by her employer brought into focus once again the violence migrant workers have to face in an alien country. Kusumawathie, a 43-year-old from Kelankutiya, a village near Kekirawa in the North Central Province of Sri Lanka, was one of an estimated 100,000 housemaids who are working overseas, mainly in Middle Eastern countries. She has been scarred for life and has to survive on liquids as her esophagus has been completely destroyed by the acid. This is just one of the many instances of violence against women which take the form of rape, torture, sexual harassment as well as harsh working conditions and inhuman treatment.
>
> Some like Kusumawathie return to Sri Lanka maimed, crippled, scarred and battered. Some others come back in a coffin.[75]

---

73   Email to f-agenda discussion list, 26 October 2005, quoted with author's permission, with a request for anonymity.
74   Email to f-agenda discussion list, 26 October 2005, quoted with author's permission, with a request for anonymity.
75   <http://www.cenwor.lk/migrantwomen.html>.

In Kuwait:

> According to newspaper reports a Sri Lankan housemaid was tortured and killed by her employer in Kuwait. The victim is still unidentified.
> Driven by poverty, Sri Lankan housemaids slave in Middle East homes despite insults, ill treatment, torture, and harassment by members of the employers' households. The families of the housemaids are dependent on their earnings.[76]

Under the present international economic system, women from poor nations will continue to take risks in search of relief from poverty for their families. As one of the Filipinas quoted above put it: "What else can Filipinas do in this sick and poor country? The poverty is being pushed to women to bear and find ways how to survive." While the poor put their lives in danger, with little attention given by employers or governments to their working conditions, the rich are the ones who reap the most benefit under current international trade and economic systems.

Sweatshop workers

Sweatshops have been a concern of unions, feminists and other human rights groups for many years. Well-organised campaigns by groups operating under various names, such as No Sweat, Sweatshop Watch, FairWear, Wal-Mart Watch and United Students Against Sweatshops, have had some degree of success with individual manufacturers. The emphasis on globalisation and international trade agreements, however, has seen a rise in oppressive and unjust working conditions by major companies around the world. When challenged by factories wanting to do the right thing by their employees, they simply withdraw their business and take it offshore to countries where sweatshop conditions are tolerated.

> In 1995, the exposure of two sweatshops operating in and for the United States put the spotlight back on the issue of sweatshop labour. Julie Su, labor rights activist and founder of Sweatshop Watch, led the fight to free 72 Thai garment workers who were enslaved for years in an apartment complex in El Monte, California, and served as lead counsel in a federal lawsuit against the manufacturers and retailers involved [Su 1997].[77]

On the ZNet website, David Swanson reported on a sweatshop workers' tour of US colleges, designed to raise the awareness of students and staff. Writing on 26 February 2006, he said:

---

76 <http://www.cenwor.lk/housemaid.html>.
77 <http://www.everyhumanhasrights.org/julie-su>.

> Josefina Hernandez Ponce is a worker and union leader from the Mex Mode factory (formerly Kukdong) in Puebla, Mexico. Hernandez Ponce said that when companies come to what they call third-world countries, the governments there, including hers in Mexico, do not require that they obey the nation's labor laws.

She told students at the University of Virginia: "It would take half our salary to buy one of the sweatshirts we produce". For every University of Virginia sweatshirt sold at a cost of $39.99, the worker gets 20 cents in pay. Hernandez Ponce told the students that when Mex Mode began responding to union demands to increase salaries and reduce their exploitation of workers, Nike reduced its orders.

> ... Mex Mode was doing well until a year ago, when Nike reduced its orders from 100,000 pieces per month to 25,000. Nike argues that Mex Mode is too expensive. When the WTO's quota system ended in January of 2005, Nike and others began shifting more work to China and Vietnam, and other countries that openly violate workers' rights. Nike has work in 152 factories in China and 12 in Mexico. In 11 of the factories in Mexico, workers have few if any rights.[78]

A major report titled "Sweatshops and Globalisation: An Activist Response", prepared by No Sweat in Britain, has a section on female sweatshop workers. The focus on women begins with the example of Sonia, "a garment worker and union organiser in El Salvador", who lives with her five-year-old daughter who needs expensive medicines to deal with certain health problems.

> Sonia works from 6.45am to 4pm for the minimum wage, $30 per week. Usually she can buy rice, beans, sugar, vegetables and soup. Occasionally she can afford a little chicken. When it was cheaper, she used to be able to buy milk ...
> Sonia's company, Apple Tree, a Korean-owned company, forbids workers to talk to each other or to leave the production area. The toilets are disgustingly dirty and the workers are only allowed to use them twice a day.
> Women, the majority of the workforce, are vulnerable to verbal and physical abuse. They must undergo forced pregnancy testing ... and sexual harassment from managers, including demands for sex.[79]

---

78 <http://www.zmag.org/content/showarticle.cfm?SectionID=19&ItemID=9804>.
79 <http://www.nosweat.org.uk/files/Sweatshops_&_Globalisation.pd>.

In Australia the FairWear campaign, operating under the slogan "Stopping the exploitation of homebased outworkers", pushes for fairer working conditions and also "encourages Australians to think critically about where the clothes we wear are produced and under what conditions". They report:

> Homeworkers are mostly women who make clothes at home in Australia for as little as $2 to $3 an hour. They often work up to 18 hours a day, 7 days a week. Homeworkers make clothes for our major retailers, designers and even suppliers of school uniforms. It is estimated that there are 300,000 outworkers in Australia today.[80]

Sweatshops in the United States, the United Kingdom and Australia usually rely on women from newly arrived immigrant communities who can be easily exploited. "Racism, language, and insecure immigration status are used to keep them isolated and unable to fight back."[81]

Women and men who are desperate for work usually operate on the assumption that low-paid work is better than no work at all, and are unwilling to complain about the exploitative practices of employers. Wherever large companies choose to operate sweatshops, in wealthy countries with migrant workers or in developing countries, they know that the desperate personal circumstances of workers will ensure their silence and cooperation.

Present-day international trade and economic imperatives are designed to favour wealthy nations, companies and individuals, while the poor are locked into poverty through unemployment, under-employment and exploitative working conditions. The daily struggle for survival guarantees their silence.

The language of corporate governance

This relatively recent form of silencing, discussed in more detail in Chapter Four, is mentioned here because it is one of the "new" tactics used quite effectively today to silence women.

Women working in areas which have come to be known as the "women's sector"[82] always interpreted their role as offering support, counselling, advice, information and a safe place for women who contact their service for help. Also, in line with the democratic principle of "equal participation", government funding bodies encouraged workers to advocate on behalf of

---

80 <http://www.fairwear.org.au/engine.php>.
81 <http://www.nosweat.org.uk/files/Sweatshops_&_Globalisation.pd>.
82 The women's sector has historically included services aimed at responding to the needs of women, such as women's refuges and shelters, sexual assault support services, domestic violence support services, women's health centres, women's information and referral services. These NGOs have been established and staffed mainly by women who are feminist, or at least committed to working with women according to feminist principles.

those who use their services and to lobby politicians so that governments could be kept informed of the situation of women in need.

All that changed in Australia. During the years of the Howard government, federal and state governments funded women's services only to respond to women's immediate needs. Advocacy or political lobbying on behalf of the poor or homeless or victims of men's violence was discouraged and could have resulted in the defunding of a service. Then, after the federal government under Kevin Rudd had been in office for more than twelve months, the constraint against advocacy was removed. On 29 April 2009, Prime Minister Rudd launched "Time for Action", the report of the National Council to Reduce Violence against Women and Children. In his speech, he called for a "national conversation". He said: "Silence can no longer be tolerated because violence can no longer be tolerated. And violence prospers in the silence". Calling on everyone to work together, he continued: "The challenge for all of us, government at all levels, you in the community sector and each one of you as the young people and as the future of our nation, lies in this—to act together to make a difference. Personally, socially, institutionally, politically, in all that you do and all that you say". [83]

While the Rudd government has moved to reinstate the role of advocacy, the continued dominance of market forces means that governments of all persuasions still favour the corporatising of human services and such services are still required to operate according to "a corporate model of governance". This requires that "the delivery of social and human service outputs are defined and quantified in ways that blame charity organisations for not doing more with less" (Bonisteel and Green 2005, p. 2). Canadian researchers Bonisteel and Green explain that the requirement to "do more with less" results in the silencing of service-users as well as service-providers.

> Poverty and lack of access to basic commodities such as housing and adequate food, divert people from criticizing government agendas, even if temporarily. Add the silencing of their advocates and the result is the replacement of the social justice community with insular policy makers [2005, p. 13].

Because the language of corporate governance does silence all who work for or seek help from NGOs, not only those in the women's sector, Chapter Four discusses this form of silencing in more detail.

---

[83] See <http://www.fahcsia.gov.au/about/news/2009/Pages/TimeforActiontoReduceViolenceAgainstWomenandChildren.aspx>.

In the name of community and cultural solidarity

Silencing on the basis of "gender" always exists alongside the silencing which occurs on the basis of race, class, ethnic origin, physical and mental ability, age, sexual preference and so on. As discussed in the Introduction and in Chapter Five, there are always debates about which area of oppression is central for someone who is, say, female, Indigenous and poor. Radical feminists believe that her oppression as a woman is central; socialists and other human rights activists focus on poverty; Indigenous men, some Indigenous women and some non-Indigenous human rights activists focus on race. While not wanting to be diverted into a full discussion of that debate here, it seems important to draw attention to the analysis by Australian feminist Denise Thompson, who points out that the main weakness in most race, class and gender debates is that any reference to domination has been deleted.

> There is no identifiable ruling class; the debate focuses exclusively on categories of the oppressed who are subjected to power relations which are never located in the vested interests of the powerful. If, in contrast, we enter the debate by recognizing the existence of male supremacy in the first place, then it is possible to identify the social system of meanings and values by which domination is maintained [2001, p. 126].

Thompson points out that the politically neutral word "gender" is problematic because it fails to draw attention to the fact that men have a monopoly on power and, as a consequence, women are rendered powerless. She sees a problem, too, with "entering the debate from the standpoint of resistance to capitalist domination or to racial supremacy", the problem being that both perspectives suffer from "ignoring or subordinating the interests of women". "Bringing feminist insights to bear on race and class domination keeps political attention focused on women, attention which is too easily diverted given the ongoing reality of the male monopolization of who counts as 'human'" (2001, pp. 126, 127).

Indigenous Australian academic and activist Jackie Huggins comes at the debate from a totally different perspective. She is highly critical of what she calls the white middle-class feminist movement and acuses feminists of wanting to divert the attention of Indigenous women away from their central oppression, which is "racial domination". After an article by Diane Bell and Topsy Napurrula Nelson titled "Speaking about Rape is Everyone's Business" was published in *Women's Studies International Forum*, Huggins was one of twelve Indigenous Australian women who signed a letter to the editor of the journal objecting to the article:

> We continually find we are being jockeyed into the position of fighting and separating from our men and we will not. We are women and men together who have suffered grave injustices by the white invaders. We have all suffered ... Sexism does not and will never prevail over racial domination in this country [Huggins et al. 1991, p. 506].

Huggins has more recently acknowledged the existence of intra-racial violence against women, but the demand for racial and cultural solidarity is still strong among oppressed Indigenous communities. Although such a demand is understandable, it often means that women who want to speak out about men's violence against them and about the sexual abuse of children by men in their communities are silenced. Also, Indigenous women such as Boni Robertson from Griffith University in Brisbane, who headed a Women's Task Force on Violence (Queensland Government 1999), are often accused of betraying their own people, and attempts are made to silence them.

Similarly, women from newly settled migrant or refugee families are counselled by elders in their communities to be silent about their experiences of domestic violence and rape. When a woman who has come to Australia under the Integrated Humanitarian Settlement Scheme from, say, Sudan, complains to the police or seeks assistance from a domestic violence service about her husband's violence toward her, she is generally counselled by members of the Sudanese community to keep the problem within their own community. She is to take her complaint to the community's elders so that they can help sort out the issues between the couple. There are two problems with that suggestion. One is that a man's violence against his partner is usually not a sign of relationship problems which can easily be sorted out with the intervention of others, but rather a sign of the man's need to dominate and willingness to use violence to get his own way. The other problem is that the governing elders in any African cultural group will most likely be men (who could, in fact, be perpetrators of violence in their own homes). It follows that, if a woman succumbs to the silencing and shares her concerns only with community elders, she will most likely be counselled to stay with the perpetrator where, statistics show, the violence will continue.

The necessary first step for women wanting to be free of the cycle of violence against them is, as always, to find the courage to break the silence. In the case of women from countries where men's violence against women is culturally sanctioned, however, this is no small step to take. Cultural solidarity is a powerful force in the lives of those who find themselves in a strange land, and the threat of disapproval and ostracism from their own community is enough to silence even the strongest women. For many women, however, the desire to be free of violence and subordination by breaking their silence is even stronger.

Another form of silencing occurring in the name of community or cultural solidarity is that which says "not yet". The experience of women around the world who have joined their brothers in the fight for independence (for instance, for Zimbabwe from Britain and East Timor from Indonesia) is that they were continually advised to wait till independence was achieved before expecting the issue of women's equality with men to be discussed. When independence was finally achieved, however, no such discussions ever took place. The spoils of the battle—positions in the new government and the privilege of being involved in decision-making—went to the men. Apart from one or two token women, those women who fought as hard as the men for independence were simply brushed aside.

In Afghanistan, as already quoted, one of the women chosen to be on the transitional government silenced women activists with the words: "Let the men get along first, then we will get involved ... Until our country has been rescued, the women's issue is a non-issue" (quoted in Nawa 2002, p. 177).

Another example of the "not yet" form of silencing was described in a flyer handed out all over Israel by member organisations of the Coalition of Women for Peace on the thirty-seventh anniversary of Israel's occupation of Palestinian lands. It is quoted by Israeli peace and human rights activist Gila Svirsky in her article "Working to Break the Silence", and demonstrates the "not yet" tactic for silencing women when war is the main agenda:

Shhhhhhhh, security!

They tell us not to speak of unemployment,
because the security situation is so bad.

They tell us not to talk about the municipal
workers who haven't received their salaries, or
sexual violence, or hungry children, not right now,
because we're at war and there's no one to talk to.

And not about the corruption of politicians,
because we'll soon be leaving Gaza.

And not about selling the country to the
World Bank at end-of-season prices,
because who knows anything about that bank and
anyway we're in the midst of war.

And not about foreign workers,
racism,
clean air and water,
selling women into bondage,
road accidents,
or breast cancer.

WE ARE FURIOUS
ABOUT THE OCCUPATION

and about

The capitalists who create this war,
The generals who continue to sleep well at night,
And the governments of occupation that bring us
more and more
destruction, killing, and hate,

37 YEARS OF OCCUPATION AND OPPRESSION ARE

37 YEARS TOO MANY! [Svirsky 2004]

The silencing of women in the name of community and cultural solidarity can be interpreted, in almost every instance, as the preferencing of the agenda of men over that of women.

In the name of anti-racism and cultural inclusiveness

Men and women who position themselves on the left of politics or advocate for human rights are often ridiculed by those on the right as being "politically correct" or "PC" for their attempts to address the needs of racial and ethnic minorities for equality and justice. Working to bridge the gap between the haves and have-nots, between the powerful and powerless, between mainstream and minorities is an honourable endeavour but, at times, those who attempt to be culturally inclusive are criticised, also, by others on the left and groups within the cultural communities they are seeking to support.

Radical, political feminists in Australia (both Aboriginal and non-Aboriginal) are highly critical of attempts to support Aboriginal traditional "law" when such traditional law supports and perpetuates men's right to abuse women and girls. Human rights advocates who insist that Aboriginal tribal law be considered alongside mainstream law when judging the behaviour of Aboriginal people, seem happy to turn a blind eye to the suffering caused to victims of certain so-called "traditional" behaviours.

A glaring example of injustice in the name of cultural inclusiveness is the leniency with which a Supreme Court judge treated a 55-year-old Aboriginal tribal elder who raped and sodomised a 14-year-old Aboriginal girl in the Northern Territory in 2004. Following the assault, the girl reported her four-day ordeal to police, who subsequently arrested the man. When the case came to court in August 2005, Northern Territory Supreme Court Chief Justice Brian Martin heard the facts of the case against the elder referred to as GJ.

It was June 18, 2004, in school holidays. The girl was in Year 9 and had a boyfriend her own age. Word spread about the community that the boy and girl had stayed together that night and, perhaps, had sex. This appeared to give rise to an urgency among the involved elders to fast-track and consummate the girl's promised marriage. The girl's grandmother told her she had to go with a person she barely knew and considered to be "an old man".

The girl's grandmother and GJ went and found the girl the next morning. The grandmother took the girl outside of the house where she was staying; GJ struck the girl hard over the shoulders and back with a pair of boomerangs.

It was decreed the child would be taken to GJ's outstation. The child did not want to go and pleaded with the grandmother that she not be sent away with GJ. "Rather than help the child," said Martin, "the grandmother packed personal belongings for her, including her school bag, and insisted that the child go with you [GJ]. The child was forced to get into your car, where she sat with your first wife and two other persons. The child was crying and shaking."

That evening, at the outstation, GJ dragged the child by the leg and into a bedroom. GJ's wife and children went to another room [Toohey 2005].

The court heard that GJ beat her with a boomerang, pushed her on to a mattress, turned her so that she was lying on her stomach, and then had anal intercourse with her. All the while leading up to the rape, the child "kicked and screamed and resisted". In his summing-up the judge said:

> While the child was lying on her stomach you had anal intercourse with her. During intercourse the child was frightened and crying. She was in pain. You injured the child. You caused a deep laceration at the edge of her anus. The child was later seen by a doctor and the examination also revealed painful areas over the child's body ...
>
> The child later told the police that she was "at that old man's place for four days", and that she was crying "from Saturday to Tuesday". She knew that she was promised to you in the Aboriginal traditional way, but she did not like you. In the words of the child, "I told that old man I'm too young for sex, but he didn't listen" [Toohey 2005].

While the charges against this perpetrator should have been for serious assault and rape of a minor, he was actually charged with the lesser crimes of unlawful assault and unlawful sexual intercourse. In sentencing him, the judge appears to have bent over backwards to show respect for Aboriginal law and culture (even though there is nothing in Aboriginal law which condones anal intercourse, let alone anal rape). He said: "I have a great deal of sympathy for you and the difficulties attached to transition from traditional Aboriginal culture and laws as you understood them to be, to obeying the

Northern Territory law ... The shortest period I can see fit to impose is that you serve one month" (Toohey 2005). One month's gaol for serious assault, imprisonment for four days, rape and anal rape of a minor surely represents a gross miscarriage of justice by a well-meaning judge intent on displaying his anti-racist and culturally aware credentials. The girl's pleas for justice were ignored and silenced by the judge's need to support a man for whom he felt "sympathy". Subsequently, the case was sent to the Court of Appeal and the sentence increased to three years with a mandatory eighteen months to serve.[84]

Another example of the silencing of women in the name of anti-racism and cultural inclusiveness is that highlighted by a group of Muslim women at the World Social Forum in Porto Alegre in January 2005 (referred to in Chapter Two). The international solidarity network Women Living Under Muslim Laws called on left-wing forces in the West, including feminists, to stop the trend toward supporting the fundamentalist agenda. Any support for fundamentalism in an effort to prove one's anti-racist stance and cultural awareness, they explained, is support for the silencing of women.

---

84   See Law Council of Australia 2006.

SILENCING DISSENTING VOICES 4

The silencing of women, described in some detail in the previous chapter, is part of a larger system designed to silence anyone who challenges the values of the dominant group in any given society. Politicians, media owners and business leaders whose hold on power is threatened by "noisy" dissenters, work to punish, exclude and silence anyone who dares to speak out against them. Indeed, those whose increasing power and wealth depend on war, economic globalisation, the exploitation of workers or the violation and subordination of women, collude with each other to silence those who raise their voices in protest. Such protesters include peace activists calling for non-violent solutions, anti-globalisation activists demanding a fairer distribution of the world's wealth, trade union activists fighting for the rights of workers, as well as feminist activists agitating for justice for women and children.

While the rhetoric of governments in so-called democratic countries supports the principle of freedom of speech as the cornerstone of democracy and all sections of the media demand freedom of the press, there is a certain degree of hypocrisy in their relationship to such freedoms. On the one hand, governments and media express the view that censorship is unacceptable in a democracy;[85] on the other hand, they have no hesitation in censoring those who hold views that differ from their own.

In this chapter, I will discuss the two main strategies used by those in power to silence dissenting voices: systematic silencing through manipulation of the minds of the general population, and targeted silencing.

Systematic silencing

Systematic silencing through mind manipulation, thought control or indoctrination is a serious accusation when levelled at governments that claim to be democratic but, as will be seen, there is plenty of historical evidence to support the accusation in relation to countries such as the United States, the United Kingdom and Australia. In line with the discussion in Chapter One on the dumbing-down of society, governments intent on keeping power firmly

---

85 In line with the argument for truth, all ideas, opinions and behaviours are to be allowed in the "marketplace". See Chapter One.

in their own hands devise strategies aimed at manipulating the minds of the masses with the express purpose of minimising the potential for dissent. This is done mainly through the use of propaganda, fear and carefully constructed language, three activities which are so intertwined and interdependent as to defy their discussion as separate entities. For our purposes here, however, it is important to consider each of them separately in an attempt to analyse and understand them as the foremost ingredients of mind manipulation.

Propaganda

There are three main players in the production and distribution of propaganda for the purpose of controlling the masses: the government as producers of propaganda, the media as reporters of propaganda, and industry as both producers and financial supporters of propaganda. "Controlling the general population has always been a dominant concern for power and privilege", says Noam Chomsky, who goes on to illustrate his point with examples from history. In seventeenth-century England, those who enjoyed power and privilege referred to themselves as "men of best quality" and to the masses who were agitating for a greater say in the affairs of the country as a "giddy multitude of beasts in men's shapes". Three centuries later, in the early years of the twentieth century, US President Woodrow Wilson expressed similar ideas. By then, though, the elite sector in both the United Kingdom and the United States realised that the crude, blatantly repressive techniques of the past would no longer work and that "it would be necessary to devise new means to tame the beast, primarily through control of opinion and attitude" (Chomsky 2003, pp. 5, 6).[86]

How does propaganda work? Governments intent on swaying entire populations and bringing them around to accepting the views of the power elite usually follow a similar course. First, they set up a top-level committee or ministry within government, or alternatively purchase the services of public relations companies or approved think tanks and charge them with the task of working closely with government to create and manage propaganda. Second, they appropriate and attach their own meanings to terms already in use, repeating them over and over to ensure that the government's way of thinking penetrates the minds of all citizens. Other strategies employed by politicians which seem mandatory if propaganda is to be effective include: never admit a mistake; perfect the art of diverting attention from issues the public may find unpalatable; and be prepared to lie and deceive.

---

[86] For more on the situation in the seventeenth century and Wilsonian idealism, see Chomsky 1991a, 1999.

Set up (official or unofficial) arms of government to manage propaganda
The discussion here relies heavily on the writings of Noam Chomsky whose influential work in this area has inspired much-needed analysis of the role of propaganda in society.

Throughout recent history, there are many examples of committees, commissions, ministries and institutions established and supported by governments for the purpose of manipulating the minds of citizens. The United Kingdom led the way early in the twentieth century, setting up a Ministry of Information whose task it was "to direct the thought of most of the world". In the United States, Woodrow Wilson established a Committee on Public Information whose first task was to "coordinate wartime propaganda" with the aim of "whipping the population into war fever". One member of Wilson's committee was leading American journalist Walter Lippmann. In his essays on democracy, Lippmann had introduced the term "manufacture of consent" to describe the need for the power elite to conduct propaganda campaigns so that "responsible men" who are the proper decision-makers could "live free of the trampling and the roar of a bewildered herd" (in Chomsky 2003, p. 6).[87] Chomsky, in *Media Control: The Spectacular Achievements of Propaganda*, defines the phrase "manufacture of consent" as "to bring about agreement on the part of the public for things that they didn't want by the new techniques of propaganda" (1991, pp. 14–15).

In 1988, Edward Herman and Noam Chomsky borrowed Lippmann's phrase and titled their book on the analysis of the role of the mass media in the dissemination of propaganda, *Manufacturing Consent: The Political Economy of the Mass Media* (1988). A central concern expressed by the authors in the preface is:

> If ... the powerful are able to fix the premises of discourse, to decide what the general populace is allowed to see, hear, and think about, and to "manage" public opinion by regular propaganda campaigns, the standard view of how the system works is at serious odds with reality [p. lix].

Most people think they know "how the system works" and are content to trust their leaders, but the insidious nature of propaganda is such that most have no awareness of how their thoughts and emotions are being manipulated. Any suggestions that things might not be as they seem are readily criticised by the trusting majority as "conspiracy theories".

When President Ronald Reagan took office in 1981, his administration established the Office of Public Diplomacy whose task, according to Chomsky, was "to manufacture consent for its murderous policies in Central America" (2003, p. 8). One of their first moves was to label it a "war on terror" and to

---

87 See also Lippmann 1921.

present the "offending" Central American countries as rebels and terrorists who needed to be brought under control. The United States was then able to "come to the rescue" and President Reagan was hailed by US citizens as a strong and decisive leader.[88] Even though the "record of murder, torture, and devastation was extensively reported by human rights organizations, church groups, Latin American scholars, and many others..." (Chomsky 2003, p. 9), the truth was largely hidden from the general population.

How was it possible to hide the truth from US citizens when the atrocities being inflicted in their name were occurring just south of them in Central America? As Chomsky explained in an interview with David Barsamian, hiding the truth from the people was and is made possible by a very effective propaganda machine: "...one of the main purposes of the indoctrination system [is] to prevent the population from understanding what they are participating in indirectly through the institutions that they support" (Chomsky 1992, p. 17).

Atrocities committed or supported by the United States have continued under successive presidents (both Democratic and Republican), a fact which, thanks to powerful propaganda machines and a burgeoning public relations industry, has been effectively hidden from the American public. After the tragedy of 9/11, distraught and bewildered individual US citizens were heard to ask: "Why do they hate Americans so much? What have we ever done to them?"

When George W. Bush became president in 2001, he chose to recycle many of the neo-conservatives from the Reagan and Bush I administrations.[89] They became a powerful "inner circle" responsible, with the help of the media and public relations personnel, for generating propaganda. In Australia the government of John Howard relied heavily on the right-leaning media as well as on a right-wing, corporate-funded think tank called the Institute of Public Affairs (IPA) for the creation and distribution of propaganda.

The media

In a critique of the close association between the media and the Howard government, political journalist Margo Kingston pointed out that Australia has "the narrowest media-ownership profile in the Western world", dominated as it is by two individual proprietors, Rupert Murdoch and Kerry

---

88 These tactics were so successful that they were employed again by President George W. Bush to justify the post-9/11 wars against Afghanistan and Iraq.

89 Bush I refers to the presidency of George H.W. Bush, Bush II to that of his son, George W. Bush. One member of the inner circle was Donald Rumsfeld, Reagan's "special envoy to the Middle East during the first phase of the war on terrorism". In George W. Bush's team, as secretary of defense, he was "running the military component of the second phase of the war on terrorism" (Chomsky 1991b, p. 71).

Packer (2004, p. 99).[90] In the United States, Rupert Murdoch's Fox News was called the "number-one American propaganda outlet" when a former employee, Charlie Reina, exposed the direct link between President Bush's administration and the Murdoch news. He revealed that, every morning, an "Executive Memo" would be distributed electronically, telling newsroom personnel which stories would be covered and how. "The Memo was born with the Bush administration early in 2001..." (Kingston 2004, p. 95).

Focusing on Rupert Murdoch's influence in Australia, Margo Kingston explains:

> Here he controls 70 per cent of our newspapers, including our only national daily, and with Kerry Packer now jointly owns Foxtel, Australia's only viable pay TV network. Packer in turn owns Australia's commercial TV powerhouse, the Nine Network [2004, p. 99].

In the introduction to a collection of essays called *Do Not Disturb: Is the Media Failing Australia?*, Robert Manne expresses a "growing unease at the active complicity of some parts of the mainstream media" in what he calls "a creeping conservative counter-revolution in public sensitivity" occurring in Australia for more than a decade. One of the reasons for this unease, he says, is "the almost ludicrous dominance over the metropolitan press that Rupert Murdoch's News Corporation has been allowed to assume" (2005, pp. 1, 2).

Guy Rundle, in the same anthology, comments on the noticeable shift which occurred in Murdoch's politics and, consequently, in his approach to his newspapers:

> By the mid-1990s it was clear that he had taken on many of the values of the right ... Increasingly his papers began to propagate a world-view that combined economic neo-liberalism with social conservatism and to adopt a tone that was less inclined to foster a debate between contending social visions than it was to assert its own plain "common sense" against a range of whacky ideas [Rundle 2005, p. 34].

Throughout the term of the Howard government, journalists with the Murdoch press continued to present their own conservative slant on events as "common sense" and criticise dissenting minorities as "whacky" and "out of touch".

---

90 Following the death of Kerry Packer in December 2005, control of the Packer media empire passed to his son, James Packer who, in October 2008, proceeded to sever his links with his late father's media empire by resigning from the board of PBL Media. See <<http://www.guardian.co.uk/media/2008/oct/27/mediabusiness-pressandpublishing>>.

The Institute of Public Affairs

In addition to the right-wing media, Prime Minister John Howard and his cabinet relied heavily on the IPA in the creation and distribution of propaganda. Based in Melbourne, it has close historical links with the Liberal Party and its key policy positions were reflected in those of the Liberal Party under Howard: "advocacy for privatisation, deregulation, reduction in the power of unions and denial of most significant environmental problems, including climate change".[91]

The IPA was established in 1943 by Charles Kemp and a group of businessmen who had a degree of influence on Robert Menzies during his years as leader of the Opposition and then during his second term as Australia's prime minister from 1949 to 1966. Its influence diminished under successive governments till the 1980s when Charles Kemp's son, Rod Kemp, became leader. It was then that the agenda of the IPA was transformed from a conservative to a neoliberal one, "funded mainly by big business groups, and pursuing a hard-right, pro-free-market, pro-privatization, pro-deregulation and anti-union agenda" (SourceWatch website).[92]

As guest speaker at the IPA's sixtieth C. D. Kemp Lecture on 19 May 2004, John Howard used the opportunity to justify Australia's involvement in the war on Iraq. In that speech he congratulated the IPA for the work they were doing and admitted that "the Institute has played a role in shaping, as well as articulating, our nation's values".[93]

One of the tactics of the IPA was to establish non-profit front groups to carry out their agenda, including: the Australian Environmental Foundation, "which campaigns for weaker environmental laws"; Independent Contractors of Australia, "which campaigns for an end to workplace safety laws and a general deregulation of the labour market"; and Owner Drivers Australia "which campaigns against safety and work standards for truck drivers".[94]

---

91 See SourceWatch, <<http://www.sourcewatch.org/index.php?title=Institute_of_Public_Affairs>. The Howard government changed its attitude toward climate change in the second half of 2007, in the lead-up to the federal election when it became obvious that the majority of voters rated it as a serious environmental issue.

92 Rod Kemp and his brother David were both Liberal Senators and both held ministerial portfolios at various times in Liberal coalition governments.

93 <http://www.ipa.org.au/events/index/year/2004>.

94 SourceWatch, <http://www.sourcewatch.org/index.php?title=Institute_of_Public_Affairs>. The IPA's use of words such as environmental, independent and owner drivers is a classic example of right-wing groups' appropriation of the language of the left for their own conservative ends.

One high-profile project of the institute during the Howard years was their Non-Government Organisation Project, aimed at influencing government to defund those NGOs engaged in advocacy and political activism. This is discussed in some detail in the next section of this chapter.

Another high-profile project was their Murray River project, which aimed to persuade the government to drop its plans to increase the flow of water for the purpose of rescuing the Murray from its present level of pollution. Dr Jennifer Marohasy, director of the IPA's Environment Unit, argued in a paper called "Myth and the Murray: Measuring the Real State of the River Environment" that the river environment was healthy (2003, p. 1). She blamed environment groups for spreading "false" information about the river, in partnership with scientists and the media:

> Many local communities believe a vocal environmental lobby has formed a partnership with scientists pursuing funding. They regard this partnership as having hijacked the debate and, through exploiting an ill-informed media, given city-dwellers the wrong impression that the Murray is facing a crisis. Local communities generally reject the idea that the river is dying and many reject the various proposals to take additional water from irrigators [2003, p. 2].

While the IPA is always reluctant to disclose its funding sources, it was revealed in June 2004 that Australia's largest irrigation company, Murray Irrigation Limited, contributed $40,000 to the work of the institute.

Environmentalists explained that because the significance of the Murray–Darling Basin to the wellbeing of Australia as a whole could never be overstated, many Australians were concerned about the apparent collusion between the IPA and the Howard government to minimise the crisis facing the area. The basin, which derives its name from its two major rivers, the Murray and the Darling, covers 1,061,469 square kilometres or approximately 14 per cent of the total area of Australia. The website River Murray describes it:

> It contains over 40% of all Australian farms, which produce wool, cotton, wheat, sheep, cattle, dairy produce, rice, oil-seed wine, fruit and vegetables for both domestic and overseas markets ...
>
> Three-quarters of Australia's irrigated crops and pastures are grown in the Basin. While agricultural production is vital to our economy, the Murray–Darling Basin is much more than simply a "food basket". It has an important place in the cultural heritage of all Australians and includes many significant natural heritage features.[95]

---

95 <http://rivermurray.com/html/about_the_murray/murray_darling_basin.html>.

The Save the Murray campaign stressed the basin's geological, agricultural and cultural significance and that millions of people were being directly affected by the impending death of the Murray. "Two million people live and work within the Basin or depend on it for their water supply. Another one million people living outside the basin are also heavily dependent on its water".[96]

The way the Murray River issues were handled provides a clear example of the close association between the Howard government, business interests and the propaganda-generating IPA. By creating and articulating neoliberal propaganda, the IPA provided the government and business corporations with the "research" required to justify their pro-business, anti-union, anti-environment, anti-welfare stance and, in this instance, the depletion of the Murray River system was the result.

Repeat carefully selected terms till they become part of everyday vocabulary

An effective element of propaganda is language: words and phrases carefully selected and repeated often enough to ensure that they penetrate the minds of the population at large. Chapter One discussed the terms "in the national interest" and "national security". As propaganda, such terms are powerful. While citizens are aware that the government is not telling them important "secrets", they are meant to be lulled into a sense of security by the assurance that whatever the government is doing is in the national interest and in the interest of national security. The more these phrases are repeated, the more likely it is that citizens will keep out of the affairs of the nation and trust the power elite to make decisions on their behalf. Noam Chomsky, who has contributed much to the understanding of how propaganda programmes use language, calls this "vulgar propaganda":

> We are inundated with [vulgar propaganda] every moment of our lives. Many of us internalize it ... These are the ways in which our intellects are dulled and our capacity for thought is destroyed and our possibility for meaningful political action is undermined by very effective systems of indoctrination and thought control that involve, as all such systems do, abuse of language [1992, pp. 3–4].

Since business corporations and governments of wealthy nations have joined together to push the concepts of a free market and global financial initiatives, the words free and freedom have become part of the everyday mantra of politicians and market leaders. We hear the terms free trade, free market

---

96 <http://www.savethemurray.com/facts_history_of_the_murray.php>. Articles and speeches by protesters can be found on <savethemurray.com>. The papers delivered at a symposium organised by Diane Bell and Gloria Jones are highly recommended reading: Bell and Jones 2007.

and free enterprise repeated over and over. We hear that poverty brought about or exacerbated by global trade policies is a kind of freedom because free enterprise has opened up the possibility for the poor to pull themselves up out of poverty.

In an attempt to justify the horrendous wars visited on Afghanistan and Iraq by George W. Bush's Coalition of the Willing, we heard and continue to hear that democracy must be forced on such countries in order to bring them freedom. We were told repeatedly that our military personnel bombed Afghanistan and Iraq killing many of their citizens in order to free them. As bizarre as it sounds, the majority of citizens particularly in the United States and Australia, believed it. Very few questioned the spin churned out by their leaders. Propaganda works.

As mentioned earlier, another phrase that was used effectively by the Reagan administration and then by the administration of George W. Bush is "war on terror". Whenever it suits the political or economic purposes of the United States to visit war on another country, they do so, provided two questions can be answered in the affirmative: Is it a war we can win? And, will we be able to bring the public along with us? Noam Chomsky observed that any target of a US war must have the following characteristics:

1. It must be virtually defenseless.
2. It must be important enough to be worth the trouble.
3. There must be a way to portray it as the ultimate evil and an imminent threat to our survival (2003, p. 17).

Through propaganda, the Bush II administration convinced the majority of US citizens that the wars perpetrated in their name were a necessary part of ridding the world of "evil" by conquering "terrorists" who want to eliminate the "free world". Most believed in the need for the continuing "war on terror". Australian citizens, too, were subjected to a similar barrage of propaganda aimed at convincing them that Australia's involvement in the US war on terror was "in the interest of national security".

Never admit a mistake
Another feature of a government intent on manipulating the minds of citizens through its carefully constructed propaganda is the determination to appear "right" at all times. Citizens must not be allowed to see or dwell on the mistakes politicians make. A politician who is found to have erred must deny it totally and indignantly.

The Westminster system of government requires that, if a minister of the Crown is found to have breached the code of practice, or if a senior bureaucrat in the minister's department is found to be guilty of a major misjudgement, the minister must accept responsibility and stand down voluntarily or be stood down by the prime minister. In recent years in Australia, however, this particular tenet of the Westminster system has been ignored. When a minister in the Howard government was accused of dereliction of duty or of misleading the parliament by giving information he/she knew to be false, even when those allegations were supported by sound evidence, the prime minister chose to weather the storm of protest and refuse to order the minister to stand down.

This kind of defiant behaviour on the part of prime minister and cabinet seems to be based on the curious belief that to admit a mistake is to show weakness, and that the way for any government to retain power is to show no weakness at all. Any talk of accountability or ethical standards is simply scoffed at.

One distressing feature of a government's determination never to admit a mistake is that sometimes it becomes necessary to offer up a sacrificial lamb, often in the form of a low-ranking bureaucrat. Not surprisingly, that low-ranking bureaucrat is often a woman. The devastating effect on that individual's life is of no consequence to a government whose aim is to retain power at any cost.

Perfect the art of diverting attention

Another tactic employed with varying degrees of success is that of diverting attention from an incident or event the public may object to. A common diversion since the terrorist attacks of 2001 has been to make an announcement aimed at stoking the fear which lies just under the surface of everyone's consciousness. When serious questions were being asked by more and more Australian citizens about their government's treatment of asylum-seekers, and it looked as though the Howard government would lose the 2001 election because of it, lies were invented about asylum-seekers throwing their children overboard to gain attention as their boat came closer to the Australian coast. Immediately, all eyes were on these "evil" people who treat their children so badly. Of course, these "potential terrorists" had to be locked up with all other asylum-seekers while the government processed their applications for refugee status.

The tactic of diverting the population's attention usually works. In this case the majority of people were convinced that the government's tough (many would say, inhumane) tactics were necessary. At the next election (2001), they voted John Howard's government in for another term.

Be prepared to lie and deceive

Propaganda, by its very nature, is concerned with dressing up situations, often by the use of lies, deceptions and half-truths, in order to make them acceptable to entire populations. Two of the really big lies in recent history were those invented in the United States by the Bush II administration and enthusiastically adopted by allies the United Kingdom and Australia: that the invasion of Iraq was a necessary part of a "war on terror" following 9/11; and that Iraq had weapons of mass destruction which they were planning to use.

War on terror
In September 2002, the Bush administration launched a propaganda campaign:

> to depict Saddam Hussein as an imminent threat to the United States and insinuate that he was responsible for the 9–11 atrocities and was planning others. The campaign, timed to the onset of the midterm congressional elections, was highly successful in shifting attitudes [Chomsky 2003, p. 3].

Saddam Hussein was a "terrorist" or, at least, supported and provided a haven for terrorists, so the propaganda went. Therefore, US plans to invade Iraq were justified as a necessary part of the global war on terror. The United States' first war on terror, in the 1980s, focused on Central America and on the Middle East, while the immediate targets of their second war on terror were Afghanistan and Iraq, with suggestions by President George W. Bush that North Korea and Iran were also in their sights.

When the propaganda offensive was launched, it encountered serious opposition from intelligence officers and academics, particularly in relation to its plans to invade Iraq. One experienced intelligence officer in Washington said: "This administration is capable of any lie … in order to advance its war goal in Iraq". Two international relations scholars added that the president's claims about the threat Iraq posed to the United States "should be viewed as transparent attempts to scare Americans into supporting a war..." (in Chomsky 2003, p. 18).

Political analyst Anatol Lieven analysed the September 2002 propaganda campaign which succeeded in convincing nearly 90 per cent of Americans that Saddam Hussein's regime "is aiding and abetting terrorists who are planning future strikes against the US". He commented that most Americans had been "duped … by a propaganda programme which for systematic mendacity has few parallels in peacetime democracies" (2003, pp. 18–19).

Weapons of mass destruction
In addition to the lie about Iraq's involvement in terrorism, there was the other lie concerning weapons of mass destruction. The US administration alleged that Saddam Hussein's government, in defiance of a UN Security Council ruling, had a large stockpile of weapons of mass destruction which it planned to use against the West. With a view to raising the level of fear in the minds of US citizens and thus winning their support for the pending war, the then

national security adviser, Condoleezza Rice, "warned that the next evidence of Saddam Hussein's intention might be a mushroom cloud—presumably in New York" (Chomsky 2003, p. 18). Regardless of the failure of intense efforts by UN weapons inspectors to uncover any such weapons, then Secretary of State Colin Powell said on the eve of the US invasion of Iraq:

> The question simply is: has Saddam Hussein made a strategic, political decision to comply with the United Nations Security Council resolution [and] to get rid of his weapons of mass destruction. That's it in a nutshell ... That's the question. There is no other question [Chomsky 2003, p. 34].

One of the staunchest supporters of the lie that Iraq was harbouring these weapons was Australia's prime minister, John Howard. On 4 February 2003 he said in a speech to the federal parliament: "The Australian Government knows that Iraq still has chemical and biological weapons and that Iraq wants to develop nuclear weapons." Again on the same day he claimed in a ministerial statement: "Iraq continues to work on developing nuclear weapons—uranium has been sought from Africa that has no civil nuclear application in Iraq..." Then, in an address to the nation on 20 March 2003, as the US war on Iraq was beginning, he said:

> The Government has decided to commit Australian forces to action to disarm Iraq because we believe it is right, it is lawful and it's in Australia's national interest. We are determined to join other countries to deprive Iraq of its weapons of mass destruction, its chemical and biological weapons, which even in minute quantities are capable of causing death and destruction on a mammoth scale.[97]

Other lies

On domestic matters, too, the Australian government under the leadership of John Howard seemed comfortable using lies and deceit for the purpose of retaining power. One glaring example (referred to earlier) has come to be called the "children overboard affair" and was represented in the Opposition's website at the time as follows:

> *John Howard Lie:* "The Government's position remains that we were advised by Defence that children were thrown overboard, we made those allegations on the basis of that advice, and until I get Defence advice to the contrary I will maintain that position". John Howard, *Sunrise*, Channel 7, 9 November 2001.

---

[97] <http://www.globalsecurity.org/wmd/library/news/iraq/2003/iraq-030320-australia-pm01.htm>.

The Truth: "I left him in no doubt that there was no evidence, that there were no children thrown overboard". Mike Scrafton, former adviser to the then Defence Minister, *7.30 Report*, ABC, 16 August 2004.

John Howard Lie: "... the behaviour of a number of these people, [on (the boat) SIEV 4] particularly those involving throwing their children overboard..." John Howard, ABC Radio 774, Melbourne, 9 October 2001.

The Truth: "There is no indication that children were thrown overboard." Defence Strategic Command chronology to Department of Prime Minister and Cabinet, noon on 10 October (quoted in "Investigation into Advice Provided to Ministers on 'SIEV 4'"), 21 January 2002.[98]

John Howard Lie: "Nothing can alter the fact that I have in my possession an ONA report that states baldly ... that children were thrown in the water." John Howard, *Insight*, SBS 8 November 2001.

The Truth: "... fundamentally there was nothing to suggest that women and children had been thrown into the water." Account of private conversation Acting Chief of the Defence Forces, Angus Houston, had with Peter Reith, Minister for Defence, on 7 November 2001, evidence given to the Senate Foreign Affairs, Defence and Trade Legislation Committee, 20 February 2002.[99]

Propaganda is produced and distributed by governments, and by media outlets, public relations firms and think tanks working hand-in-hand with governments, with the aim of keeping power in the hands of a small, wealthy power elite. Propaganda by other names is mind manipulation, thought control, indoctrination. It achieves its ends through lies, deceit, diversions and a dishonest use of language. To reiterate: because of propaganda, "our intellects are dulled ... our capacity for thought is destroyed and our possibility for meaningful action is undermined..." (Chomsky 1992, p. 4).

Fear

A major feature of propaganda is the deliberate use of fear to keep the masses under control. In a critical analysis of US administration tactics, Chomsky remarked that when there are "growing domestic social and economic problems", a situation which was becoming serious during the presidency of the elder George Bush, "you've got to divert the bewildered herd" and "whip

---

98   Australian officials gave the name SIEV, or "suspected illegal entry vessel", to boats entering Australian waters carrying asylum-seekers. They usually added a number according to the order in which a particular vessel was spotted. The SIEV 4 is also referred to as SIEV X, where X indicates "unknown". <http://www.greenleft.org.au/2002/500/27880>.

99   <http://www.alp.org.au/features/lies.php>.

them up into fear of enemies". During the Reagan–Bush years, he says, "the leadership conjured up one devil after another to frighten the populace into obedience" (1991, pp. 42–3; 2003, p. 115).

In 1981, the Reagan administration chose Libyan president General Qaddafi to portray as the evil monster who had to be brought down. Qaddafi was said to have hitmen in Washington waiting for an opportunity to assassinate the president. Next, he was sending his troops across the desert to invade Sudan. Then the propaganda had Qaddafi planning to overthrow the government of Sudan. Neither Sudanese nor Egyptian intelligence had any evidence of Libya's supposed aggressive intentions, but the United States went ahead and bombed the palace of General Qaddafi anyway and the American people praised their president for putting the "monster" back in his box.

As soon as the fear generated about Libya subsided, the US administration's attention turned to Grenada and their relationship with the Russians. Russia was planning to launch an offensive against the United States from the air base in Grenada, according to the propaganda, so 6000 US military personnel descended on defenceless Grenada. Then it was the Nicaraguans, supported by Libya's Qaddafi, whose plan was to "expel America from the world" (Chomsky 1989, pp. 96–7). All of these "monsters" were invented for the purpose of exploiting the fear factor among US citizens.[100]

In more recent times, the 9/11 terrorist attacks provided the incentive the neocons in the Bush II administration needed. Fear was at an all-time high in the United States and in all Western countries. From 9/11 to the end of George W. Bush's term as president, the fear factor was massaged by propaganda about the evil Osama bin Laden, al Qaeda and Islamist suicide bombers as well as Saddam Hussein. Chomsky observed that "Manufactured fear provided enough of a popular base for the invasion of Iraq, instituting the new norm of aggressive war at will…" (2003, p. 121). Unscrupulous governments know that, when populations are whipped up into a state of fear about external monsters planning to obliterate them, and when their government appears strong in the face of such threats, they will support the incumbent government in whatever it decides to do.

Fear creates confusion and results in intellectual disorientation. There are many examples of fear campaigns waged against feminists which have created confusion and suspicion in people's minds about the agenda of feminism.

---

100 For a feminist's comment on the US invasion of Grenada, see Audré Lorde's essay "Grenada Revisited: An Interim Report", which tells of her sadness and fear during her second visit to her mother's birthplace in December 1983. Grenada had been "savaged, invaded, its people maneuvered into saying thank you to their invaders", she said. "I knew the lies and distortions of secrecy surrounding the invasion of Grenada by the United States on October 25, 1983; the rationalizations which collapse under the weight of facts" (1984a, p. 177).

US evangelist Jerry Falwell, for example, referring to the September 11 terrorist attacks, said: "the pagans and the abortionists and the feminists and gays and lesbians … you made this happen" (cited in Hawthorne 2002b, p. 354).

Fear is useful for governments on the domestic front, too. Fear of crime and fear of drugs are the two which are used prior to every election. Even when statistics show the crime rate to be low, citizens are encouraged to be aware that they or their children could be accosted in the street or that criminals could break into their homes and terrorise them or steal their property. There are drug-dependent people everywhere, too, citizens are warned, and they feel safer knowing that their government is "tough" on drugs and drug-related crime.

Because of the propaganda used to increase fear, mainstream citizens of Western nations harbour within themselves not only fear of crime and drugs but also fear of anyone who is different from themselves: Indigenous people, migrants, refugees, anyone of Middle Eastern or Asian appearance, lesbians and gay men, as well as those who are poor and/or homeless.

Fear is the great silencer. If the power elite in any society can whip up a sufficient degree of fear, they can be assured that the majority of the population will go about their lives inwardly focused, satisfied to let government, business and community leaders make decisions about social, national and international matters on their behalf.

Language

The use of language as a tool to control the thoughts of entire populations is a huge issue which deserves special attention here. Chomsky remarked that, when language is debased and distorted to serve the cynical purposes of politicians, it "undermines the possibility of independent thought" (1992, p. 49). Deliberate and well-organised exercises aimed at confusing citizens through language-distortion, result in the majority being robbed of any possibility of clarity of thought and perception.

Feminists have long been aware of the power of language and the ways in which language has been distorted to serve the purposes of those intent on creating confusion and keeping women in a subordinate position. Jane Caputi, in "Cuntspeak: Words from the Heart of Darkness", writes about the silencing that occurs in relation to the language used to refer to women's genitals and the need for women to reclaim those words. Girls are likely to learn the words for men's sexual parts before they know about their own, she says. Girls and women who have suffered rape and other forms of sexual abuse often feel disconnected from their sexual selves and have no language to describe those parts of their bodies that have been violated. For example,

Eve Ensler, creator of *The Vagina Monologues*, explained that the writing of the monologues helped her reclaim the word vagina, from which she had felt disconnected since being raped as a girl (in Caputi 2004, p. 371).

Language of war

The distortion of language to portray the horrors of war in a positive light is commonplace. While some are able to decipher such language, it still has the effect of white-washing and sanitising extreme acts of violence and murder. In one section of Marilyn French's *The War Against Women*, she drew attention to the incomprehensible distortions inherent in military language. The murder of ordinary citizens in bombing raids is called "collateral damage". Not the real targets. They just happened to be "in the way of the important business" (1992, p. 161). "Friendly fire" is the name given to accidents in which military personnel or civilians are killed by their own side. "Surgical strikes" are counterforce attacks on the enemy's weapons or military installations. The aim is to "take out" their weapons capability without causing too much damage to anything else. Defence personnel and defence analysts refer to "clean bombs" and "damage limitation weapons". The bombs that "wreaked such human horror on Hiroshima and Nagasaki were [personalised with the names] ... 'Little Boy' and 'Fat Man'". An MX missile with "a destructive power about 250–400 times that of the bomb that levelled Hiroshima" was dubbed "the Peacekeeper" by Ronald Reagan (French 1992, pp. 160, 161–2).

The US National Security Strategy of 2002, which legitimised pre-emptive strikes and preventative wars, signalled the intention of the administration to attack countries it labelled "rogue states", perpetrating wholesale destruction and murder, so that the citizens of those countries could be "free" and "at peace". While such reasoning, such distortion of language, is perverse and cynical, the aim of confusing and silencing multitudes of people is usually achieved.

Language of corporate governance

Now that the global market dominates every aspect of life, public sector language and strategies have been replaced by those of the private sector. The language of care and concern which characterised the public/welfare sector has been replaced by the language of corporate governance. De Clarke demonstrates how corporate language is used to bring practices oppressive of women into the mainstream and give them legitimacy.

> Prostitutes, we are told, choose their line of work in a free market; they are rational agents. To criticise the industry which exploits them, or even to say that they are exploited, is to deny their agency. To attempt to regulate or restrict it is only to deny them "opportunities" and "choices" [2004, p. 170].

In an essay on market populism in Australia, Marian Sawer, professor of political science at the Australian National University, explains that today's market populism brings together two clearly identifiable theoretical elements which now dictate the terms and conditions of the public sector. They are the "new class theory" developed by neoconservatives in the United States in the 1970s, and "public choice theory" developed by neoliberals in the United States from the 1950s on (Sawer 2003).[101]

New class theory

Neoconservatives were critical of the "new class" which consisted of "university graduates who had been radicalised by the social movements of the 1960s and who had moved into positions in the public sector and communications industry". In March 1989 the editor of the conservative *Quadrant Magazine* in Australia wrote that "the new class with its values of environmentalism, feminism, and multiculturalism had replaced totalitarianism as the major threat to freedom" (in Sawer 2003, p. 2). Those who agitated for justice and equality were derided as the "new class elite".

Feminism was equated with political correctness, selfishness, coldness, barrenness,[102] and even terrorism. Environmentalists were seen as constant whingers, anti-union, having no concern about the people who could possibly be deprived of their livelihood as a result of their campaigns. Multiculturalism was equated with a "black-armband view of history". Calls for a national apology to Indigenous people for the Stolen Generations or stolen wages were met with accusations of "rewriting history" or "dwelling on the past", and the advice freely given to activists was to get over the past and look to the future.[103]

---

101 See also Sawer 2005, a paper prepared for the UN Division for the Advancement of Women.

102 Australia's deputy prime minister, Julia Gillard, was told by Liberal Senator Bill Heffernan that she was "unfit for leadership" because she was childless. Senator Heffernan was forced to apologise to Gillard for describing her as "deliberately barren", <http://www.theage.com.au/news/national/heffernans-gibe-hurt-australian-women/2007/05/04/1177788348405.html>. New Zealand's previous prime minister, Helen Clark, who is married but has no children, was also subject to accusations of barrenness, even being called "a barren lesbian" married to a "gay man", <http://www.flatrock.org.nz/topics/working/serving_time.htm>.

103 For instance, the Liberal member for Herbert, Peter Lindsay, responded to calls for compensation for Indigenous women and men who worked for white companies and white individuals for many years without pay, by saying "The past has happened. Just get over it". *Townsville Bulletin*, 3 April 2008.

Public choice theory

Closely related to utilitarianism, public choice theory focuses on maximising market opportunities for individuals. Those calling for equality are depicted as self-seeking, as "people who would do well out of equality". The claim is that "social justice was a mirage, and those who purported to be pursuing the public interest were really 'special interests'. Equality-seekers were rent-seekers, calculating they could do better out of the state than out of the market" (Sawer 2003, p. 2).

Soon after the election of the Howard government in 1996, changes in language to describe the public sector and the work of government-funded NGOs became evident. Similar changes had occurred in the United Kingdom and in Canada. To begin with, the concepts of the "public good" or "community" were replaced with "individual responsibility". Phrases like "user pays" and "mutual obligation" were introduced into the language, evidence that those working in the public sector were expected to take a much tougher line with those who sought assistance.

Those seeking the help of NGOs were to be called "consumers" or "customers" and dealt with according to a customer service model. Agencies providing services in domestic violence and sexual assault were to think of the women coming to them not as "survivors" but as "consumers". Objecting to the Canadian situation, Mandy Bonisteel and Linda Green remarked in a paper presented at the Canadian Social Welfare Policy Conference: "Use of the term consumer rather than survivor reflects the shift to a corporate profit-based model that blurs the rights of citizenship by equating citizenship with consumption" (2005, p. 17).

They took issue, also, with the word "stakeholder". When introducing unpopular changes to the public sector, governments are careful to emphasise the fact that they have consulted with "key stakeholders". Bonisteel and Green quote from the work of Seamus O'Tuama, who pointed out that while "Stakeholder participation in political decision-making is presented as inclusionary … the reality is that like in private corporations some of the stakeholders hold more of the shares" (O'Tuama 2002, p. 3).

The experience in Australia was that, whenever the Howard government consulted with key stakeholders on public sector matters, very few NGOs working on the ground with people who surely had a "stake" in the issues at hand, were ever included in the consultations. Representatives of the business community, conservative think tanks and mainstream charities such as the Salvation Army and the Smith Family were usually among the hand-picked "stakeholders".

Along with corporate language directly related to the everyday management of public sector business, there was language aimed at discrediting those who dissent from and criticise the dominance of market populism and the impersonal nature of corporate governance concepts.

Those dissenters who persisted in pointing out the injustices inherent in a system which operates primarily for the benefit of the mainstream were labeled "the black-armband brigade" engaging in "black-armband history". Speaking of Howard, Sawer reminded her readers:

> The Prime Minister himself has told us that elites engaging in "black-armband history" are displaying contempt for the national pride felt by ordinary Australians and that feminists promoting equal opportunity are showing contempt for the values of ordinary women. He has spoken on talkback radio of the "stridency of the ultra-feminist groups in the community" that sneer at and look down on women choosing to provide full-time care for their children [2003, p. 3].

The "new class elites" were derided also as "bleeding hearts", "politically correct", "thought police" and "tyrannising minorities". Those who spoke out for justice, insisting on a better deal for women, Indigenous people, refugees, migrants, lesbians and gay men, were said to be promoting their own special interests, "selfishly pursuing a social justice and environmental agenda" while looking down on "ordinary taxpayers who just want to pay off their mortgage" (Sawer 2003, p. 3). It is difficult to make sense of such propaganda: it seems to imply that no feminists, Indigenous activists, refugees, migrants, lesbians or gay men are taxpayers, or that they are not paying enough taxes. As curious as such reasoning is, there is no doubt that, whenever and wherever governments choose to go down that path, they are successful in influencing the majority of citizens to agree with them.

Language of postmodernism

Postmodernism is the current popular theoretical trend in institutions of higher learning and, while many of its proponents would object to its being labelled "conservative", it does provide fuel and legitimacy for the conservative political agenda. Susan Hawthorne, in a paper focused on "the political uses of obscurantism", discussed some of the ways in which postmodernism aids the process of depoliticisation:

> The problem posed by the use of postmodern theory is not just one of access and intellectual elitism, it has also been a process of depoliticisation. Postmodernism has rendered many silent, many speechless, including those whom the theorists claim to defend, namely, the dispossessed, the marginalised, the poverty stricken and the politically powerless [2004a, p. 1].

In rejecting universals, postmodernism questions the legitimacy of universal categories such as women. There is no such thing as "women", they say, because women are socially constructed and, therefore, are all different—different races, cultures, economic status. Women cannot be spoken of (as feminists have done) in a universal sense. Also, one cannot speak of the reality of women's lives because there is no such thing as "reality". Reality is different for everyone and, therefore, does not exist. It is a social construction. As Catharine MacKinnon argues: "The fact that reality is a social construction does not mean that it is not there; it means that it is there, in society, where we live" (2006, p. 56).

Instead of "women", postmodernists favour the word "gender". Thus they play into the hands of the neoconservative and neoliberal power elite, whose aim in relation to women and feminists is to render all women invisible and speechless. Hawthorne claims that the word gender is "deeply depoliticising".

> Gender is such a soft word. It is a word that asks permission to exist. It is a word without demands. Without political clout. Without power. To use a word such as gender might let us sneak past the guards at the door of the boys' cubby house, but it will not get us to the table where the decisions are being made [2004a, p. 2].

She goes on to comment on the term "gender mainstreaming":

> When gender is teamed with mainstreaming the effect is deadening. Gender does not and cannot belong in the mainstream. Gender is girls' stuff; the mainstream is where the boys swim. Gender drowns in the mainstream. Or perhaps is pushed under, held down, and drowned.
>
> Gender is the word that pretends that women can be just like men. But listen to men talk. How many men do you know who talk regularly about gender [2004a, p. 3]?

Postmodernism's declaration that society has moved into a "postfeminist" phase was vehemently rejected by radical feminists. In the introduction to their anthology *Radically Speaking: Feminism Reclaimed* (1996), Diane Bell and Renate Klein defend the long-held feminist position "of addressing actual issues as they arise in the lives of particular women". Women do exist and the reality of women's lives is that they are exploited, oppressed, excluded and silenced. Bell and Klein sum up their comparison of postmodernism and radical feminism:

> Whereas post-modernists occupy the borderlands looking out over the wastelands created by their deconstructive brilliance, radical feminists have been busy crossing boundaries in order to integrate modes of understanding. The common ground thus generated constitutes what Mary Daly has mapped as a kind of "collective feminist memory" which makes action on many and diverse projects possible [p. xxvi].

Taking their lead from Michel Foucault, many postmodernists write about power but, as Bell and Klein argue:

> Because it declines to identify domination in general and male domination in particular, post-modernism cannot contest the relations of power. The post-modern turn has depoliticised feminist theory [1996, p. xxvi].

In line with their emphasis on gender rather than women, postmodernists also prefer the terms "lesbianandgay" and "queer" rather than "lesbian". Sheila Jeffreys remarks that lesbianandgay theory is "depoliticised, sanitised and something difficult to associate with sexual violence, economic inequality, women dying from backyard abortions. It is gender reinvented as play for those who see themselves far removed from the nitty gritty of women's oppression" (1996, p. 359).

Sue Wilkinson and Celia Kitzinger remark that the term queer celebrates its own inclusiveness by incorporating lesbian, gay, bisexual, transsexual, sadomasochist and all other varieties and combinations of "sexual identities". While postmodernists and queer theorists congratulate themselves on their radical inclusiveness, however, queer theory is actually conservative and anti-feminist. "Within queer, radical feminist analyses are ignored or marginalised at best, subverted or derided at worst ... [It] is centrally antagonistic to feminism" (1996, p. 379).

In the same way as "gender" causes women to disappear, both "lesbianandgay" and "queer" conveniently cause lesbians and lesbian feminists to disappear by a process of assimilation.

Language is a powerful tool of propaganda. Whether in the hands of governments, public relations personnel, business leaders, media or academics, language can be used to silence dissent and stifle social and political movements calling for justice. Propaganda, fear and carefully constructed language combine to enable the power elite in any society to manipulate the minds of the masses and render them harmless to the elite's hold on power.

Targeted silencing

Fortunately, attempts at manipulating the minds of entire populations are never 100 per cent successful. In every society there are those who resist all efforts to turn them into compliant, harmless spectators and who courageously claim their democratic right to engage with the affairs of their nation and world. Pushing through the maze, through the deliberate attempts at mystification, they do their own independent analyses of power relations; this is followed often by behaviour designed to demonstrate their objections, namely resistance, disruption and dissent.

Knowing that there is strength in numbers, most dissenters seek the company of like-minded others with whom they can discuss and compare ideas and organise political activism. Whether tightly knit or unstructured, groups provide individuals with a much-needed sense of solidarity and support.

The response of governments intent not just on minimising dissent but on eradicating it altogether, is usually deliberate targeted silencing of individuals and groups who persist in presenting alternative views. Those groups which have been targeted for unprecedented silencing during the years of rising political and economic conservatism were non-government organisations, the trade union movement and popular social movements.

Restricting non-government organisations

The role of NGOs in Australia, Canada, the United States, the United Kingdom and New Zealand has always been understood to have two components: to "serve as essential intermediaries between community and government" keeping governments informed about the needs of a wide range of community groups; and to "provide a voice for marginalised groups ... to make claims on government between elections". A survey of NGOs conducted in 2004 by the Australia Institute was based on the assumption that, given the intermediary and advocacy roles of NGOs, they are "an essential component of a healthy and robust democracy" (Maddison, Denniss and Hamilton 2004, p. vii).

With the increasing dominance of market populism and the forced adoption of the rules of corporate governance, the survey found that NGOs were under attack as never before, living with the constant threat of having government funding withdrawn. Drawing on the findings of two important studies into the deliberate silencing of NGOs, one in Australia and one in Canada,[104] I will focus here on three tactics governments used to rein in the freedoms NGOs once enjoyed: imposing strict accountability requirements; excluding them from consultation processes; and curbing their advocacy role.

Imposing strict accountability requirements
One of the features of NGOs in the past was that most were acutely aware of the need to be accountable to the people who used their services and, more generally, to the community at large. This was acknowledged in the

---

104 Maddison, Denniss and Hamilton 2004; Bonisteel and Green 2005.

introduction to the Australia Institute report: "The legitimacy of NGOs is granted by the communities they represent and it is to these same communities that they must be accountable" (Maddison, Dennis and Hamilton 2004, p. viii). However, the move to require and enforce strict accountability to government, which is "a reversal of the role and function played by nonprofit organizations in the past as a monitor and a check on government", jeopardises their relationship of accountability to the public (Bonisteel and Green 2005, p. 19).[105]

It has long been the dream of those who interpret democracy as "rule for the people" that dissenters be stripped of their power and silenced. Conservative politicians, business leaders and academics have identified NGOs as the main sites of dissent and have consequently called for stricter accountability to be imposed on workers and boards of management.

To this end, the Australian government under Howard secretly funded the Institute of Public Affairs early in 2003 to the tune of $50,000 to do an audit of Australia's NGOs. When sections of the media found out about the secret move and began asking questions in *The Sunday Age*, the IPA issued a media release explaining that "the aim of the project was to develop a 'trial protocol' for public disclosure of relationships between NGOs and government, including the need for NGOs to 'supply information about their organisation'" (Nicholson and Hughes 2003, p. 1). Community groups were understandably upset at the government's choice of the IPA, given that Gary Johns, senior fellow of the institute, had previously targeted NGOs in a similar way to that employed by the American Enterprise Institute. In a "defund the left" campaign, the latter had insisted that "non-government organisations that gain tax benefits or funding from government ... be subjected to more scrutiny".[106]

As early as 2001 the IPA had launched a newsletter, *NGO Watch*[107] and appointed Gary Johns to head its Non-government Organisation Project. The aim, according to the online encyclopedia SourceWatch, was to reduce the influence of NGOs. To this end, the IPA proposed:

> that NGOs would have to pass a series of threshold disclosure tests before gaining high-level access to government officials, funding or inclusion on committees. Information to be disclosed to government would include "their source of funds, their expertise, their membership and the means of electing their office holders" [SourceWatch, n.d.].

---

105 See also Harvie 2002.
106 See SourceWatch, 2003. <http://www.sourcewatch.org/index.php?title=Institute_of_Public_Affairs>.
107 *NGO Watch* had a very short life. It produced its last edition in October 2002 due to lack of interest. According to Johns, there weren't enough people "buying the product".

Since the IPA had already demonstrated that it held the kinds of views the government of the day wanted to see reflected in the outcome of the audit, it was no coincidence that that particular institute was chosen in 2003 to undertake the government's work.[108]

In a move which the IPA insisted was quite separate from its proposals, Treasurer Peter Costello released draft legislation on 22 July 2003 which "threatened to remove tax exemption status from NGOs if they were deemed to be more involved in political lobbying and advocacy than in community work" (Nicholson and Hughes 2003, p. 1). The treasurer's so-called Charities Bill was aimed at preventing charities from gaining tax concessions if they advocated a political cause, supported a particular political candidate, challenged government policy, or encouraged civil disobedience. "Following a storm of protest, the Australian government dropped the proposal in early 2004, but in 2005 the Australian Tax Office passed a ruling that contained some of the most contentious elements of the proposal" (SourceWatch, n.d.).[109]

Focusing on the increasing requirement of accountability from all sectors of the community, Onora O'Neill in her BBC Reith Lectures suggested that the present situation is indicative of a culture of suspicion which has led to a crisis of trust. Speaking of the level of accountability governments currently require of the public sector in the United Kingdom, she said:

> the new accountability takes the form of detailed control. An unending stream of new legislation and regulation, memoranda and instructions, guidance and advice floods into public sector institutions ... The new accountability culture aims at ever more perfect administrative control of institutional and professional life [2002, pp. 45–6].

Some of her criticisms of the "new conceptions of accountability" were that they superimpose managerial targets, burden and even paralyse those who have to comply, obstruct the real purposes of professional practice, and damage professional pride and integrity (O'Neill 2002, pp. 18, 49, 50). She continues:

> *In theory* the new culture of accountability and audit makes professionals and institutions more accountable *to the public* ... But underlying this ostensible aim of accountability *to the public* the real requirements are for accountability *to regulators, to departments of government, to funders, to legal standards*. The new forms of accountability impose forms of *central control*... [pp. 52–3, italics in the original].

---

[108] For a hard-hitting critique of the Howard government's intention toward and treatment of NGOs, see Kingston 2004, pp. 260–88.

[109] See also Lyons 2005.

Writing about the way the new accountability requirements are affecting the women's sector, specifically the feminist anti-violence sector in Canada, Bonisteel and Green commented that "feminist groups are right to worry that they are being invited into processes and partnerships that work against the interests of women" (2005, p. 21). They were highly critical, for example, of the requirement to measure outcomes, and rejected the suggestion that "Trauma symptom inventories, a Multi-Dimensional Self-Esteem scale, and anger scales" be used in women's shelters and refuges. All such forms of outcome evaluation "identify individual women as the sites of the change that is necessary to address the problem of women being beaten and raped", when women are not the problem. When men perpetrate violence against women, feminists refuse to identify women's behaviour and attitudes as the cause of the problem. Rather, it is the perpetrators who are to be held accountable for their violence (p. 25).[110]

Another concern expressed by Bonisteel and Green is that the requirements of evaluation and accountability have the potential to interfere with the development of women's self-esteem and empowerment:

> Of great concern is the potential for interference with women's self-determination and agency under this evaluation regime, since these organizations are being directed to move individual women along trajectories of change that conform to funder-mandated organizational outcomes [2005, p. 24].

Speaking at a conference on Australia's Gold Coast in 2001, Julie Oberin, then national chair of Women's Services Network (WESNET),[111] spoke passionately about the issues later reflected in the kinds of studies quoted. I focus here on WESNET because it is an example of an NGO which refused, and continues to refuse, to be silenced. Despite the threat of defunding hanging over their heads and the subsequent actual defunding of their service, they continued to speak out for women and demand that the Howard government take violence against women seriously.

---

110 Progressive legislation in Sweden targets men who buy the services of prostitutes rather than the prostitutes themselves, an example of perpetrators being held accountable. Sweden's law came into effect on 1 January 1999 and was inserted into the Criminal Code on 1 April 2005. Buying time with a prostitute is a criminal offence described as "a gross violation of a woman's integrity", <http://www.prostitutionresearch.com/swedish.html>.

111 WESNET, established in 1992, is the national peak organisation for almost 400 women's domestic and family violence services across Australia. It was funded as a peak body by the federal Labor government under Paul Keating and defunded by the subsequent coalition government under Howard. Since being defunded, WESNET has been forced into the position of trying "to represent and coordinate its 400-member organisation relying on donations and contributions from members" (Summers 2003, p. 97).

Referring to the inappropriateness of the new rules of corporate governance, Oberin stated: "We're sick of the purchaser/provider split, the new managerialist language, the lack of coordination between [government] departments, and output based funding models rather than a focus on long term qualitative outcomes." She accused the then government of "tinkering around the edges" in relation to women's services:

> Stop pretending to do something. Halt competitive tendering. Stop the de-gendering of policies and the general thrust towards mainstreaming.
> Stop the busyness ... the work on how to unit cost domestic violence ... the redistribution of dollars and resources from one area to another to fill gaps rather than adding much-needed new dollars. And ... don't use the excuse that the pot is only so full. I don't hear ... that with regard to the defence budget [Oberin 2001, p. 4].

Oberin's overall concern and criticism was that "the voice of the women's domestic and family violence sector has been increasingly silenced and excluded from this government's agenda" (2001, p. 1). Under the subsequent national chair Pauline Woodbridge, WESNET continued to speak out fearlessly. In a media release on 27 October 2004, Woodbridge pointed out that "More than half of the people who need help [in terms of emergency accommodation] ... do not get it and are turned away because agencies lack resources." In a plea for more funding for the domestic and family violence sector, she went on to say, "...we need a government which prioritises the safety and well-being of women and children ... Don't leave [them] out in the cold again Mr. Howard" (WESNET, 2004a). Then, in a 2006 media release, responding to "alarming" new data released by the Australian Bureau of Statistics, Woodbridge repeated the familiar refrain when she asked: "When is the Australian Government going to finally treat violence against women as the serious social issue it is?" (WESNET, 2006).

Rules that rely on corporate, outcome-based models, combined with strict requirements of evaluation and accountability, saw a large number of NGOs in Australia, Canada, the United States and the United Kingdom defunded and stripped of their ability to advocate on behalf of those who once used their services. Other NGOs who made the choice to cooperate with the new rules in order to keep their funding were able to continue offering a service to those in need, but many acknowledged that they have been virtually silenced.

In addition to the threat of losing funding, another tactic used by governments determined to silence dissent among NGOs was to exclude all but a few carefully chosen groups from their consultation processes.

Managing consultation processes

Unscrupulous governments whose first concern is that of preserving their own power, go to extraordinary lengths to suppress dissent. The study undertaken by the Australia Institute identified four main tactics consistently used against NGOs by the Australian government under Howard: insult, public criticism, attacks on workers' credibility; bullying, threats, personal attacks; management of consultation processes; and the use of diversionary tactics, that is, manipulating debate so as to keep it on the government's own terms (Maddison 2004, p. 3).

Many NGOs find the tactic of micro-managing consultations particularly odious because it feigns openness and willingness to listen to all views before making decisions when, in fact, it is a process whereby governments ensure that they hear only the views they want to hear. Having "consulted", their preconceived plans for the sector can then proceed with an air of legitimacy. A notable example of this tactic in Australia was that raised in a forum on ABC television's *7.30 Report* on 12 October 1999. Discussing the funding of women's services by the Howard government, including the fact that three very conservative organisations were to receive more funding while many others were "left out in the cold", interviewer Philippa McDonald drew attention to the proposed women's roundtable consultation called by the Minister assisting the Prime Minister for Status of Women at Parliament House in Canberra. She commented that "already the number of groups invited has been cut in half", to which Anne Summers responded: "...there are 30 groups who had every expectation of being invited to this consultation who were suddenly receiving a letter ... saying unfortunately their presence wouldn't be required".[112]

At that roundtable, the future of women's services in Australia was discussed without the benefit of the experience and opinions of long-time feminist women's sector workers. Seeming not to care about the loss such a situation entailed, the government achieved its aim of silencing feminist voices and rendering them impotent.

The tactic of leaving potential dissenters out of consultation processes was also evident in the development of Australia's new family relationships centres. While churches, fathers' rights groups and other men's groups were consulted all along the way, attempts by feminists, domestic violence workers, sexual assault workers and single mothers' groups (on whom the policies have the greatest impact) to have input into the development of the new centres were largely ignored. When the required emphasis is on "happy families", the implications of men's violence against women in the home and

---

112 <http://www.abc.net.au/7.30/stories/s59370.htm>.

of sexual abuse of children in the home are conveniently set aside. So-called community consultation, when "community" turns out to be a narrow group of the government's preferred conservative NGOs, is a farce.

Australia's Labor government led by Kevin Rudd, while popular, is showing signs that it too is managing consultation to ensure that issues not of the government's choosing are excluded from the nation's agenda. In the lead-up to the election, when the Labor Party released a document outlining their social inclusion agenda, feminists remarked that one of the glaring omissions from the document was any mention of women or women's issues. Women, it seems, were excluded from consideration for social inclusion. Another sign of the exclusion of feminist concerns came after the Labor Party took office in Canberra. One early initiative was the announcement of a 2020 Summit, in which 1000 of the country's top minds would meet at Parliament House to discuss ten topics of the government's choosing. The vice-chancellor of the University of Melbourne was given the task of heading the summit and ten others were appointed as coordinators, one for each of the topics to be discussed. Alarm bells rang for feminists when they saw that, of the eleven people chosen by the government, only one was a woman. Subsequently, when one of the men had to withdraw, a woman was appointed in his place. So, in spite of the outcry by feminists and other women, the summit went ahead led by nine white middle-class men and two women (one Indigenous and one non-Indigenous). After the outcry, co-chairs were appointed, several of whom were women.

Curbing the advocacy role

Nothing revealed the strength of the Howard government's determination to silence dissent more than its deliberate efforts to forbid NGOs from continuing their historic role as advocates and spokespersons for those who, because of their life's circumstances, have difficulty speaking for themselves.[113] Bonisteel and Green quote the definition of advocacy by Betsy Harvie (2002) as "a means by which socially marginalized groups gain voice, power, and access to individual, systemic, and public benefits in a socially exclusive environment" (2005, p. 1). Maddison, too, describes the advocacy role of NGOs as providing "a voice for marginalised groups" (2004, p. 1).

The survey conducted by the Australia Institute, titled "Silencing Dissent", targeted NGOs involved in both service delivery and advocacy. Regardless of the fact that public debate is seen to be an essential aspect of a healthy democracy and that dissenting views make public debate possible, the survey found that only "nine per cent of respondents believe that the Federal Government

---

[113] The advocacy role of the union movement in Australia was also under threat as the government did all in its power to discourage workers from joining unions and thus diminish unions' power.

encourages public debate". Most (92 per cent) disagreed with the statement that "Individuals and organisations that dissent from current government policy are valued by the government as part of a robust democracy", while 90 per cent agreed with the statement that "Dissenting organisations and individuals risk having their funding cut" (Maddison 2004, p. 2).

The introduction of the Charities Bill referred to earlier and the subsequent adoption of many of its elements by the Australian Taxation Office sent a clear message to NGOs that the government would not tolerate funded organisations advocating on behalf of those who otherwise would never be heard.

Tanya Plibersek, Labor parliamentarian and then shadow minister for women,[114] in a scathing critique of the Howard government's silencing of NGOs, said: "If you help the homeless, it's OK; if you say there shouldn't be so many homeless you lose funding". In acknowledging the "valuable role" NGOs have played "in encouraging public debate" and representing "some of the poorest and least powerful people," she laments the fact that so many NGOs have lost the funding that enabled them to continue their work. In summary, she added:

> A strong democracy depends on its citizens being given a variety of ways to have their say—not just at election time but every day. This Government has done all it can to close off those channels and silence those voices [2006].

NGOs were targeted mercilessly by Howard and his colleagues, who had long harboured the view that radical activists from the 1970s had found their way into NGOs and politicised them. Church groups who voiced an opinion about poverty, environment groups who spoke of greenhouse gases, Indigenous groups who pleaded for an end to racist attitudes and women's groups who called for the elimination of men's violence against women all risked having their funding and/or their charitable status withdrawn, because advocacy on behalf of less privileged members of society was deemed to be dissent, and dissent was not permitted.

The silencing of NGOs occurred progressively over the eleven years of the Howard government through the imposition of strict accountability requirements, the exclusion of all but a chosen few from consultative processes, and the curbing of their historic advocacy role.

---

114 Tanya Plibersek was Shadow Minister for Work, Family and Community; Shadow Minister for Youth and Early Childhood Education; and Shadow Minister for Women, from 26 October 2004. In the Rudd government, she is Minister for Housing and Minister for Women.

Weakening the union movement

Noam Chomsky points to the connection between the restricting of NGOs (the "social welfare system") and the weakening of the union movement in the United States during the Reagan era. Referring to the "lowering of real wages", the "breakup of the unions", the "dismantling of the popular structures ... that would enable ordinary citizens to fight for their rights" and the "attack on the social welfare system", he says:

> All of these are part of the same effort of the dominant social groups in the United States, the owners and managers of the corporate system, to ensure their own privilege and to defend themselves against the rising domestic enemy [1992, pp. 111–12].

The "rising domestic enemy" was actually ordinary US citizens speaking out (often through social advocates in the welfare sector) and demanding their rights. This was variously referred to by the Reagan administration and the business elite as "civil disorder" and "domestic dissidence" causing a "crisis of democracy" which had to be "controlled" (Chomsky 1992, pp. 104–11).

The union movement with its emphasis on workers' rights, and on collective action as the only way to achieve those rights, has long been a target of employers and governments intent on protecting the right of the rich and powerful to ever-increasing profits. Politicians rationalise their behaviour by referring to the "trickle-down effect", the claim that if governments take care of corporations, businesses and employers, the profits will trickle down to the community in terms of more jobs and better pay and conditions for workers. Such a concept, however, fails to take account of the greed factor, or the "trickle-up effect" as it was called in a case study written by Dr K. Balachandra Kurup for the Community Water Supply Management in Kerala, India (n.d.). Most companies are only too happy to accept the privileges and incentives offered by governments but, rather than improving the pay and conditions of workers, they use the extra profits to pay exorbitant salaries to CEOs and other senior workers and to satisfy the need of shareholders to receive greater returns for their investment.

For much of the twentieth century, Australia led the world in fair work practices: reasonable working hours, higher rates of pay for overtime, three to four weeks' annual leave, 17.5 per cent leave loading paid by employers in addition to workers' holiday pay, laws to prevent unfair dismissal of workers and the establishment of the Industrial Relations Commission as an independent arbiter in disputes between employers and employees. According to the Australian Council of Trade Unions (ACTU), that situation began to change in the 1980s. Under the Hawke and Keating Labor governments (1983–96), while access to justice via the Industrial Relations Commission continued to be available, there was a noticeable increase in workers' hours.

When the conservative, pro-business Howard government came to power in 1996, workers' rights diminished markedly. The government's long-rehearsed theme of demonising unions gained momentum and they made no secret of their intention to weaken the union movement and deprive workers of the gains made on their behalf over many decades.

The Workplace Regulations Act, which took effect from 27 March 2006, was described on the Howard government's website as providing "a single, national set of rules for minimum terms, conditions, awards and agreements". The aim of the new regulations was said to be to "help employers and employees to know their rights and responsibilities under the new WorkChoices system and to make any necessary changes in their workplace". Employees were told: "WorkChoices is a national workplace relations system that provides more choice and flexibility for employees in the workplace. The system offers better ways to reward effort, increase wages and balance work and family life."[115]

The Australian Labor Party in opposition, the Australian Democrats, the Australian Greens, the ACTU and the Socialist Alliance in Australia saw it differently. Sue Bolton, the national trade union coordinator for the Socialist Alliance, in an article titled "Howard's Lies on Industrial Relations 'Reforms'", listed twelve "lies" contained in the 2006 Workplace Regulations Act. The lies amounted to a kind of sleight-of-hand, hiding the true situation in an attempt to deceive. For example, the promise that there would be "new safeguards for wages and conditions" hid the fact that the so-called safety net guaranteed only a few conditions: the minimum wage, annual leave, sick leave, unpaid parental leave and the 38-hour week. There was no longer any guarantee of "redundancy pay, overtime pay, shift-work penalty rates, weekend and public holiday pay rates, annual leave loading, work rosters, work and family rights, allowances, skill-based pay increases, and a host of other award conditions" (2005, p. 1).

ACTU president Sharan Burrow spoke out against the prioritising of individual agreements between employees and employers known as Australian Workplace Agreements (AWAs). She argued, prior to the passing of the Workplace Regulations Act, that the government's new industrial relations laws "are all about pushing workers on to individual contracts [AWAs] that can cut people's take-home pay and remove conditions like overtime, shift penalty rates, meal breaks, rostering protections and public holiday penalties" (ACTU 2005b).

Around that time, the ACTU secretary Greg Combet expressed serious concern about the Howard government's intention to "gut the Industrial Relations Commission and take away its power to increase minimum wages

---

115 Since the defeat of the Howard government in November 2007, the Work Choices website from which this information was derived has been removed.

for Australia's 1.6 million award workers". The government's plan, he said, was "to take away the Commission's power ... and to set up instead a rival body—a so-called 'Fair Pay Commission'". Combet referred to the Industrial Relations Commission as "an independent umpire" and the Fair Pay Commission as a "Government-appointed 'kangaroo court'" (ACTU 2005a).

After the passing of the Workplace Regulations Act in March 2006, the government's Fair Pay Commission was established and, while they seemed resistant to raising the minimum wage for workers, the ACTU (2006) revealed that the commissioners themselves "received a 4.4% pay rise after 5 months on the job".

Protection of workers against unfair dismissal, protection of award wages, four weeks' annual leave, the right to join a union, the right to strike, the right to collective bargaining, the right to refuse to sign an individual agreement (AWA) were in jeopardy in Australia. The Howard government's aim was to weaken the union movement by encouraging workers to reject the idea of unions and think individually rather than collectively, but this backfired. The result was a strengthening of unions and a determination to defeat the unfair workers' contracts. In the lead-up to the 2007 election the union movement ran a powerful campaign against the injustices of the Howard government, and their efforts, together with those of the Labor opposition, saw the government defeated and Prime Minister Howard actually lose his own seat.

Discrediting popular social movements

Along with NGOs and the union movement, popular social movements were also targeted for silencing by the political and corporate power elite in the Western world. Any movement which has the potential to interfere with the profit-making ability of the few is seen to be a threat and must be put down.

The feminist movement

Almost as soon as Second Wave feminism appeared in the 1960s, it was seen to be creating a "crisis of democracy", to adopt Noam Chomsky's term.[116] The Second Wave had a broad agenda, that:
- men share their power with women
- the situation of women be taken into account in all national and international decision-making
- men's violence against women and children be eliminated

---

[116] When discussing the situation in the United States described by the Pentagon in May 1967 as "domestic dissidence", Noam Chomsky adopted the term "crisis of democracy", which was a term introduced in 1975 by the Trilateral Commission. Domestic dissidence or crisis of democracy referred to "the massive civil disobedince involving ... women, youth, [and] segments of the intelligensia" (1992, p. 111).

- those in power stop condoning and encouraging men's violence as a way of keeping men in a state of perpetual preparation for war
- poverty and starvation, the victims of which are mainly women and children, be eliminated
- drug companies stop using women for experimental purposes
- the exploitation of women and children through pornography and prostitution cease.

Feminists were challenging some of the most sacred rights of men and male institutions to use and abuse women. It was not surprising, then, that there was a deliberate and sustained campaign of ridicule, lies and misinformation about the intent of feminist activism. Politicians and the media working together ensured that the movement was contained and that, to this day, dissenting feminist voices are either not heard at all or misrepresented in such a way as to reflect badly on feminism, making it an unattractive option for most women.

After being silenced for eleven years by the Howard government, feminist activists in Australia were hopeful that the new Labor government under Kevin Rudd would display a different, more open, attitude. It was presumed that it would want to hear from feminists concerned about the everyday injustices being perpetrated against women, but early indications were that feminist voices calling for radical change in male attitudes and behaviour were being ignored.

To its credit, the Rudd government moved quickly to respond to matters of injustice and neglect ignored by the previous government but, initially, there was no mention of the need to reduce or eliminate men's violence against women. Feminists were as pleased as all other fair-minded Australians with the government's attention to issues such as an apology to Indigenous people; Indigenous health issues (including closing the gap in life-expectancy between Indigenous and non-Indigenous people); binge drinking among young people; homelessness; poverty; and the restoring of democracy. Despite these efforts, feminists had grave concerns about what was missing from the Rudd agenda. There was no mention of men's violence against women, the wholesale subordination of women through pornography, the safety of women and children after separation and other issues many women deemed urgent; this was incomprehensible to feminists. However, most feminists agree that, while Time for Action, the national plan to reduce violence against women and their children mentioned in the previous chapter, was a long time coming, it is a welcome indication that the Rudd government strongly supports efforts to eradicate men's violence against women and children.

While Prime Minister Rudd was careful to choose strong women as ministers in his government and a well-qualified feminist lawyer as governor-general,[117] it was apparent that he was also careful to ensure that real power remained in the hands of men. The 2009 cabinet reshuffle actually saw women's representation reduced by one parliamentary secretary.

Movements for the liberation of racial minorities
The various movements protesting against the second-class status accorded to racial minorities in Western countries have also been targeted by political and economic conservatives. The preferred images of Indigenous women and men presented by the media are those of drunken groups sitting around in parks, young people roaming the streets in gangs, and people battered and bruised due to the violent behaviour of some toward family members and/or strangers. From the early days of the Black Liberation Movement in the United States and the Freedom Rides by Aboriginal activists in Australia in the 1960s, there has been a concerted campaign to discredit those who speak out about the injustices which are a daily reality in the lives of racial minorities.

Discrediting can take the form of accusations that Indigenous community councils or NGOs have mishandled public money; of implications that violence is more prevalent in Indigenous homes than in non-Indigenous homes; and of suggestions that activists are encouraging ongoing welfare dependency in Indigenous families. Those who speak out against such accusations point to the fact that criticism by governments and mainstream communities are rarely accompanied by any serious attempt to lift the standard of living and provide job and lifestyle opportunities for Indigenous women and men.

In April 2004, the federal government in Australia announced that the Aboriginal and Torres Strait Islander Commission (ATSIC), a federal body charged with overseeing the work and funding of Indigenous services throughout the country, was to be abolished.[118] It also announced that Indigenous programmes would be mainstreamed and that a group of distinguished Indigenous people would be formed (chosen and appointed by the minister) to advise the government on matters pertaining to Aboriginal and Torres Strait Islander people. While some ATSIC officials were not without fault and some criticisms of their priorities seemed justified, the dismantling and defunding of the whole commission and its replacement by

---

117 Women are a small numerical minority in the Rudd government. Out of twenty ministers in cabinet (including the prime minister), only four are women. The outer ministry consists of ten ministers, of whom only three are women. Of twelve parliamentary secretaries, since the 2009 reshuffle, only two are women. Queensland Governor Quentin Bryce AC, a prominent lawyer, academic, women's rights activist and former federal Sex Distrimination Commissioner, was chosen by the prime minister as governor-general of Australia, taking office in September 2008.

118 All of ATSIC's affairs were wound up by 30 June 2005.

an appointed body was a serious blow to Indigenous people nationally. It sent a clear message to them that the concerns of Indigenous leaders and activists were of no special consequence to the government.[119]

Prime Minister Howard coined the phrase "practical reconciliation" to indicate that political and social justice issues like land rights and the need for positive discrimination were off the agenda; the only concerns the government would listen to were those related to practical issues like health, housing, employment and policing.

Some state governments, too, downgraded their focus on Indigenous issues. After the 2006 Queensland government election, Labor Premier Peter Beattie announced that there would no longer be a portfolio devoted to Indigenous Affairs in his cabinet. Instead, Indigenous issues would be incorporated into the Communities portfolio, which already included communities, disability services and seniors. This move confirmed the suspicions of Indigenous leaders in Queensland that the government's attitude toward the Indigenous population was "out of sight, out of mind".

As mentioned earlier, there was no doubt that, in Australia, the policy of assimilation was back in vogue federally and in some states. With the focus on mainstream society, Indigenous people were given to understand that they must assimilate into the mainstream and take their chances alongside other Australians as equals. That racism and racial discrimination will never afford them equality was apparently not a consideration. Under assimilationist policies, dissent is silenced and Indigenous women and men disappear from the landscape. Indigenous leader Patrick Dodson warned of the Howard government's "assimilation agenda" in his response to the federal intervention into Indigenous communities in the Northern Territory:

> The tragedy of the Howard Government's eleven-year hold on power is that Indigenous policy has focused on destroying the potential for this nation to respect and nurture the cultural renaissance of traditional Indigenous society. Public policy that celebrates Indigenous culture has been shunned
>
> ...
>
> The current battleground of the assimilation agenda is located on that vast new region of northern and central Australia where Indigenous people maintain their languages, own their traditional lands under Western legal title, and practise their customs whilst seeking to survive on public sector programs whose poor design has resulted in entrenched dependency [Dodson 2007].

---

119 When the Rudd Labor government came to office, the contrast between it and the previous government on attitudes toward Indigenous people was marked. One of the first acts of the new government was to issue a formal apology to Australia's Indigenous people for past offences against them. Also, it initiated community consultations with a view to establishing a new national body for Indigenous affairs.

While the Rudd Labor government is proving to be much more humane in its dealings with issues affecting Indigenous people, its determination to continue with the Northern Territory intervention is reminiscent of the assimilationist policies of the previous government. Following the 2020 Summit in April 2008, Dodson was reported as calling for "a change to the 'assimilationist ethos' which he said underpinned Aboriginal affairs. [He stressed] the need for a 'new national dialogue'" (*Townsville Bulletin*, 21 April 2008, p. 7). The Indigenous voices receiving favourable attention by the Rudd government are the same as those heard by the previous government. They are the voices that recommend punishment for Indigenous people who do not measure up to the white standards imposed on them. While it is agreed that problems of alcoholism, violence and neglect of children need to be addressed urgently, Indigenous social justice activists insist that tactics such as withholding welfare benefits from families already living in serious poverty, or sending children out of their communities and away from their families in the hope that they will receive a better education, will only exacerbate the oppression.

As with dissenting feminist voices, few dissenting Indigenous voices were heard at the Rudd government's 2020 Summit. While there were some excellent advocates for social justice among the Indigenous nominees chosen to participate, there were also those who support punitive measures in an attempt to force a greater degree of assimilation on Indigenous families and communities.

Other racial minorities, those who had come to Australia as migrants or refugees, were also required to assimilate during the Howard years. Some politicians expressed the view that the term multiculturalism belongs in the 1970s and should be dropped from the community's vocabulary. "It's time to talk about the things that unite us", one Queensland politician said. The call to ignore differences is a call to focus on mainstream, and anyone from a non-mainstream racial group must do their best to assimilate or integrate.[120]

Since 9/11, men thought to be of Middle Eastern appearance are vulnerable to attack and discrimination by other citizens and their movements are subject to scrutiny by the Australian Federal Police as potential terrorists. Women and girls who wear the veil as a symbol of their Muslim faith are also subject to attack, ridicule and ostracism from other Australians. Muslim leaders and other human rights activists who speak out for justice for racial minorities are discredited and silenced.

---

120 On 18 August 2007, Australia's then minister for immigration, Kevin Andrews, announced that his government was cutting back on its intake of African refugees coming to Australia under the Humanitarian Settlement Scheme and suggested that Sudanese refugees in particular were having "integration problems", <http://www.abc.net.au/news/stories/2007/10/03/2050315.htm>.

The peace movement

During the Vietnam War, peace activists were largely responsible for the domestic dissidence that had the US administration and the Pentagon really concerned. In Australia, the peace movement was so strong at that time and had such an impact on the general population that the conservative government which had been in power for several decades was defeated by the Labor Party under Gough Whitlam, who had campaigned on the promise to bring Australia's troops home from Vietnam. Prime Minister Whitlam, appointed on 2 December 1972, did just that. The last of Australia's troops were brought home by the end of that year.

At the beginning of 2003, the peace movement again became a force to be reckoned with in many Western nations. Protesting against the US-led invasion of Afghanistan and the planned pre-emptive strike on Iraq, millions of people in the United States, Canada, Europe, Australia and New Zealand, marched and demonstrated for peace. Unbelievably, the strength of the peace movement was ignored by those intent on war, and even though protests continued well after the war had started, the power elite had a great deal of success in their efforts at discrediting protesters. Those involved in continuing demonstrations for peace were accused by politicians and the media of "not supporting our troops". The implication was that individual soldiers and their families who had given up so much to fight for "freedom for the Iraqi people" were being maligned by peace protesters. While the protests were never about individual soldiers, but rather about the decision by governments to visit war on another sovereign nation, the lies had the desired effect. The message of the protests was all but lost at peace rallies as speaker after speaker bent over backwards to assure everyone that they were not against individual soldiers. Also, many protesters, afraid of being seen in that light, pulled back from their protests.

The one group of peace activists which has consistently demonstrated for peace is Women in Black. Small groups of women around the world continue their vigils as a way of expressing publicly their opposition to war in Afghanistan, Iraq, the Middle East, Sudan and other places where the slaughter of human beings continues in the name of war. CODEPINK is another group of women formed in the United States in protest at the number of American troops killed in the Iraq War which, in their view, was an unnecessary and senseless war.[121]

---

121 For Women in Black, see <http://www.womeninblack.net/>. For CODEPINK, see <http://www.codepink4peace.org/>.

The environment movement

The discrediting of those involved in activism on environmental issues also continues without pause. Greenpeace and other green activists are often criticised for their methods of protest. Disparagingly referred to as the "loony left", they are accused of loving trees or fish or animals more than people. Those who act to protect old-growth forests from destruction by timber companies are said to be anti-development, anti-industry and uncaring about ordinary, hard-working people in the timber industry whose jobs are placed in jeopardy.

The growing concern about global warming and the call for developed nations to cut greenhouse emissions is still met with ridicule by some in politics and business. The Kyoto Protocol—a commitment to reducing greenhouse gases—was signed by all except the United States and Australia. Indeed, some in the Australian government during the Howard years jeered at the Kyoto Protocol, referring to it as a "slogan". Regardless of all the scientific evidence available, they tried to paint a picture of alarmist environmentalist activists inventing a slogan in an attempt to slow down the progress of industry and development. What's the point of committing to a slogan? they asked.

In the latter part of 2007, however, when the Australian government had to admit that global warming was shaping up to be a serious election issue, they began to present themselves as committed environmentalists, deeply concerned about global warming. The United States and Australia still refused to sign the Kyoto Protocol, but instead supported an alternative plan designed to sustain economic growth while investing in a "in a new, cleaner energy structure".[122]

In the lead-up to the 2007 federal election, the Labor Party opposition campaigned heavily on issues of climate change and concern about global warming. They made a commitment to the Australian people that, if they won the election, one of the first things they would do would be to sign the Kyoto Protocol. When they took office they were quick to add Australia's signature, leaving the United States as the sole nation out of step with the rest of the developed world.

The anti-globalisation movement

Ever since the Multilateral Agreement on Investment was mooted in the 1980s, dissidents have worked to uncover details of secret negotiations between multinational corporations and governments of the world's wealthiest nations.[123]

---

122 <http://www.newscientist.com/article/dn1932.html>.
123   See Clarke and Barlow 1997.

Suggestions by international finance and trade institutions that dominance of the global market by (mainly) US companies will eradicate poverty and hunger in poorer countries is scoffed at by anti-globalisation activists, who quote one example after another of subsistence farmers being forced off their land by multinational corporations and into unemployment, homelessness and deeper poverty than they have ever experienced before.

World social forums, national social forums, demonstrations timed to coincide with meetings of top-level government, finance and trade meetings reveal that the anti-globalisation movement is extremely well organised and determined to have an impact. Consequently, the power elite have worked hard to discredit it by claiming that demonstrators are violent, that they have no concern for those living in poverty, that they are against business and development taking place in underdeveloped countries, that their actions exacerbate poverty and starvation, and that their only concern is for themselves and their own selfish interests.

The fierce nature of the attempts to discredit the anti-globalisation movement is due, no doubt, to the fact that their words and actions expose and threaten to undermine the comfortable relationship which exists between the politically and economically powerful.[124] Individuals and groups targeted for special silencing are those who resist and reject their government's programmes of mind-manipulation, thought control and indoctrination and who see the power elite's propaganda for what it is.

While the individuals involved in NGOs, unions and popular social movements often pay a high price in terms of personal stress, rejection and feelings of hopelessness and helplessness in the face of powerful opposition, their determination to continue the fight for social justice makes a huge contribution to any society. Activists speaking out for the rights of less privileged members of society, of workers, women, Indigenous people, communities of people from non-English-speaking backgrounds, lesbians and gay men, those speaking out for peace, for the environment and for the poor are all engaging in a fight, not simply for justice for the people they represent but, also, for the very survival of democracy.

Following my analysis of the tactics used to silence women (Chapter Three) and those used to silence dissent generally (this chapter), we turn now to an analysis of the ways in which women, including feminists, silence each other.

---

124 There are also problems of male domination in the anti-globalisation movement. Feminists who have tried to address certain glaring inequalities have been met with attitudes of impatience and silencing. See Hawthorne 2007, pp. 125–38.

WOMEN SILENCING WOMEN 5

Any discussion of women silencing women must address the complexity of the issues involved. Without a doubt, silencing does occur between women and the central aim of this chapter is to explore that phenomenon. Along with actual silencing, however, there are also *perceptions* of silencing and *accusations* of silencing.

Also, there is the question of what it is that represents silencing. Does criticism or disagreement equal silencing? Then there is the question of intent. If it was not my intention to silence you but you *felt* silenced by what I said or did, does that mean that I silenced you? Must I take responsibility for how your perception of my words and actions made you feel?

While this chapter will give some attention to the ways in which women from all walks of life silence other women, the main focus is on the silencing which occurs of, by and among feminists. Before addressing the actual silencing of women by women, including the silencing of lesbians, radical feminists, Indigenous women and women from ethnic and religious minorities, I want to discuss and illustrate the kinds of false accusations levelled at feminists. Some of those accusations come from the genuine perceptions of women who feel inside themselves that they have been put down by feminists. Others come from observers of women's behaviour, journalists and other commentators who seem to delight in finding examples of feminists supposedly excluding and silencing other women.

Perceptions of silencing

From the early days of Second Wave feminism to the present, some women have expressed the feeling that feminists have shunned and criticised them when, from the perspective of the movement itself, that was not the case. It is common, even today, to hear women express the opinion that "feminists criticise me because I choose to be a stay-at-home mum", or "feminists don't approve of the fact that I love my husband and family and put them first in my life", or "professional women look down on me because I'm just an administrative assistant".

While it may be true that there are incidents of individual feminists passing these judgements on other women, it is fair to say that such criticisms do not reflect the philosophy of the feminist movement nor the attitude of the majority of feminists.

The emphasis in feminism—indeed, the stated objective of the feminist movement—is to push for justice for women, usually expressed by Western liberal feminists as "equality with men". In practical terms this means that a woman must have the freedom to be who she wants to be and the freedom to make her own decisions.[125] Liberal feminists emphasise the need for equal opportunity in education and employment for those who choose to pursue further study and/or to work outside the home, the need for equal pay for equal work and for total control over one's own body. While such issues are central to the feminist struggle and liberal feminists are active in pushing government and business leaders to acknowledge their responsibility to bring about a greater equality between the sexes, radical feminists emphasise other issues, issues which stand in the way of equality ever being realised.[126] Radical feminists insist that there is no point in agitating for equality without also challenging society's condoning of such practices as men's violence against women in the home, rape of women and children, prostitution, pornography, restrictions on women's freedom in the name of religion and the use and abuse of women's bodies for harmful medical experimentation.

In their vocal criticisms of such practices, radical feminists are also critical of the women who support them. Therefore, it is important to ask: Does such robust criticism represent silencing? Prostitutes who argue that it is their right to choose to work in the "sex industry" often express the view that they are being silenced by feminists who criticise the "choices" that they have made. Also, some Muslim women question the right of Western feminists to criticise their "choice" to wear the veil, and feel silenced by such criticism. The issue of what constitutes silencing is addressed below under the heading "Actual silencing".

---

125 Liberal feminists working for women's equality with men are confronted with a conundrum. How is it possible for individual women to achieve to the same degree as men when patriarchal societal structures constrain women in every way?

126 It is this difference in emphasis which has created the perception that liberal feminists are positive and radical feminists are negative. For liberal feminists, a victim of rape is a "survivor" who should be empowered to leave the past behind and get on with her life. For radical feminists, she is a "victim/survivor" who should be encouraged to be angry at her rapist and to join with other women in maintaining the rage and insisting on a change in men's attitudes toward women. It is only through acknowledging that she is a victim, expressing her anger and seeking justice, either through the courts or in some other way, that she will be able to become a survivor in the true sense of the word. For more on a radical feminist analysis of the central role justice plays in the restoring of mental and emotional health, see McLellan 1995, pp. 64–70.

Accusations of silencing

False perceptions of the silencing of women by women are often formed as a result of the deliberate misrepresentation of feminists by those whose aim is to present feminism in the worst possible light. The remark by former Prime Minister John Howard, quoted in the previous chapter, that strident "ultra-feminist groups in the community … sneer at and look down on women choosing to provide full-time care for their children" (Sawer 2003, p. 3) is one such blatant misrepresentation designed to cause mischief. False perceptions are formed from false accusations.

One of the noticeable features of opinion pieces in the mainstream print media is the continued criticism of feminists by certain journalists. Rarely do opinion pieces by radical feminists or supporters of feminism's call for justice for women globally and nationally see the light of day but, when someone expresses yet another "clever" slant on the evils of feminism, it is snapped up by the editor and printed immediately.

In the *Sydney Morning Herald* in July 2006, a piece headed "A Shameful Silence on Women's Rights" had an editorial subtitle designed to grab readers' attention: "Paul Sheehan asks why Western feminists are mute on the plight of their Islamic sisters". In his article Sheehan attempts to link two issues to illustrate how Western feminists have let Muslim women down on both counts. One is the gang-rapes of dozens of young women in Sydney by Muslim men. The other is the treatment of Muslim women by fundamentalist men in Muslim cultures around the world. While Sheehan admits the extreme complexity of the "cultural clash" between fundamentalist Muslims and the Western world, he nevertheless finds someone to blame for the violence some Muslim men perpetrate against Muslim and non-Muslim women. Ignoring his own and other men's inaction, he says:

> In the midst of this cultural and moral struggle one element has been conspicuously missing—the feminists—the authors, academics and commentators who rose to prominence as advocates of women's rights. In Australia and Europe, their response to the growing levels of sexual intimidation, harassment or suppression of women by Muslim men has either been a deafening chorus of silence, or denial and blame-shifting [2006a].

A moment's examination of Sheehan's article shows that, in his enthusiasm for accusing Western feminists of remaining silent about the plight of women under Islam, he has actually skewed the facts on both issues. First, the gang-rapes in Sydney were perpetrated by Muslim men against non-Muslim women, so the accusation that Western feminists were "mute on the plight of their Islamic sisters" hardly applies. Second, none of the female Muslim authors he quotes to support his claim that Western feminists have deserted them actually blames feminists. They criticise leftist intellectuals from the West but not specifically feminists. Ayaan Hirsi Ali blamed "the adherents to the gospel of multiculturalism" for deliberately overlooking aspects of Muslim culture that oppress women (2006). Irshad Manji blamed "Western liberals" for their double standards, although it ought to be acknowledged that Manji is far more positive about the West than negative. Indeed, a major theme of her book is expressed in the chapter title "Thank God for the West" (2003, pp. 211–24). Taslima Nasreen called for an end to the double standards of "liberal Western intellectuals" who adhere to cultural relativism.[127] None of the authors actually blames feminists, but Sheehan chooses to leave his readers with the impression that they do.

Sheehan's opinion piece—which, incidentally, received widespread attention in Australia—is at best a sloppy piece of journalism, and at worst a deliberate misrepresentation of the facts in order to present Western feminists in a bad light.[128]

False accusations against feminists abound in the media, with feminists themselves being granted few opportunities to respond. Among their regular critics in the Australian media are a number of women, including Janet Albrechtsen, Bettina Arndt and Miranda Devine. By far the most persistent of those critics is the right-wing journalist Albrechtsen who, with monotonous predictability, criticises feminists at every turn. Her favourite theme in recent years has been the way "selfish, self-centred, self-indulgent" Western feminists have ignored the plight of women from other cultures. In an opinion piece on 6 September 2006, in which she supported Prime Minister Howard's latest initiatives designed to curb the violence of some Muslim men, Albrechtsen mocked Australian feminists by accusing them of being "obsessed with glass ceilings, pay discrepancies and men not changing the right number of nappies" rather than showing some concern about the violence perpetrated against Muslim women (2006). If glass ceilings, pay discrepancies and equality in the home were the only issues feminists focused on, one would have to agree with her criticism. She chose to focus narrowly on a very small group of liberal women and ignore the overwhelming majority of feminists who consistently rage against men's violence in all its forms.

---

127 For more on the thoughts of Taslima Nasreen, see Nasreen 2005.

128 It must be said that Sheehan's article took many feminists by surprise because he had previously been very supportive of women and women's rights. In Girls Like You, published at around the same time in 2006, he wrote movingly about the Sydney rapes and expressed considerable anger at the way the women victims had been treated in the courts. Feminists still see him as an ally in the fight for justice for women but are confused by the accusatory tone of his July 2006 opinion piece.

Earlier, Albrechtsen referred to the gang-rapes of young women in Sydney and, like Sheehan, asked: "Where was the feminist outcry?" Implying that feminists were more interested in appearing culturally sensitive than speaking out against violence against women, she said: "the silence of the feminists and others on egregious cultural issues is having devastating consequences for women" (2005). In the same article, Albrechtsen raised the matter of the 14-year-old Aboriginal girl, mentioned in Chapter Three, who was bashed and raped by a 55-year-old elder to whom she had been promised under customary Indigenous law. Again, Albrechtsen accused Australian feminists of caring more about culture than about the violence perpetrated against a 14-year-old girl: "And who were the leading critics of this case? Chris Ellison (a white man), Warren Mundine (a black man) and a few indigenous women. But where was the white feminist outcry?" (2005).

One wonders how much research journalists like Albrechtsen do before blaming feminists. Do they bother to ask feminists working in rape crisis centres and other women's services around the country how many of them write letters to the editor following such horrendous events, letters which are rarely published? Do they ask feminist academics, writers and activists how many of them write opinion pieces that are simply ignored by the mainstream media? Do they go into the many internet blogs where feminists and other women discuss these difficult and perplexing issues in an attempt to find ways for their protests to be heard in the wider community? Do they ask politicians how many contacts they receive from feminists demanding that initiatives are put in place to change men's violent attitudes and behaviour toward women? Do they inquire about the number of feminist groups in Australia, the United States and Europe who work with and support women's groups in Afghanistan, Iraq, Palestine, Pakistan, Bangladesh, Sudan and other predominantly Muslim countries? It seems not. Journalists whose personal agenda is to ridicule and criticise feminists and feminism do not seem to feel the need to do genuine research and the concept of journalistic integrity seems not to apply.

The phenomenon of women journalists who verbally attack and falsely accuse feminists and other women was analysed by leading Australian psychotherapist and commentator, Stephanie Dowrick, in her 2004 book, *Free Thinking*:

> There is a kind of awesome monotony with which they return to their insistence on women's capacity for manipulation, revenge, selfishness, narrow-mindedness and plain nastiness. This far from pretty view is augmented by a view of men that casts them into almost equally dreary and limited roles as victims, dupes and martyrs [p. 60].

In response to her own question, "What drives a woman to write so negatively and obsessively about other women?", Dowrick concludes:

> The answer closest to hand is that most women who don't like other women lack a secure and reliable sense of identity, however "assertive" they may appear. Gender is fundamental to the creation of a secure sense of self. That means it's mighty hard to feel good about yourself while also feeling contempt and mistrust for your own sex. The same is true for men. Yet there are fewer "men-haters" among men ... [pp. 60, 61].

Her conclusion is that "no woman can grow in self-respect while publicly or privately doing other women down" and that, while there is nothing wrong with "looking critically" at one's own sex, there is a distinction between criticism aimed at healing and that aimed at harming (p. 62).

Accusations that feminists ignore the plight of women who are victims of men's violence, victims of a system which despises and uses them up, are so far from the truth as to be almost laughable. The frustrating truth is that feminists are ignored and silenced by the media and then criticised by representatives of the media for not speaking out.

Actual silencing

While false perceptions and false accusations of silencing abound and feminists have no choice but to live with the frustration of having their words and intentions misunderstood and misrepresented, it is also true that actual silencing of women by women, feminists by feminists, does occur. Historically, Second Wave feminism is littered with examples of deliberate attempts at silencing women who are outside mainstream feminism.

It can be argued that the feminist movement is a microcosm of society and, as such, reflects the prejudices and conflicts of society in general. Although some feminists might reject such an unflattering assessment, I suspect that there is a great deal of truth in it. The feminist battle against injustice and prejudice is always waged from within the culture which produces those injustices and prejudices and which all citizens internalise through the process of socialisation. As with all social justice activists, the feminist commitment to changing the way cultures around the world subordinate and oppress women involves a commitment to unlearning the negative attitudes learned through socialisation and replacing them with positive, more inclusive and transformative attitudes. Radical feminists, both lesbian and heterosexual, have succeeded in these endeavours as shown by the consistency with which they reject systematic injustices against women and demand a transformation of society's patriarchal institutions and attitudes—not just a trimming around the edges, but complete transformation.

While both radical and liberal feminists have had some significant successes in the West, resulting in a slight easing of the burden for many women, it must be said that there have also been some serious failures. The exclusion and silencing of diverse groups of women by mainstream feminists is one such failure and, while it is a difficult and painful issue for white middle-class feminists to face up to, it is a discussion we need to have.

Before focusing on the silencing of groups such as lesbian feminists, radical feminists, Indigenous women and women from culturally and linguistically diverse backgrounds, we must look at the issue of what represents silencing.

When I raised this matter at the beginning of the chapter, I asked two questions. First, does criticism or disagreement equal silencing? No, it does not, even though women often choose to interpret it as such. The truth is that many women wilt in response to criticism or disagreement and become silent, which is quite different from saying that they have been silenced. If criticism and disagreement did equate with silencing, women could never enter into free-flowing discussions and robust exchanges of opinions and ideas. In a healthy democracy, women and men alike are able to express opinions, present rational arguments, offer judgements based on research, impressions or emotions and generally throw ideas back and forth. Most people accept at a rational level that there must be differences of opinion but, in reality, many people (women and men) want others to agree with them all the time and feel threatened when someone disagrees. Men's response is often to become abusive or to retreat into silence, while women's response is usually to retreat and resolve not to express their opinions so freely in the future.

In their own defence, "silenced" women often explain that it is not criticism or disagreement *per se* which causes them to feel that they have been silenced but, rather, the tone with which the criticism or disagreement is delivered. Feminists who have developed a healthy confidence and assertiveness sometimes forget to take into account the fact that other women/feminists may not have developed that same level of confidence. In all our interactions, whether with other women, with children or with men, it seems crucial, as a matter of common courtesy, that we tailor the tone of our responses to fit our audience.[129]

The foregoing brings us to the second question: Am I guilty of silencing another person simply because she feels silenced by my words or actions? If it was not my intention to silence her, must I take responsibility for the feeling elicited by her perception of my intentions? The answer is a qualified "no". In

---

[129] Some criticise this approach as patronising; others see it as an important concession to living harmoniously together as people from different backgrounds and with different life experiences.

the 1980s the "no" would have been clear-cut. When the emphasis was on individual human potential, on personal empowerment, on the individual's right to do and say whatever they liked regardless of the consequences to another person, it was deemed acceptable to say: "I'm not responsible for how you choose to interpret what I've said. I can say what I like, and how you feel about what I've said is your own responsibility." At that time, such an attitude was lauded by some as a sign of an individual's advanced personal development, whereas today there is more chance of its being seen as arrogant, insensitive and devoid of any understanding of what it means to be a member of a community.

While students of psychology and sociology have moved past the focus on the individual as the be-all and end-all, global politics still operates according to that philosophy. It took politicians, business leaders and financial institutions a little while to catch up, but once they grasped the potential for greed and dominance and manipulation inherent in the liberal/libertarian philosophy, they took hold of it with both hands. Unscrupulous and arrogant political leaders believe that they can do as they like, regardless of the effect their actions may have on poorer and militarily weaker nations, as well as on their own citizens. Business and financial institutions do as they like within the constraints of the law regardless of the effect their actions may have in terms of creating more poverty, malnutrition, ill-health and homelessness for more and more people. Similarly, religious fundamentalists do as they like regardless of the effect their actions may have on women or men.

Radical feminists and other social justice activists work to replace the harsh, individualist philosophy of neoliberalism with one that takes account of diversity, the need for community and the sharing of wealth and opportunity. Must I take responsibility for the effects of my words and actions on others? When seen in the light of global hegemony, the answer is "yes". When seen in the light of an individual's feeling silenced by words not intended to silence, the answer is "no" because there was no intention to silence, but "yes" in the sense that living in a community demands a certain level of sensitivity.

Having established that, in personal interactions between women, criticism and disagreement do not equate with silencing and, also, that a woman's perception of having been silenced (when that was not the intention of the speaker) does not automatically equate with silencing, it is time now to move into a discussion of how certain groups of women are silenced by other women.

Relationships between groups of women (including groups of feminists) reflect the dynamics of society at large. White middle-class women whose behaviour is within the bounds of patriarchal acceptability are afforded a degree of power in society not available to non-mainstream women.

Although mainstream women only have access to as much power as men will allow, they nevertheless have more power than non-mainstream women. As discussed in earlier chapters, power brings with it the privilege of speech and the ability to silence the speech of others. Within the feminist movement, there is evidence of deliberate silencing and also of silencing by omission. Attempts to silence lesbians and radical feminists have been deliberate, while the silencing of Indigenous women and culturally and linguistically diverse women has occurred in the most part through ignorance and insensitivity to difference. My discussion of the actual silencing of women by women will touch on the silencing of each of these groups by feminists whose power is relative to their connection with, and acceptability to, the mainstream.

Lesbian feminists

The campaign by heterosexual feminists to silence lesbian feminists during the 1970s and 1980s, even though the movement was driven from its beginnings by the energy and commitment of lesbians, is a fact of history. In a speech to a small group of lesbian feminists in New York in 1977, Adrienne Rich painted a picture of the invaluable contribution lesbians had made to the women's liberation movement:

> In this country, as in the world today, there is a movement of women going on like no other in history. Let us have no doubt: it is being fueled and empowered by the work of lesbians. Lesbians are running presses, starting magazines and distribution systems, setting up crisis centers and halfway houses for rape victims and battered women; creating political dialogues; changing our use of language; making a truly lesbian and female history available for us for the first time; doing grassroots organizing and making visionary art [1979, p. 228].

This fact has been acknowledged and reiterated by feminist historians ever since. There is no doubt that lesbian feminists "fueled and empowered" the feminist movement that emerged in the late 1960s. How is it, then, that lesbians within the movement were the victims of silencing and exclusion by heterosexual feminists from the earliest days? For lesbian feminists, the struggle was not only against men and patriarchal systems that oppressed women, but also against other feminists who were embarrassed by their presence in the movement and sought to be rid of them.

In the introduction to a small but powerful book titled *Lesbianism and the Women's Movement* (1975), the editors Nancy Myron and Charlotte Bunch refer to "the straight–gay splits of 1970–71". Lesbian feminists, they explain, were attacked by feminists "for being 1) lesbian chauvinists, 2) into oppressive sex roles, or 3) divisive to the women's movement" (p. 11).

Lesbian chauvinism

Jill Johnston in *Lesbian Nation: The Feminist Solution* (1973) expressed the opinion that the term "lesbian chauvinist" was "an easy invention by association to further discredit the lesbian as the upsetting gadfly in the feminist movement" (p. 148). Myron and Bunch commented that the label was simply an excuse to dismiss issues around heterosexuality that made some feminists uncomfortable. In response to the accusation that lesbians wanted to "guilt-trip women about their personal lives", they said:

> analyzing heterosexuality necessarily raises questions about women's lives. So too does analysis of almost any issue impacting women: motherhood, marriage, etc. Are we to abandon our insights into these institutions of male supremacy in order to avoid making each other uncomfortable? Political thought and change do not develop by avoiding conflict and refusing to question what we have been taught is "natural" or "personal". What is feminism about if it is not continually challenging and changing our lives? [1975, p. 11].

Several of the early lesbian feminist writers refer to "heterosexual privilege" and the perception that lesbians in the movement would threaten that privilege. In Adrienne Rich's words, many feminists feared that they would be "'discredited' if perceived as lesbians" (1979, p. 202) or if the movement was seen as questioning, in Sheila Jeffreys' words, "the naturalness of heterosexuality" (1993, p. xii).

Coletta Reid, in her personal account of "coming out in the women's movement", said that she was not prepared for the hostile reaction she received from her heterosexual feminist sisters.

> I had expected joy and jubilation, since I was choosing myself, other women, and strength. The non-committal attitude turned to outright hostility whenever I discussed the political implications of my choice …
>
> I slowly left the women's movement or more accurately I was slowly pushed out. I had never envisioned myself a lesbian/separatist when I left my husband. The women's movement had given me the ideas, strength and support to do something I thought best for me and womankind; I had no idea it would reject me once I had done it [in Myron and Bunch 1975, pp. 94–5].

Since "male chauvinism" was the term used by early feminists to criticise the dominance of men over women, the term "lesbian chauvinism" was no doubt invented for the purpose of inflicting hurt on lesbians and driving them out of the movement.

Oppressive sex roles

The second criticism by heterosexual feminists, mentioned by Myron and Bunch, was that lesbians were involved in playing out oppressive sex roles. There is no doubt that many lesbians, in the early 1970s, were into butch–femme roleplaying because the only examples available to them were those of heterosexual relationships where the man was dominant and the woman passive. Unhappy with their analysis of the power dynamics in male–female, butch–femme sex roles, however, lesbian feminists began experimenting with new, more equal ways of being in relationships.

Sheila Jeffreys' important article "Butch and Femme: Now and Then" discusses the history of the butch–femme phenomenon; she points out that in lesbian feminist circles in the 1970s "lesbians avoided identifying themselves as butch or femme" (1993, p. 158). At one point she quotes Del Martin and Phyllis Lyon describing

> the process they worked through before they had a feminist analysis, away from butch femme roles which didn't seem to fit the reality of their relating in any way, toward "acting as people, as ourselves, as women rather than as caricatures in a heterosexual marriage. But it took us a while" [p. 173].

Divisive to the women's movement

The charge that lesbian feminists were creating division in the movement seemed to come from the perception that lesbians were "demanding that every woman be a lesbian". According to Myron and Bunch, this was not true:

> We are less concerned with whether each woman personally becomes a lesbian than with the destruction of heterosexuality as a crucial part of male supremacy. Lesbians have been the quickest to see the challenge to heterosexuality as necessary to feminists' survival [1975, p. 12].

The concern expressed by many lesbian feminists was that "women remaining tied to men prevents them from seeing the function of heterosexuality and acting to end it". Whoever was causing the division in the women's movement (whether lesbians or heterosexual women), Myron and Bunch declared: "We won't get beyond this division by demanding that lesbians retreat, politics in hand, back into the closet" (pp. 12–13).

Sadly, the persistent criticisms of lesbians in the movement did have the effect of silencing many of them. When the two-pronged battle became too much—the battle for justice for women at social and political levels and the battle for justice for themselves within the movement—some lesbians retreated into the relative safety of suburbia, some became separatists and some put their energies into the "gay" movement.

Those who retreated to suburbia chose to live somewhat solitary lives with their lesbian partners and a small circle of friends. They withdrew from the political scene to focus on the individual and private pursuits of establishing a home, having babies, succeeding in employment and, generally, mimicking the lives of heterosexual couples. Mimicking the heterosexual lifestyle also allowed them to feel more "normal".

Those who retreated to become separatists saw separatism as a political choice when, in fact, many worked at creating a life where they did not have to engage politically. Many lesbian separatists worked at establishing their own exclusive communities where the focus was on organic farming, healthy living and offering support and sustenance to each other. Commenting on the separatist phenomenon, Jeffreys said:

> There are some lesbian feminists who, feeling exhausted and disillusioned by the struggle to persuade heterosexual feminists to take lesbians seriously into account, have chosen to drop the title feminist. They call themselves radical lesbians or just separatists. I do not see how the interests of lesbians can be separated out from the interests of women as a class ... [1993, p. xiii].

Writing a few years earlier, Janice Raymond referred to separatism as "dissociation from the world". While she understood women's reasons for choosing to dissociate, she, like Jeffreys, questioned its helpfulness in terms of making the world a better place for women.

> Because women have been the eternal victims of male tyranny ... many women have developed a dissociation from the world.
>
> The difficulty ... is that when dissociation becomes a prominent mode of existence ... female existence becomes segregated from the rest of the world. Philosophically this can make women narrow in vision; politically it can make them very vulnerable ...
>
> The politically dissociated feminist plays the revolutionary in a community of other like-minded women but does not really impinge on the dominant male ethos [1986, pp. 153–4].

While a retreat into total separatism is seen as an unproductive stance by feminists who give high priority to engagement with the world, degrees of separatism have been seen as crucial to the survival of women in a world dominated by men, male images and male demands. Susan Hawthorne's distinction between separation and separatism is important. Separation "is used as a tool of oppression by the powerful", while separatism "is a political strategy used by the dispossessed to counter the oppressive social system".[130]

One of the priorities of the women's liberation movement in the 1960s and 1970s was the development of "women-only" spaces where women could meet and discuss issues affecting their lives. Time out from the requirement to be constantly cognisant of the needs of men proved to be refreshing and empowering for women. Separatism as retreat for the purposes of rejuvenation, inspiration and building strength continues to be a high priority for feminists, both lesbian and heterosexual. Right from the start, women had to fight to keep the women-only spaces they created on university campuses, women's centres and other places because reaction from the mainstream was sometimes fierce. In recent years, however, with the influence of postmodernism and the emphasis on "gender", many women-only spaces and programmes have disappeared. Lesbian-only spaces, too, have been under serious attack by those who insist that lesbians welcome into their spaces male-to-female transpeople who identify as lesbians. This issue is raised again when discussing the "postmodern emphasis on gender" later in this chapter.

Those lesbian feminists who retreated into the gay movement made a choice to focus on gay rights rather than women's rights. Undeterred by the gay movement's almost exclusive focus on gay men's issues, many lesbians were happy to invest their energies in supporting safe-sex campaigns and caring for men with AIDS. In recent years, the gay movement has become the queer movement where lesbian issues continue to be subordinated not only to gay men's issues but also to those of transsexuals, bisexuals and intersexuals. Even though many lesbians in the queer movement are used up in the service of others, they continue to bring an enormous amount of energy to the task.

While many lesbians did retreat from the women's liberation movement in the early years, others were determined to stay on because the feminist battle for women's rights was far too important to them to allow it to be taken over and, some feared, watered down by women who had a vested interest in pleasing men. Lesbian feminists formed the nucleus of that branch of the movement which became known as radical feminism.

---

130 Email to f-agenda discussion list, 24 October 2007, quoted with permission from the author.

Radical feminists

Lesbians who stayed in the feminist movement were known as radical feminists because of their insistence on confronting the root cause of women's oppression which, in their view, was male domination. All feminists, both lesbian and heterosexual, who see "sexism as the fundamental inequality" (Jaggar and Struhl 1978, pp. 118–27) and the central task of feminism as that of fighting for justice for women in an overwhelmingly oppressive patriarchal system, are happy to call themselves radical feminists.

As outlined in the Introduction, the feminist movement in the 1970s had already developed several philosophical strands as identified by Jaggar and Struhl: liberalism, traditional Marxism, radical feminism and socialist feminism. Liberal feminists saw inequality of opportunity between the sexes as the fundamental oppression; Marxist and socialist feminists focused on class; while radical feminists focused on sex and sexism, basing their activism on the belief that the fundamental oppression in society is men's dominance over women.

Shulamith Firestone, in *The Dialectic of Sex* (1970), used the terms "sex class" and "sex war", and spoke of the need for a feminist revolution aimed at eliminating female oppression. Such a task, she warned, would not be easy:

> For feminist revolution we shall need an analysis of the dynamics of sex war as comprehensive as the Marx–Engels analysis of class antagonism was for the economic revolution. More comprehensive. For we are dealing with a larger problem, with an oppression that goes back beyond recorded history ... [p. 12].

Charlotte Bunch wrote that sexism, the domination of women by men, is the first and deepest form of oppression. The "original imperialism", she said, "was male over female: the male claiming the female body and her service as his territory (or property)" (in Myron and Bunch 1975, p. 32). This original oppression was followed by men's domination on the basis of race, class and national identity and, while the feminist task is to concentrate on fighting men's dominance over women, Bunch adds that women's "war against male supremacy does ... [also] involve attacking the latter-day dominations based on class, race, and nation" (pp. 32–3).

Denise Thompson, in *Radical Feminism Today* (2001), reiterates the point that male supremacy/domination is the fundamental problem and that oppression on the basis of race or class cannot be properly understood without a prior understanding of the "male supremacist ideology that only men count as 'human'" (p. 95). She explains:

> Feminism cannot afford to give priority to the politics of race or class while ignoring male supremacy ... to ignore male supremacy is to empty feminist politics of its central meaning. With that central meaning in place, the political challenge to pernicious distinctions based on race and class takes on a different appearance [p. 92].

Starting from the premise that oppression on the basis of sex is the fundamental oppression, radical feminism maintains its focus on identifying and opposing male domination (Thompson 2001, p. 3) and refuses to soften or change that focus. Catharine MacKinnon was correct to call it "feminism unmodified" (1987, p. 16).

It is because of this refusal to be diverted that radical feminists have suffered criticism and ridicule over many years from other feminists, in particular from those who adhere to liberal and postmodernist philosophies.

Renate Klein, internationally known Australian radical feminist, spoke at a conference in Townsville (2002) of the dilemma she experienced when the dust finally settled after several years' battle to save the women's studies course at Deakin University in Geelong and Melbourne. Eventually the battle was lost and hundreds of students who had chosen Deakin University precisely because of the radical nature of its women's studies area were left feeling puzzled and deceived by the university. Klein's dilemma was between not wanting to speak out against other (liberal) feminists, while at the same time not wanting to contribute to the disappearance of years and years of radical feminist work (2002, p. 12). Such has been the dilemma experienced by most radical feminists since the mid-1980s. Knowing that male dominance affected all women and that a favourite tactic of patriarchy was to weaken groups that opposed them by encouraging division in their ranks, they were reluctant to engage in public criticism of those feminists they privately referred to as "sex liberals" and "reproductive liberals". However, the ferocious nature of some of the attacks against them convinced radical feminists that they ought to fight back, precisely for the reason Klein highlighted—that not speaking out comes at a price, and the price is that of "contributing to invisibilising ... years of radical feminist work" on any given issue (p. 12).

Radical feminists had worked tirelessly to prevent the use and abuse of women's bodies through reproductive technologies and other enterprises of the medical and pharmaceutical industries, as well as through pornography, prostitution and trafficking. They had worked to convince governments and lawyers of the need for law reform to criminalise men's violence against women in the home; to highlight the fact that rape can and does occur in marriage and should be treated as a crime; and to strengthen laws against rape of women and children by men known to them as well as by strangers. Also, they had worked to establish safe places for traumatised women and children, such as women's refuges, women's centres and rape crisis services, where they could be assured that no man would intrude on their private, healing space.

According to radical feminist researchers and commentators, the liberal emphasis on "individual choice" and the postmodernist emphasis on "gender" have seriously undermined efforts to achieve justice for women.

The liberal emphasis on individual choice

Liberal feminists preach the doctrine of "choice". They believe, for example, that individual women ought to be allowed the "choice" to participate in reproductive technologies, to "donate" eggs for stem cell research, and to "work" as porn stars and prostitutes. The propaganda coming out of the reproductive technology industry, and supported by liberal feminists, emphasises sentiments such as "every woman has a right to a child"; "stem cell research will save lives"; and young women who donate their eggs will be "contributing to life-saving medical science". Medical experimentation is touted as inherently good, regardless of the cost to so many women who do not actually end up with a baby after years of IVF or who suffer health problems as a result of having their eggs "farmed" on a regular basis. Misleading propaganda coming out of the pornography and prostitution industries, too, is that "sex work is a matter of choice" and "sex work in all its forms is empowering for women".

Radical feminists who speak out against such oppressive practices as IVF, pornography and prostitution are criticised by liberals as "depriving women of agency". Clearly, to liberal feminists, an individual woman's right to "choose" to be exploited is more important than the exploitation itself.

Also, on the issue of violence against women, the liberal emphasis on equality encourages and supports sentiments such as "women are violent too" (as if the 3 per cent of domestic violence perpetrated by women equates with the 97 per cent perpetrated by men); and "men can be raped too" (as if the smaller percentage of men raped, usually by men, equates with the much larger percentage of women raped by men). The use of language such as "a violent relationship" or "sex between father and daughter" is meant to cover up the fact that, in most cases, it is men who are violent and men who rape their children.

The postmodern emphasis on gender

Postmodernists, encouraging the use of the word gender, support the closing of women's studies programmes in universities and replacing them with gender studies programmes; the aim is to depoliticise the sex debate by giving equal attention to women and men. Government funding for research in primary and secondary education is awarded to projects focusing on boys in reaction to a perceived bias in favour of girls. Domestic violence services, established originally to assist women who were victims of men's violence in the home, are now required to focus on family violence, playing down the fact that the vast majority of violence in the home is perpetrated by men against women. Services receiving government funding are required to develop perpetrator programmes to assist men in addition to supporting and empowering women and children.

The emphasis on "gender" dismisses decades of radical feminist research which reveals that men's violence against women is complex and requires more than simple anger management courses or mediation sessions if the problem is to be addressed effectively. Far from collapsing both sexes into one and calling it "gender", the radical strategy begins with an appropriate focus on the situation of each player, perpetrator and victim. It then calls for the immediate protection of the victims (usually women and children) from the perpetrators (usually men) while, at the same time, addressing the deeper, more entrenched problem of men's and patriarchy's negative attitude toward women.

Another serious problem for women is that caused by the belief, supported by postmodernism, that male-to-female transsexuals ought to be given access to women-only spaces. As mentioned earlier, radical feminists have worked hard to convince governments of the need for safe spaces where men are not permitted entry, but now queer enthusiasts insist that transsexuals living as females (even though not biologically female, even after surgery) ought to be treated as women and given access to all the places where women have hitherto felt safe. While it is not disputed that transpeople living as females do need support and access to safe spaces, lesbian feminists insist that that should not be at the expense of spaces created by and for women-born-female.

In a paper titled "Sappho had a Party and ...", presented at the International Feminist Summit in Townsville, Australia, in 2007, Spiderlily Redgold reiterated this point when she spoke of the need for lesbian feminists to search for "a positive way forward as allies of transpeople ... without relinquishing lesbian gender identity rights" (2007, p. 1).

To sum up, radical feminists have watched while many of the gains they made for women in the 1970s and 1980s have been systematically rolled back by liberal and postmodernist feminists working hand-in-glove with conservative politicians, universities, the media and industry leaders.

While the division between radical and liberal feminists was there from the beginning of Second Wave feminism, it only became obvious and public in the early 1980s. Four events, and the debates surrounding them, stand out in the history of feminism as signalling the huge split, the unbridgeable division, which developed between the two philosophically opposed groups of feminists.

The Feminist Ordinance against Pornography (1983)

The decision by Andrea Dworkin and Catharine MacKinnon to write a "sex equality law" outlining the reasons why pornography is a violation of women's civil rights was a milestone in the history of feminism (see discussion in Chapters One and Two; Dworkin and MacKinnon 1988). It was lauded by feminists as a huge step toward justice for women but, in what MacKinnon calls "an act of extraordinary horizontal hostility" (1990, p. 9), a group of women who called themselves feminists opposed it. Reflecting on the situation, MacKinnon said:

> To no one's surprise, especially ours, it was opposed by many people. It was opposed by conservatives who discovered that they disliked sex equality a lot more than they disliked pornography. It was opposed by liberals, who discovered that they liked speech—i.e., sex, i.e., women being used—a great deal more than they liked sex equality. Then came the opposition from a quarter that labeled itself feminist: from FACT, the Feminist Anti-Censorship Task Force. At this point, for me, the women's movement that I had known came to an end [p. 9].

FACT members went to great lengths to argue that pornography represents sex equality. One member wrote in her brief to the court that pornography can be a source of erotic pleasure for women as well as for men. It can free a woman to explore her sexuality. "A woman who enjoys pornography, even if that means enjoying a rape fantasy, is, in a sense, a rebel", she said. MacKinnon commented that "the FACT brief did what pornography does: it makes harm to women invisible by making it sex" (1990, pp. 9, 11).

A significant point in the article by Catharine MacKinnon was her lament that, at that time, when the women of FACT fought so hard (in the name of feminism) to protect men's right to exploit women through pornography, "the women's movement that I had known came to an end" (1990, p. 9). Expanding on that point later in the article, she said:

What is the difference between the women's movement we had and the one we have now ...? I think the difference is liberalism. Where feminism was collective, liberalism is individualistic ... Where feminism is socially based and critical, liberalism is naturalistic, attributing ... women's oppression to women's natural sexuality ... Where feminism criticizes the way in which women have been socially determined ... liberalism is voluntaristic, meaning it acts like we have choices that we do not have ... [p. 12].

As already discussed, the sex equality law, the ordinance outlawing pornography, was lost due in no small part to the actions of the group of liberal feminists who called themselves the Feminist Anti-Censorship Task Force.

Test-Tube Women: What Future for Motherhood? (1984)

Another event that drew attention to the split between radical and liberal feminists was the publication of *Test-Tube Women*, edited by Rita Arditti, Renate Duelli Klein and Shelley Minden, and the subsequent reaction from liberal feminists. The book was a hard-hitting appraisal of the reproductive technology industry and its use and abuse of women for experimental purposes in the guise of giving infertile women the chance of having babies. Liberal feminists—or "reproductive liberals", as radical feminists labelled them—sprang to the defence of the industry and accused radical feminists of wanting to deny infertile women the "choice" of having a baby when, in their view, it is every woman's "right" to do so.

Based on the belief that "women are being used as living test-sites for drugs and new techniques" (Klein 1989, p. 2), the Feminist International Network of Resistance to Reproductive and Genetic Engineering (FINRRAGE) was established in the Netherlands in 1984 for the purpose of resisting technologies such as in vitro fertilisation (IVF), embryo transfer, surrogacy and sex predetermination.[131]

In the early 1990s, FINRRAGE members' opposition to reproductive technologies expanded to include long-acting hormonal contraceptives known to have the potential to be harmful to women's health. While liberal feminists rejected the radical stance on IVF in the 1980s, they are totally outraged by the more recent stand radical feminists have taken against contraceptives such as the five-year implant Norplant and the abortion pill RU486, claiming that women in developed and developing countries are being deprived of the "right to choose" whether or not to become pregnant and/or continue with their pregnancy.

---

131 FINRRAGE was originally called FINNRET, Feminist International Network on New Reproductive Technologies, but changed its name in the early 1990s to reflect more accurately the breadth of the members' concerns.

In a critique of "reproductive liberalism" and its claim to give women freedom of choice in reproductive matters, Janice Raymond contends that "reproductive liberalism provides women with a supposed liberty that requires women to give up more freedom than we get". It offers "a concept of choice that is reduced to the option to consume" (1994, p. 77).[132]

FINRRAGE members oppose the notion that women hand over control of their bodies and their reproductive capacities to an industry bent on using women for experimental purposes. Their position is based on medical and biological research which offers no assurance that long-acting hormonal contraceptives and reproductive procedures are safe for women. As Raymond explains:

> Opposition to these technologies is based on the ... political feminist perspective that *women as a class have a stake in reclaiming the female body ... by refusing to yield control of it to men, to the fetus, to the state, and most recently to those liberals who advocate that women control our bodies by giving up control* [1994, p. 91; emphasis in the original].

For more on the radical feminist position, see books such as *Test-Tube Women* (Arditti et al. 1984), *The Mother Machine* (Corea 1985), *Man-Made Women* (Corea 1987), *Made to Order* (Spallone and Steinberg 1987), *The Baby Machine* (Scutt 1988), *Infertility* (Klein 1989), *RU486* (Raymond et al. 1991), *Living Laboratories* (Rowland 1992), *Depopulating Bangladesh* (Akhter 1992), *Women as Wombs* (Raymond 1994) and *Resisting Norplant* (Akhter 1995).

On the other side of the debate, liberal feminist texts include *Reproductive Technologies* (Stanworth 1988), "My Body, My Property" (Andrews 1986), *Is the Future Female?* (Segal 1987), "Alternative Modes of Reproduction" (Andrews 1988), "Surrogacy: Feminist Notions of Motherhood Reconsidered" (Zipper and Sevenhuijsen 1988), "Victorian Values in the Test-Tube" (Rose 1988), "The Feminist Debate on Reproductive Rights and Contraception in Bangladesh" (Rozario 1997). Postmodernist texts focusing on the body include Butler 1993; Grosz 1994; Bell 1994; Grosz and Probyn 1995; and Gatens 1996.

The Sexual Liberals and the Attack on Feminism (1990)

A conference organised by radical feminists to challenge liberal feminists' acceptance and support of sexual libertarianism was held on 6 April 1987 at the New York University Law School. *The Sexual Liberals and the Attack on Feminism* contains the papers presented at that conference. In the introduction Dorchen Leidholdt described the powerful impact of

---

132 For a brief but excellent discussion of choice as consumption, see Raymond 1994, pp. 85–8.

the conference. The presentations "reverberated throughout the women's movement", she said. Eight hundred people packed the auditorium, "while hundreds more sat riveted to television monitors outside", anxious to hear major radical feminist thinkers challenge "an ideology and a program that, they asserted, was undermining feminism in the guise of being its best friend" (Leidholdt and Raymond 1990, p. ix).

The focus was on liberalism and, more specifically, on the damage sexual liberals were doing to women and to the feminist movement through their support of pornography, prostitution, reproductive technology, sadomasochism and other sexual and medical practices harmful to women. While liberal and libertarian feminists[133] today continue their support for such practices, bolstered by the approval of the male leaders of a multibillion-dollar sex industry, radical feminists continue articulating their resistance. Part One of this important book includes papers that dealt directly with the clash between radical and liberal feminists, while the rest of the book is divided according to the topics dealt with at the conference: rape of women and children, prostitution, reproductive technologies, sexuality, and pornography. In Part One, liberal feminism is discussed in terms of "The Death of Feminism", "Antifeminism" and "Woman-Hating".

Catharine MacKinnon's article "Liberalism and the Death of Feminism" has already been mentioned. Sheila Jeffreys, in "Sexology and Antifeminism", pointed out that the attack on feminism was coming not only from liberal feminists but also from left-leaning libertarian men and women, gay men and some lesbians. She rejected the so-called sex reforms lauded at the 1984 Barnard Conference accusing the proponents of "eroticizing … dominance and submission":

> The libertarians have an agenda on sexuality that is in fundamental opposition to that of feminists. Where feminists seek to transform sexuality in the interests of keeping women and children safe and ending women's inequality, the libertarians seek to promote and legitimize the traditional sexuality of dominance and submission. They eroticize practices that rely on power imbalance, such as sadomasochism, butch and femme, and so-called erotica that display women's humiliation and degradation [p. 25].

---

133 The terms sexual liberals and sexual libertarians were defined by Sheila Jeffreys: "Sexual liberals are those who subscribe to the 1960s' agenda of sexual tolerance, to the idea that sex is necessarily good and positive, and that censorship is a bad thing. Sexual libertarians have a more modern agenda and actively advocate the "outer fringes" of sexuality, such as sadomasochism, with the belief that "sexual minorities" are in the forefront of creating the sexual revolution" (1990, p. 15n).

Andrea Dworkin, in her article "Women-Hating Right and Left", pointed out that neither the right nor the left seems to understand what feminists are on about:

> Feminists are trying to destroy a sex hierarchy, a race hierarchy, an economic hierarchy, in which women are hurt, are disempowered, and in which society celebrates cruelty over us and refuses us the integrity of our own bodies and the dignity of our own lives [p. 28].

She states unequivocally that those who support woman-hating practices such as pornography and prostitution are not feminists.

> Anybody who fronts for those who hate women, who produce woman hating, who produce pornography, who celebrate woman-hating sex, those people are not feminists.
>
> I would like to see in this movement a return to what I call primitive feminism. It's very simple. It means that when something hurts women, feminists are against it. The hatred of women hurts women. Pornography is the hatred of women. Pornography hurts women. Feminists are against it, not for it [pp. 39–40].

Radically Speaking: Feminism Reclaimed (1996)

The fourth event that drew attention to the split between radical and other feminists was the courageous, some would say audacious, confrontation with postmodernism by radical feminists Diane Bell and Renate Klein in the production and publication of *Radically Speaking*. Their stated aim was to "interrogate" postmodernism because it was, in their view, an affront to feminism. "The Post-modern turn is apolitical, ahistorical, irresponsible, and self-contradictory; it takes the 'heat off patriarchy'"(1996, p. xix).

In bringing these radical feminist voices together (68 contributors in all), they sought first to tell the story of radical feminist theory and activism, a story of *"passionate determination to create a better world for women"* where there is *"justice, dignity and above all safety from all forms of violence"*. The other aim in bringing all these radical voices together in one publication was to point to the undermining of radical feminism by other feminists.

> *Radical feminists' knowledge of the past has been misrepresented, fragmented, and indeed abused in the retelling by others, such as liberal and Marxist feminists, post-modernists, the right and the media. Furthermore, our ability to act in the present is being severely curtailed by the post-modern insistence that there are no subjects, with the consequence that woman has been virtually erased as the author of her own life. Women, reduced to an assemblage of texts and multiplicities of identities, no longer exist as a sociological category. From this perspective, women's*

on-going multifaceted oppressions by men as a social class are deemed at best irrelevant, at worst non-existent. Thus, envisaging a feminist future is rendered impossible: woman disappears [Bell and Klein 1996, p. xx, emphasis in the original].

This important volume was met with virtual silence from liberal and postmodernist feminists while, as Klein said in her 2002 conference paper, "the assault on radical feminists continues unabated" (p. 8).

It should be noted here that, while the split between radical and liberal feminists receives most attention in the mainstream media, it is by no means unique. In most social movements, divisions occur based on philosophical adherence. There are internal battles in the environment movement—for example, between those who insist on the need to preserve old-growth forests in their natural, pristine state and those who want to negotiate with the forestry industry with the aim of reaching a compromise. There are those who reject the idea of eco-tourism and those who promote it. In one debate within the movement for Indigenous rights, one side insists that justice must be done before any reconciliation between black and white is possible while the other side urges the integration of Indigenous people into white society with the aim of reaping the rewards of that society. In all political parties, too, there is division within on the basis of philosophical differences and the degree to which human rights ought to be preserved.

On some social and political issues, divisions occur between left, right and centre.[134] Those on the left and the right are usually motivated by anger at injustices they see occurring. They resist the existing system and are determined not to waver till justice is done. Alternatively, those at the centre almost always advocate compromise. They look for common ground and advocate working within the existing system for the good of the individual. Radical activists point out that any attempt at working within an unjust system is tantamount to condoning the injustice. Experience confirms that those who benefit from an unjust system are not usually interested in hearing criticism from within or without, but will gladly use whoever chooses to come on board. Radical feminists and other radical activists refuse to come on board, and for that reason suffer the consequences of being silenced, criticised, maligned and misrepresented.

---

134 On issues such as prostitution, pornography, stem-cell research and cloning, those on the right and on the left are united against the centre. The anything-goes attitude of liberalism, libertarianism and postmodernism means that their proponents are quite comfortable being at the centre, sitting on the fence, not having strong ethical opinions either way. Because they emphasise the individual and an individual's right to do as he/she pleases, they don't have strong ethical judgements either way on most issues. In contrast, those on the left and on the right *do* base their beliefs and actions on solid ethical standards and often find themselves in agreement, albeit for vastly different reasons.

Indigenous women

As this discussion reveals, the silencing of lesbian and radical feminists by liberal, libertarian and postmodernist feminists has been and continues to be deliberate. This section argues that, while the silencing of Indigenous women and women from culturally and linguistically diverse backgrounds by white feminists has been less deliberate, it is equally reprehensible. Ignorance and insensitivity as "excuses" for the silencing of women from other racial and cultural backgrounds do not extinguish one's responsibility.

The analysis of racism, undertaken by black and white feminists in the United States in the 1970s and early 1980s, is a helpful place to begin in our quest to understand the silencing of Indigenous women by both radical and liberal feminists. While African Americans are not indigenous to the United States and their experience of racism is different from that of Indigenous First Nations people, the work of feminists Adrienne Rich and Audré Lorde reveals many similarities. White American feminist Adrienne Rich writes that, while racism is a product of patriarchy and ruling white males have a history of attempting to divide black and white women against each other,[135] white women are, nevertheless, not entirely innocent. She charges that, whether passively or actively, white women have been instrumental in "the practice of inhumanity against black people" (1979, p. 285).

African American feminist Audré Lorde said in a statement about the relationship between black and white feminists: "As outsiders, we need each other for support and connection and all the other necessities of living on the borders. But in order to come together we must recognise each other" (1984b, pp. 69–70).

It is true, in the context of this discussion about the silencing of Indigenous women, that white feminists have, for the most part, failed to "recognise" Indigenous women. Reasons for that include ignorance on the part of white women, discomfort with difference, an intense personal focus, fear of confronting their own racism, and concern that the accommodation of Indigenous women's issues would necessitate a less intense focus on confronting white men and white male-dominated institutions. When the central battle is against sexism, any focus on racism is seen by some as a diversion from the main game.

---

[135] On the issue of suffrage in the nineteenth century, while Sojourner Truth, Susan B. Anthony and others were insisting on universal suffrage, the government made it clear that it was considering granting the vote to "either black men or women [black and white] ... but not both—thus playing off sex against race" (Rich 1979, p. 286) and creating the potential for black and white women to turn against each other.

My intention here is not to engage in *mea culpa* but to focus on the silencing of Indigenous women by white women with a view to promoting understanding of the existing dynamics.

As mentioned earlier, it is not true that white feminists in general have deliberately ignored and excluded the experiences of Indigenous women. However, in many instances they have, through ignorance and self-obsession, been arrogant and insensitive. Since being made aware of the white-centredness of the feminist movement in Western countries, white feminists have tried desperately to "fix it up", but in all their attempts to make up for their neglect of Indigenous women, the one thing most white feminists still do not do very well is listen. There is much organising, helping, being "inclusive" and telling black women what is good for them, but not a lot of room for listening. If they genuinely listened to Indigenous women, they would hear them tell of their particular experience of oppression and would realise that it is very different from the way white women experience it. If white feminists listened, their knowledge and their recognition of Indigenous women would increase and open up the potential for genuine dialogue and the experience of solidarity.

Because white feminists do not listen enough, they often get it wrong. With the best will in the world, many continue to silence Indigenous women by excluding them, theorising about them and trying to fix the "problem".[136]

Excluding Indigenous women

US feminist Barbara Smith, writing in the late 1970s, criticised white feminists for excluding non-European women from their research and writing. She is quoted by Adrienne Rich as saying that "much feminist scholarship has been written as if black women did not exist, and many a women's studies course or text pays token reference, if any, to black women's lives and work" (in Rich 1979, p. 281).

While it would be less than constructive and, indeed, cumbersome for black or white feminist writers to attempt to include all racial groups every time they write on any issue, white writers do have a responsibility to seek out work by non-dominant writers.[137] This would go a long way toward avoiding

---

136 It must be said that there are notable exceptions among white feminists. For example, Australian anthropologist and feminist Diane Bell has worked alongside Indigenous women in South Australia for decades and is respected by them for her willingness to listen and empathise and, then, to join with them in their political endeavours. Zohl de Ishtar, also, has lived with and listened carefully to the voices of Indigenous Australians, as discussed later in this chapter.

137 The same is true of male writers. They have a responsibility to seek out the research and writing of women (as well as that of writers from other disempowered groups) in an attempt to portray a more balanced view of society.

the presumption that the experience of white women is the experience of all women. As Lorde says: "Assimilation within a solely western european herstory is not acceptable" (1984b, p. 69).

Theorising about Indigenous women

When white feminists were made aware of the fact that they had excluded Indigenous and all other non-European women in the same way as men had excluded women, instead of committing themselves to listening to women of colour, they began trying to be more inclusive by doing research and developing theories about them. Indigenous women, in particular, express the view that the only interaction many white sociologists, psychologists, historians and anthropologists seem to want to have with them is that of researcher to subject.[138] White feminists have, for the most part, been seriously troubled by the realisation of their own racism and have tried, in various ways, to address the situation. However, researching and theorising about Indigenous women from one's own non-Indigenous perspective leaves a lot to be desired. As Adrienne Rich explained:

> Even where racism is acknowledged in feminist writings, courses, conferences, it is too often out of a desire to "grasp" it as an intellectual or theoretical concept; we move too fast, as men so often do, in the effort to stay "on top" of a painful and bewildering condition, and so we lose touch with the feelings black women are trying to describe to us, their lived experience as women [1979, p. 281].

Trying to fix the "problem"

In their efforts to fix the problem, white feminists sometimes forget that the "problem" is not that Indigenous women feel excluded and that they must therefore remember to include them. The "problem" that needs fixing is white women's racism. When white feminists start from that premise, there is more chance that arrogance will be replaced by humility and recognition of the need to listen, observe and take in what Indigenous women are telling them.[139]

This does not mean that the research and writing of white feminists will cease; it means that those academic pursuits will be undertaken from

---

138 In the words of one Indigenous Australian woman: "We are the most researched, the most investigated group of people on earth, and still our situation continues. We know what the issues are. We've been trying to tell government for years. We need action now": quoted in Queensland Government 1999, p. xxxiii.

139 This does not mean that there will be no disagreement with Indigenous women. Indeed, anti-feminist views expressed by Indigenous women should never be supported. Those who express the view that issues of sexism, violence against women, rape, sexual abuse of children, etc. are secondary to issues of racism must always be challenged. For white feminists to remain silent in such circumstances would be both dishonest and patronising.

a different vantage point, that is, from an attempt to empathise with the experience of Indigenous women; and for a different reason, that is, to connect with Indigenous women at a deeply personal level in a way that will enrich the lives of Indigenous and non-Indigenous women alike. White feminists will continue to do practical things, such as giving prominence to Indigenous women in marches and rallies, acknowledging prior ownership of the land and being sensitive to racial issues at all times. But those practical, somewhat superficial actions will be endowed with deeper meaning as non-Indigenous feminists connect with Indigenous women.

To reiterate, if white feminists are serious about addressing their racism and genuinely connecting with Indigenous women, they must speak less and engage in serious listening; stop theorising in superficial ways about racism; stop trying to fix the "idea" of racism; and try to identify with Indigenous women's lived experience.[140] The tasks, therefore, are: to acknowledge and interrogate their own racism; to support Indigenous women in the ways they identify as important to them; and to challenge white power structures designed by whites to privilege whites with a view to changing their racist nature.

- ***Acknowledging and interrogating one's own racism.*** Allowing oneself to become aware of one's own racism is a painful but crucial first step in a white feminist's determination to connect with Indigenous women. Zohl de Ishtar, a white Australian radical feminist, decided a few years ago to make a proposal to the women of a remote Indigenous community in the desert region of north-west Australia, with whom she already had a personal connection. Her aim was to "listen" to Indigenous women, to experience their culture and share their emotional journey. After making contact with the women elders and gaining their support, she travelled to the edge of the Great Sandy Desert in the Kimberley and was received into the traditional women's camp just outside the community of Wirrimanu. She lived with the women of the Kapululangu Aboriginal Women's Association and took part in their day-to-day rituals (as invited) for two years (de Ishtar 2005, p. 14). Prior to this, de Ishtar had "lived and worked within Indigenous communities for over twenty years", but following her experience of living full-time with the desert women of north-west Australia, she admitted: "The biggest problem I confronted was, to my horror, my own racism" (p. 58). Racism is so deeply ingrained in the dominant white class that they should never treat the matter lightly and certainly never presume that they are innocent of racist attitudes.

---

140 The oppression experienced by white women in many areas of their lives affords them an advantage as they seek to identify with the lived experience of Indigenous women.

- **Supporting Indigenous women in the ways they identify.** There is a growing recognition among white feminists that their urgent task is not to organise around Indigenous women's issues but, rather, to support the issues Indigenous women themselves have prioritised. Consequently, increasing numbers of non-Indigenous radical feminists are responding to invitations to attend marches, rallies and community meetings organised by Indigenous Australians to protest against issues such as black deaths in custody, the Stolen Generations, stolen wages, and domestic and family violence.
- **Challenging the racist nature of white power structures.** Whether white people admit it or not, the power structures in all white-dominated societies have been designed by whites for the benefit of whites and all who are white have access to the privileges reserved for the dominant race. The most important thing whites can do from their position of privilege is confront and challenge white institutions, calling on them to cease their oppression of Indigenous women and men (McLellan 2006, p. 2).

Indigenous women themselves are divided on issues of racism and sexism. Some seem to buy into "hierarchies of oppression" and insist that racism is more oppressive than sexism. They agree with the sentiments expressed by men on the left during the 1970s who desperately looked for ways to criticise and quash the emerging feminist movement. Adrienne Rich draws attention to the men's criticism and quotes them as saying that white middle-class feminists "are despicable creatures of privilege whose oppression is meaningless beside the oppression of black, Third World, or working-class women and men" (1979, p. 289).

Radical feminists reject the sentiments of Indigenous Australian academics such as Aileen Moreton-Robinson and Jackie Huggins who accuse white feminists of being racist for prioritising sex over race. Moreton-Robinson argues that while white women theorise about "difference and incommensurability" they, in fact, seek to reconstruct Indigenous women according to their own "middle-class white woman feminist" ideology (2000, p. xxiv). Using the language of postmodernism, she advises white feminists to stop theorising about Indigenous women and begin to look at their own subject position.

> I argue that feminists need to analyse and interrogate this subject position and its relationship to the dominant white male centre of Australian society in order to understand how such a subject position is represented, complies with and maintains the racial order [pp. xxiv–xxv].

She reiterates this point later in her book, charging that many white feminists are complicit in "the colonial project" and that their middle-class subject position "remains invisible, unmarked and unnamed" in their work. Ignoring years of white radical feminist discussions of these issues, she continues: "The exercising of white race privilege is not interrogated as being problematic, nor is it understood as part of the power that whiteness confers; instead it is normalised within feminist texts and practice" (p. 123).

Jackie Huggins, too, is adamant that oppression on the basis of race is the greater oppression. She argues in her essay "A Contemporary View of Aboriginal Women's Relationship to the White Women's Movement" that white feminists have tried to silence Indigenous women who prioritise racism over sexism (1994, pp. 75–6).

Other Indigenous women leaders, however, emphasise the need for a dual focus—confronting racism and sexism at the same time. They argue, for example, that men's violence against women ought never to be excused on the basis of racial oppression. The writing of African American feminist bell hooks supports such a view. She disagrees with those who say that black women should not be involved in the feminist struggle and who claim that "racism empowers white women to be exploiters and oppressors" to support their stance. Speaking of the "interlocking systems of domination—sex, race, and class", hooks argues, without any intention of hiding the ugly face of racism, that sexism is equally damaging and ought to be railed against by "black women and other women of color":

> Feminist struggle to end patriarchal domination should be of primary importance to women and men globally not because it is the foundation of all other oppressive structures but because it is that form of domination we are most likely to encounter in an ongoing way in everyday life.
>
> Unlike other forms of domination, sexism directly shapes and determines relations of power in our private lives, in familiar social spaces, in that most intimate context—home—and in that most intimate sphere of relations—family [1989, p. 21].

Boni Robertson, chair of the Aboriginal and Torres Strait Islander Women's Task Force on Violence, and all the women involved in doing the research and consultations for that project were of the view that racism and sexism were equally problematic. One woman expressed the feeling of all the Indigenous women involved when she said: "All we want is for the violence to stop. We don't want our men to go to jail. But by the same token we as a community have to try to address the issues of alcohol, drugs and violence" (quoted in Queensland Government 1999, p. ix).[141]

---

141 The contributors' names are listed in the report: Queensland Government 1999, pp. xviii–xix.

Indigenous women who base their activism on the view that sex, race and class are "interlocking systems of domination" are only too pleased to call themselves feminists but, at the same time, insist that their white sisters be mindful of the privilege that a racist culture confers on them as white women and give priority to listening to Indigenous women's particular experience of oppression. Indigenous feminists fight oppression on at least two fronts—sex and race—and call on their white feminist sisters to join with them in condemning racism and its destructive effects.

Women from culturally and linguistically diverse backgrounds

Many of the issues of contention raised in the previous section between Indigenous women and white feminists apply to the relationship between CALD women[142] and white feminists, but there are also concerns specific to CALD women.

Here I will raise some of the current criticisms of white middle-class Western feminists by CALD women and by women from non-Western countries on the global stage. First, it will be helpful to look at an early but significant publication by "women of color" in the United States: *This Bridge Called My Back: Writings of Radical Women of Color* (1981), edited by Cherrie Moraga and Gloria Anzaldua, with a foreword by Toni Cade Bambara. Describing how the publication came together, the editors say that in 1979 they wrote to many women of colour in the United States outlining the purpose of their project and asking for contributions. They include a paragraph from their "original soliciting letter":

> We want to express to all women—especially to white middle-class women—the experiences which divide us as feminists; we want to examine incidents of intolerance, prejudice and denial of differences within the feminist movement. We intend to explore the causes and sources of, and solutions to these divisions. We want to create a definition that expands what "feminist" means to us [1981, p. xxiii].

They go on to explain: "What began as a reaction to the racism of white feminists soon became a positive affirmation of the commitment of women of color to our own feminism" (p. xxiii). Later they remark that, although the

---

142 Various terms are used to describe women from different racial, cultural and linguistic backgrounds. In the United States the term "women of color" is used. In Australia, "Non-English-speaking background" (NESB) has been largely replaced by "culturally and linguistically diverse" (CALD) and "diverse cultural and linguistic backgrounds" (DCALB).

anthology started out to be an attempt "to make a connection with white women, it feels now more like a separation" (p. 61).

In a section of the book which the editors say is an attempt "to describe, in tangible ways how, under the name of feminism, white women of economic and educational privilege have used that privilege at the expense of Third World women" (p. 61), they comment on the power dynamics implicit in racism. Racism gives to certain sections of the community the power to implement racist ideology, they argue, and comment on the relationship between women of colour and white women:

> Women of color do not have such power, but white women are born with it and the greater their economic privilege, the greater their power. This is how white middle-class women emerge among feminist ranks as the greatest propagators of racism in the movement. Rather than using the privilege they have to crumble the institutions that house the source of their own oppression—sexism, along with racism—they oftentimes deny their privilege … [p. 62].

Women from culturally and linguistically diverse backgrounds in Australia, while still attempting to work together with white feminists on many issues, nevertheless wonder why middle-class white feminists do not give higher priority to the particular kinds of oppression CALD women are faced with.

- *Men's violence against their CALD partners.* Violence perpetrated by Australian men in relationships with women from other countries is as common as in white relationships. While women's refuges try to give adequate attention to the problem, more could be done to highlight the special circumstances surrounding the plight of CALD women, many of whom have been enticed to a foreign country to marry and then find themselves victims of physical, sexual and emotional violence.
- *Sex tourism.* Australian men make up a large proportion of the men from wealthy nations who travel to Thailand and other Asian nations for sex with women and also with children, both girls and boys. Speaking out about the issue, shaming the perpetrators, lobbying governments to criminalise such sex tourism has not been high on most white middle-class feminists' list of priorities. Some have embraced the issue and fought hard to have politicians and other community leaders publicly condemn such abuse of women and children, but more needs to be done by more feminists.
- *Prostitution.* As state governments develop a more libertarian attitude toward prostitution and pride themselves on the legalisation of brothels and so-called sex work, women from Asian countries are being trafficked into Australia in increasing numbers to service the growing demand

from men for more, and more "exotic", sex. While a strong feminist voice protests against the use of CALD women by the prostitution industry, much more needs to be done.[143]

- **Outworkers.** Almost all of the people being exploited by multinational and other companies to work out of their own homes for very low wages are women from migrant families. As mentioned in Chapter Three's discussion of sweatshop workers, some migrant women in Australia are working for $2 to $3 an hour for up to 18 hours a day, every day of the year. Although some white feminists have protested long and hard to raise awareness of the plight of outworkers, it has not received widespread attention throughout the feminist movement.

There is no doubt that women from culturally and linguistically diverse backgrounds in Australia and in other wealthy nations would appreciate the support of white feminists in giving higher priority to the particular forms of oppression they are faced with on a daily basis and to join with them in their fight for justice.

On the global stage, too, feminists living under Muslim laws, feminists from African countries, from Asian countries, from Palestine, Afghanistan, Iraq, indeed from all countries suffering as a result of Western imperialism, have called upon Western feminists to take their plight seriously. They implore all feminists to stop supporting oppressive practices such as female genital mutilation, the wearing of the veil and other forms of violence against women, in the name of cultural sensitivity. Most radical feminists have heeded the call and refuse to support any cultural practices that oppress women, but some feminists are still ambivalent in relation to the establishment of sharia law. There is a feeling that, in the name of respecting other cultures, it ought to be supported wherever and whenever Muslim communities call for it. As mentioned previously, the group called Women Living Under Muslim Laws urges all Western feminists to open their eyes, to see how oppressive and destructive sharia law is to Muslim women, and to demonstrate wholeheartedly against its establishment.

Feminists in the Philippines and Japan continually agitate against US military bases on their soil and against the relative freedom granted to US military personnel to rape, abuse and violate women. For years Japanese and Filipina feminists have been urging Western feminists to join them in their struggle for justice in this respect. More recently the problem has expanded to include some of the Pacific Islands. Since John Howard, during his term as Australia's prime minister, took on the role of "Deputy Sheriff" to George W. Bush, with a particular brief to act as aggressor in relation to Pacific Island

---

143 For an excellent discussion of this, see Sullivan 2006.

nations, there are similar issues arising for Pacific Island women as Australian military personnel and Australian police set up bases on their islands and the Australian government interferes in the affairs of their nations. Concerned Pacific Island feminists are in regular discussions with white Australian feminists urging that more be done to influence the Australian government to stop interfering.[144]

In Africa, feminists continue to express amazement that white Western feminists seem to be unmoved by the enormous crisis of HIV/AIDS in Africa, even though the majority of victims are women. Speaking at a forum in 2002, Sisonke Msimang asked "why HIV/AIDS seems not to be on the global feminist agenda" when it is clearly a feminist issue. AIDS used to be a gay men's issue but today, she says, "the face of AIDS has changed".

> It looks like mine. It is now black, female and extremely young. In some parts of Sub-Saharan Africa, girls aged 15–19 are six times more likely than their male counterparts to be HIV positive. Something is very wrong.

Emphasising the effect the feminisation of AIDS has on all African women, she continues:

> As older women are increasingly called upon to care for children, and as life expectancy shrinks to the 40s and 50s, we face the prospect in Africa of a generation without grandparents, and an upcoming orphan and vulnerable children crisis that will effectively leave kids to take care of kids. As the orphan crisis deepens, child abuse is on the rise. Girls without families to protect them are engaging in survival sex to feed themselves and their siblings ... [Msimang 2003, p. 111].

Expressing deep concern about "the relative silence from our Northern sisters", Msimang urges the mainstream feminist movement across the globe to "get on board". She concludes her paper with an urgent challenge:

> Our sisters in the North need to develop a consciousness about the fight against AIDS as a feminist fight. We need civil society and feminist voices in developing countries to challenge their governments to tackle HIV/AIDS as a health issue, as a human rights issue, and as a sexual and reproductive rights issue. If we lose this fight, it will have profound effects on the lives of girls and women into the next century [2003, p. 113].

My desire to discuss the silencing of women in an honest and comprehensive way has required this chapter on the silencing of women by women, including the silencing of feminists by feminists. While feminists can easily agree with

---

144 Through the Pacific Women's Information Network, Pacific Island women regularly discuss issues of concern with Australian and New Zealand women.

the claims in Chapters Three and Four that women's voices and dissenting voices in general are deliberately silenced by a male-focused power elite nationally and globally, it is not so easy for them to accept that they too are guilty of silencing other women.

This chapter has faced that phenomenon and attempted to uncover some of the dynamics at work. The silencing of lesbian and radical feminists by mainstream liberal and postmodernist feminists was described as a deliberate tactic by those whose preference is to align themselves with the status quo. The silencing of Indigenous women and women from CALD communities, on the other hand, was seen as less deliberate, more the result of ignorance and insensitivity on the part of white feminists. It was argued, however, that the "excuses" of ignorance and insensitivity do not make the silencing of Indigenous and CALD women by white feminists any less reprehensible.

White middle-class feminists were urged to stop trying to "make it right" and begin listening to the lived experience of Indigenous women and CALD women in Western countries, and to women on the global stage whose lives are diminished as a result of Western imperialism and the support some feminists give to repressive cultural practices. Freedom of speech for all women is dependent, in the first instance, on the degree to which white middle-class feminists are willing to acknowledge the power which their race and class status affords them, challenge the racism inherent in their own white-dominated cultures, and listen to and identify with the lived experience of all other women.

Part III
SPEAKING THROUGH THE SILENCING

SPEAKING THE UNSPEAKABLE 6

In this feminist ethical analysis of the silencing of women, one question remains. What is the appropriate feminist ethical response to the silencing of women and other minorities in these early years of the twenty-first century? Radical feminists declare that the only appropriate response is to speak through the silencing, to persist in speaking out against injustices regardless of criticism, ridicule, misinterpretation and misrepresentation. This chapter focuses on the ethical implications of that kind of response, while Chapter Seven will look at the practical face (present and future) of such a response.

Looking back at the tactics of silencing discussed in Chapters Three, Four and Five, we can see the lengths to which members of the power elite in every society are prepared to go in order to keep speech for themselves and silence all others. Freedom of speech, touted as a universal right in democratic societies, has been revealed to be enjoyed only by the powerful, that is, by those at the top of business corporations, industries, global trade and financial institutions, the media and governments. They are the ones with enough power and wealth to buy speech and to dictate who should be listened to and who should be silenced. Power plays also exist among the less powerful in any society. Those who have more power than others, even though they themselves may be relatively weak in comparison with the power elite, are able to silence those less powerful than themselves. Men silence women. Mainstream women and men silence non-mainstream women and men. Those who are articulate and confident about voicing their opinions silence those who are not.

Chapter Three identified ongoing core tactics as well as the contemporary tactics used in the silencing of women. Chapter Four discussed at length the tactics used by powerful governments to silence all dissenting voices while Chapter Five illustrated the ways in which women, including feminists, join in the silencing of other women.

The concept of fair speech discussed in Chapter Two suggested that women and men alike need to examine both their speech and their speech acts, that is, what they say and what they do with what they say, and make a conscious effort to ensure that their speech is fair and just.

Feminist speech rendered unspeakable

Before turning to the ethical implications of the decision to speak through the silencing by "speaking the unspeakable", we will revisit the work of Rae Langton. My contention in this present chapter that radical feminism has been rendered unspeakable has been adapted from Langton's work (1994) outlined in Chapter Two. Langton uses the word "unspeakable" to refer to the incidence of women's words being turned around and used against them. She gives examples of women's "no" being interpreted as "yes" and of women's protests being made to look like the exact opposite of the protest that was intended. Here I use the word more broadly, in that the perlocutionary and illocutionary aspects of speech are included. By being ignored, feminists' words are robbed of their perlocutionary ability to enlighten and influence others; by being misrepresented, feminists' words are turned around and used against them in what Langton calls "illocutionary disablement".

Certain radical forms of feminist speech have been rendered unspeakable because such speech is "forbidden" in societies dominated by neoliberalism. While it is not actually possible or legal to forbid dissenting speech in democratic societies, those in power have overcome that problem by employing subtle, but still effective, tactics. By ignoring and misrepresenting feminist words they rob those words of their intended force.

Every generation of feminist activists finds it difficult to understand and come to terms with the fact that their speech is rendered unspeakable. Until they are able to understand that feminists are among the groups of people whom Arundhati Roy refers to as the "preferably unheard" in society (2004b, p. 1), they struggle to understand why they are not being heard and how they can improve their performance so as to command attention. A greater understanding of the dynamics between men and women, between the powerful and the less powerful, usually brings a degree of relief to the earnest activist. It is not that feminists are not speaking, not speaking enough, not articulating adequately or not aiming their speech correctly. It is that their speech, no matter what they say or how they say it, has been rendered unspeakable by being either ignored or misrepresented. To be ignored is to be treated as if one has not spoken, and to be misrepresented is to have one's words turned around and used against one.

Ethical implications of continuing to speak

Bearing in mind the sometimes vicious response on the part of those intent on preserving their own power, radical feminists must give serious thought to the ethics involved in the decision to speak the unspeakable. The following question is, therefore, crucial: What are the ethical implications of continuing to speak in a situation where one's speech is deliberately ignored and/or misrepresented? Some social and political activists seem to enter into activist pursuits after little consideration of the implications of their actions. They see it as a game to be enjoyed or a competition to be won. While not wanting to imply that activism excludes fun, enjoyment, "dancing at the revolution", I do want to emphasise the need for activists to be aware of the ethical implications of their actions. For radical feminist activists determined to speak the unspeakable, the implications for women in general as well as for the speaker/activist herself must be taken seriously.

Implications for women in general

To date, the speech of feminists has had both positive and negative effects on the women whose lot they have sought to improve, and all indications are that that situation will continue. An ethical dilemma exists in situations where speaking out against entrenched systems oppressive to women might endanger the safety or livelihood of some individual women. In such situations there are no easy answers, but feminists for whom silence is not an option must at least understand the implications and possible effects of their speaking. As we will see under the heading "Improving the situation of women", there is an abundance of evidence to show that women's situation has improved as a direct result of feminist speech, and such results are to be celebrated. However, the other side of the story is that there are negative implications. These will be discussed as: handing over women's issues to the mainstream; exacerbating the violence perpetrated against women; exacerbating the sexual subordination of women and girls; and challenging the speech of other women.

Improving the situation of women

The ultimate aim in the discipline of ethics, as stated in the Introduction, is to transform societies with a view to bringing about more effective and inclusive social justice systems. Thanks to the constant activism of feminists in every generation—analysing, researching, writing, demonstrating, rallying, lobbying, speaking out—the lives of women in Western countries have improved. Feminist historians and other commentators acknowledge that there have been significant gains for women in countries like the United States, Canada, Europe and Australia.

A huge step forward occurred at the end of the nineteenth and the beginning of the twentieth century, when the battle for women's suffrage was finally won in most Western countries. For the first time, women were permitted to vote on issues which affected their lives. The struggle began in the mid-nineteenth century and continued for half a century before the dreams of Elizabeth Cady Stanton, Lucretia Mott, Susan B. Anthony, Emmeline Pankhurst and others were realised. Two world wars later and married women had been manipulated from dependent wives (before the wars) to independent workers (during the wars when they were needed to fill the gaps in industry) and back to dependent wives (after World War II). Then there began what Betty Friedan called a "strange stirring" in women in the 1960s (1963, p. 13). Women started verbalising dissatisfaction with the second-class status assigned to them by the male hierarchy. Consciousness-raising groups were formed in many local communities across the Western world and evidence of the extent of women's oppression and the depth of their dissatisfaction came to light.

In her history of the feminist movement in the United States, *In our Time: Memoir of a Revolution* (1999), Susan Brownmiller begins by discussing her own experience of consciousness-raising groups in the 1960s and moves on to discuss the machinations inside the US movement as they fought for women's rights on many different fronts. Gains were made for individual women in equal opportunity—education, employment, politics, the military and business. In other areas, huge battles were fought against rape, battery, sexual harassment and pornography. While there were many gains along the way, US feminists admit that there is still a long way to go.

Two significant battles which have taken centre stage for US feminists over several decades have still not been won. They are the Equal Rights Amendment to the constitution and access to abortion. According to Brownmiller, "Women's Liberation found its first unifying issue in abortion, and abortion became the first feminist cause to sweep the nation", but she admits that the fierce and sustained counterattack by opposing forces has meant that "abortion remains our most important and pivotal issue, the linchpin, then as now, of women's struggle for equality and reproductive freedom" (1999, pp. 102, 135). Finishing her memoir on a positive note, Brownmiller sums up her history of the feminist struggles in the United States by saying:

> Rarely in history have women been able to set aside their other concerns and political causes, their divisions of class, race, religion, ethnicity, their geographic boundaries and personal attachments, in order to wage a united struggle, so revolutionary in its implications, against their basic, common oppression. Indeed, a full century passed between the struggle for suffrage and what is often called the second wave. But when such a coming-together takes place, when the vision is clear and the sisterhood is powerful, mountains are moved and the human landscape is changed forever [p. 330].

While Brownmiller presented a realistic picture of a movement which, while making huge gains, also had some losses, Naomi Wolf in *Fire with Fire* painted a positive picture of a battle won. She describes Second Wave feminism in the United States as a "genderquake" and urges feminists to stop focusing on the negatives and begin counting the gains, calling on them to move into the future believing that women now have equal power with men. Describing the genderquake, she says:

> Twenty-five years of dedicated feminist activism have hauled the political infrastructure into place, enough women in the middle classes have enough money and clout, and most women now have enough desire and determination to begin to balance the imbalance of power between the sexes [Wolf 1993, p. xvi].

The problem, as she sees it, is with women themselves. She laments that "women lack a psychology of female power to match their new opportunities" (p. xvi).

Feminists working in the areas of rape, battery of women in the home and the effects of prostitution and pornography, as well as those studying the effects of the deliberate subordination and exclusion of women from most areas of power and influence, are critical of Wolf's call for women to focus on the positive and ignore the negative. Feminists have a choice, Wolf says: either to "understand that we are in the final throes of a civil war for gender fairness in which conditions have shifted to put much of the attainment of equality in women's own grasp" or to continue "clinging to an outdated image of ourselves as powerless" (1993, pp. xv–xvi).

While Brownmiller and many other feminist writers call for a more balanced view than that of Wolf in terms of the gains won and the battles still to be fought for women, feminists in the United States and other parts of the Western world nevertheless agree that there have been some important gains in the situation of women.

In *Ten Thousand Roses*, Judy Rebick writes about the gains made for women as a result of the women's movement in Canada. She admits that she was prompted to write her history of the movement after reading Brownmiller's *In our Time* and realising that "the Canadian women's movement was way more interesting than the American women's movement, and way broader and more successful" (interview, O'Keefe 2005).

Rebick discusses the multiracial nature of the Canadian women's movement and the fact that working-class women and socialist feminists maintained leadership in the movement. Because of this, issues of race and class were always included in the fight for justice for women. One of the big successes in Canada was on abortion, she says. "We've ... fundamentally won the right to abortion in a way that they weren't able to in the United States." The other big success came when the Canadian government voted to include women in the nation's charter. In the United States, the long drawn-out battle for the ERA calling for equality for women to be enshrined in the constitution has been lost but, in Canada, women have legal equality.

Although the situation of women in Canada has improved beyond measure, Rebick reminds her readers that the most basic issue, that of men's violence against women, persists. When asked, in her interview with O'Keefe, about challenges facing the women's movement today, she said:

> The key issues to me are violence against women ... and figuring out how to stop violence against women, which I think requires a big, big discussion about masculinization. You know, what in the socialization of men creates this rage toward women in our culture. I think we need a big debate and discussion about that with men, because while we've made big improvements, violence against women has not been abated at all [O'Keefe 2005].

The picture Australian feminist historian Marilyn Lake paints in *Getting Equal: The History of Australian Feminism* is that of a nation in which women have made tremendous gains while still having to participate on men's terms.

> Women have taken on the world, but the world is still, by and large, structured on men's terms. Women have won equal opportunity and the formal right of equal pay, but the organisation of the workplace is still geared to the masculine experience of autonomy, mobility and freedom from domestic responsibilities [1999, p. 278].

Pronouncing feminism as a mass politics which "succeeded in winning so many political, civil, economic and social reforms", Lake goes on to list the gains:

> These reforms include political rights; mothers' custody rights; age of consent legislation; infant and maternal welfare centres; women's hospitals;

maternity benefits; the appointment of women JPs, police and magistrates; the appointment of women to juries; the criminalisation of rape in marriage; government-subsidised child care centres; the establishment of female refuges and rape crisis centres; the supporting parent's benefit; equal pay; and affirmative action programs [1999, pp. 15–16].

The situation of women around the Western world has improved due to the efforts of feminists through the ages. While most disagree with Naomi Wolf's suggestion that the battle is over and equality between the sexes has been achieved, there is agreement that many things have changed for the better for women. The attitude of most feminists is that, while things have improved, there is much more to be achieved and the battle for justice must continue.

As feminists continue their fight for justice and equality, the potential for negative outcomes is real, as the following discussion of a variety of ethical dilemmas faced by feminists will demonstrate.

Handing over women's issues to the mainstream

An ongoing dilemma for feminist activists lies in the knowledge that little will change for women unless so-called women's issues are brought into the mainstream. But as soon as an issue achieves mainstream status, it is taken out of the hands of social justice proponents and delivered into the hands of those who hold political and economic power. From that position, it almost always takes on a different look. The issue of men's violence against women is a case in point. Whenever governments have been persuaded to focus on men's violence against women, it invariably changes into something else. Instead of focusing on masculinisation or, more particularly, on "what in the socialization of men creates this rage toward women", as Judy Rebick put it, the focus is placed on alcohol or drugs or, in the case of violence by Indigenous men, on their social oppression. The message coming through clearly is that men in their right minds, i.e., not affected by alcohol or drugs or oppression, would not act in that way, when decades of feminist research shows that they very often do. As early as 1983, Jocelynne Scutt's study of 312 families, reported in *Even in the Best of Homes: Violence in the Family*, began to dispel some of those myths (1983, pp. 109–18).

When federal and state governments in Australia decided to take on domestic violence as a mainstream "project" in the late 1990s, domestic violence (which is the term used in Australia for men's violence against women in the home) became known officially as "family violence". Feminists, workers in women's services and men speaking out against other men's violence were strongly encouraged to drop the term "domestic violence" in favour of "family violence". Those in power preferred the broader term because it took the focus off men as the main perpetrators and allowed the argument that "women are violent too" to be raised to equal status. Then, with research still indicating that approximately 95 per cent of perpetrators are men and 5 per cent are women, violence in the home was able to be presented as if the ratio were 50:50.

The mainstreaming of this central issue of feminist outrage has resulted in the watering down of the demand for men to change their attitudes and behaviour toward women. Violent men are provided with excuses for their behaviour and encouraged to seek help for a "condition" which has been pathologised. Meanwhile, the violence continues.

The sexual abuse of children is another issue which has been mainstreamed after decades of feminist speech and activism. Again, once it became a mainstream issue, childhood sexual abuse took on a different look. While feminists had always insisted that sexual abuse of children by anyone, under any circumstances, was wrong and must always be treated as a crime and punished, a two-tier response began to emerge. Sexual abuse of children by strangers, teachers, sports coaches, priests, was called "paedophilia" and punished severely, while the sexual abuse of children in the home—by fathers, step-fathers, grandfathers, older brothers—was more often than not treated as an aberration or an occasion for therapy.

Whenever an issue being fought for by feminists and other activists gains recognition by those in power and is given status as a mainstream issue, it is taken over and reinterpreted with little reference to those who did the research and fought for the issue to be recognised. Once the mainstream takes ownership of an issue, there is a different analysis, different interpretations and a different response to the one the activists had hoped for. On the other hand, to prevent the mainstreaming of an issue so as to keep the analysis and interpretation in one's own hands is to defeat the purpose of social activism, which is to have an impact on society to the extent that changes will be made. Most feminist activists deal with this particular ethical dilemma by continuing to push for mainstream to recognise inequities and injustices and, once an issue achieves mainstream status, to continue to push for an accurate interpretation and a just response. One frustrating outcome, however, is that persistence is often met with indifference and a claim that the issue has already been satisfactorily dealt with.

Exacerbating the violence perpetrated against women

If there is one thing feminists have learnt from the experience of Second Wave feminism, it is that many men interpret talk of equality between the sexes as a threat to their position of privilege and something which must be put down. What feminists hoped would be a reasonable discussion between mature adults resulting in a more just and equitable arrangement for both women and men quickly became a competition in which women calling for a different, a more cooperative, relationship with men were constructed as the enemy. From that time on, anything feminists said or did was interpreted as part of a battle which men were determined to win. Those individual men who responded favourably to the themes of women's liberation were just as astounded as feminists were at the irrational response of their brothers and the many women who supported them. But the battle had begun and individual men and women intent on preserving the status quo, as well as those in charge of male-dominated institutions and power structures, all lined up in opposition to feminist demands.

Patriarchy's deliberate tactics of silencing and subordinating women outlined in earlier chapters of this book are part of the overall battle strategy and, in the personal arena, violence is often one of the tactics.

A serious ethical dilemma for feminists working in women's services exists between the desire to help empower women who have been victims of domestic violence and the knowledge that every step toward greater strength and independence for some women places them and their children in greater danger. Much of the violence and many of the murders perpetrated against women and children have occurred after a woman has found the personal strength to leave her violent spouse.

The Domestic Violence Prevention Centre on the Gold Coast in Queensland reflects the findings of all reputable research conducted in Australia:

> Often after the relationship has ended violence may continue, this can be a very dangerous time for the victim because the perpetrator may perceive a loss of control over the victim and may become more unpredictable. During and after separation is often a time when violence will escalate leaving the victim more unsafe than previously.[145]

In the Australian component of the International Violence Against Women Survey appearing in the *Australian Domestic Violence Clearinghouse Newsletter*, Jenny Mouzos reported on the matter of violence against women after separation and compared it to violence by a current partner: "the levels of violence experienced from a former partner ... were much higher than from a current partner ... Women who experienced violence from former partners were also more likely to sustain injuries and feel that their lives were in danger" (2004, p. 2).

---

145 <http://www.domesticviolence.com.au>. See also Australian Bureau of Statistics 1996; Victorian Community Council Against Violence 2003; Strang 1996.

Similarly disturbing facts are reported in the United States. The Clark County Prosecuting Attorney's office in Indiana warns that "Domestic violence does not end immediately with separation. Over 70 per cent of the women injured in domestic violence cases are injured after separation."[146]

An online initiative called AARDVARC (An Abuse, Rape and Domestic Violence Aid and Resource Collection) reiterates this point:

> leaving does not usually put an end to the violence. Batterers may, in fact, escalate their violence to coerce a victim into reconciliation or to retaliate for the perceived rejection or abandonment. Those who believe they are entitled to relationship with their victim or that they "own" their partner, view the victim's departure as an ultimate betrayal which justifies retaliation.

They go on to say:

> Battered women seek medical attention for injuries sustained as a consequence of domestic violence significantly more often after separation than during cohabitation; about 75 per cent of the visits to emergency rooms by battered women occur after separation.
>
> About 75 per cent of the calls to law enforcement for intervention and assistance in domestic violence occur after separation from batterers. One study revealed that half of the homicides of female spouses and partners were committed by men after separation from batterers.[147]

The Women's Emergency Services Network (WESNET) in Australia also reports on homicides after separation: "35 per cent of children who were victims of homicide in Australia between 1989 and 1993 died as a result of family violence, killed by a male offender and usually relating to the termination of the parent's relationship" (WESNET, 2004b).

Reports of violence, threats and murders after separation give feminist activists pause to reflect on their belief that women who are victims of their partner's violence should leave rather than stay in a situation of increasing violence. However, feminists working in the area seem to agree that supporting a woman to leave is still the safest option, so long as there is a safety plan in place. AARDVARC says:

> Because leaving may be dangerous ... does not mean that the victim should stay. Cohabiting with the batterer is highly dangerous both as violence usually increases in frequency and severity over time and as a batterer may engage in preemptive strikes, fearing abandonment or anticipating separation even before the victim reaches such a decision.

---

146 Clark County Prosecuting Attorney's Office, Indiana. n.d.
147 <http://www.aardvarc.org/dv/sepviolence.shtml>.

> Although leaving may pose additional hazards, at least in the short run, the research data demonstrates that ultimately victims can best achieve safety and freedom apart from the batterer.
> Leaving will require strategic planning and legal intervention to avert separation violence and to safeguard victims and their children. Work on your safety plan!

The Australian group Women's Safety After Separation was formed to provide practical and legal information to women choosing separation, and works to "help women to negotiate safety for themselves and their children". The group stresses the need to support women in their decision to leave as well as in developing a safety plan because "research indicates that survivors of violence and abuse begin recovery when their exposure to danger has stopped and they are able to re-establish safety".[148]

The history of domestic violence is full of stories of courageous women who endured endless beatings, some of which ended in murder, as a result of their attempts to grow stronger and speak out. The ethical dilemma for feminist activists remains: Is it ethically sustainable to speak and encourage other women to speak through the silencing about domestic violence when the result could well be that the violence worsens?

Members of oppressed groups everywhere usually learn the lesson that giving in to the will of their oppressors leads to a quieter, more manageable life and that challenging the attitudes and behaviour of one's oppressor often leads to harsh and cruel punishment. Conservative voices call on feminists to stop rocking the boat and begin supporting women in learning how to live with violent partners as obedient and faithful wives so that marriages will stay intact and children will continue to have the influence of both parents. Feminists, on the other hand, insist that women have a right to live without violence, that the safest option for women and children is to leave a partner who is violent and that safety after separation must be the focus of any plan to leave.

Exacerbating the sexual subordination of women and girls

Another ethical dilemma receiving the attention of feminist researchers in recent times is that prompted by the increasing sexualisation of women and girls in Western societies. In a classic example of illocutionary disablement, the feminist call for the empowerment of women has been turned around and made to mean the opposite of that which was originally intended.

When feminists called for the empowerment of women and a recognition in society of the need for greater equality between the sexes, the clear intention

---

148 <http://www.ncsmc.org.au/wsas/welcome.htm>.

was for women and men to be given equal respect and equal opportunity in terms of education, employment, power and influence, so that women's voices would be heard alongside those of men in decision-making on national and international affairs. The theme of empowerment, however, was quickly taken up by those who saw it as an opportunity for exploitation and profit, and now empowerment is interpreted as "sexy" and "sassy". Women involved in prostitution, pornography, lap dancing, pole dancing, stripping, etc. are called "empowered" and sometimes even "feminist".

Rosalind Gill from the London School of Economics and Political Science describes how the media went about turning around the 1970s feminist protest against the sexual objectification of women. Sexual objectification, she says, has become sexual subjectification. The re-sexualisation of women's bodies in the media represents women as choosing and enjoying the attention. The new images are "organized around sexual confidence and autonomy". The message is that women are not being acted upon; rather, they are the actors. Describing the modern phenomenon, Gill says:

> what is novel and striking about contemporary sexualised representations of women in popular culture is that they do not (as in the past) depict women as passive objects but as knowing, active and desiring sexual subjects. We are witnessing, I want to argue, a shift from sexual objectification to sexual subjectification in constructions of femininity in the media and popular culture [2003].

In *Gender and the Media* (2007), Gill tackles the media for its confusing messages about women. Describing the "extraordinary contradictoriness of constructions of gender", she says:

> confident expressions of "girl power" sit alongside reports of "epidemic" levels of anorexia and body dysmorphia; graphic tabloid reports of rape are placed cheek by jowl with adverts for lap-dancing clubs and telephone sex lines; lad magazines declare the "sex war" over, while reinstating beauty contests and championing new, ironic modes of sexism; and there are regular moral panics about the impact on men of the new, idealized male body imagery, while the re-sexualization of women's bodies in public space goes virtually unremarked upon [p. 1].

Commenting on the way the media has coopted feminist ideas for its own purposes, she observes that "feminist ideas have become a kind of common sense, yet feminism has never been more bitterly repudiated" (p. 1).

Maree Crabbe, coordinator of projects promoting healthy relationships in Warrnambool, Victoria, provides some on-the-ground examples which support Gill's pessimism. In an opinion piece in *The Age* newspaper and online, Crabbe says: "Advertising and media regularly present women as sexual objects to be looked at and used", with the result that teenagers, both male and female, "display attitudes that suggest that women are things of disrespect and humiliation, and that a woman's role in sexual relationships is about fulfilling men's desires and wishes" (2007). She speaks of "girls as young as 13" beginning their sex lives "by performing oral sex on boys". She quotes child psychologist Michael Carr-Greg as saying that "girls who were just beginning puberty were copying sex acts, including group and anal sex, that they see on the internet, believing that such behaviour is normal". A disturbing example given by Crabbe is that of eight boys who pleaded guilty in the Children's Court in 2007 to making a film which "showed them forcing a 17-year-old girl to perform sex acts with two of the boys while others spat on her and set her hair on fire". Crabbe concluded that "this incident is an extreme manifestation of a set of attitudes towards women that remain prevalent throughout our society" (2007, p. 1).

At the centre of the shift from sexual objectification to sexual subjectification is the notion that women have agency. Those media outlets and advertising companies involved in using women for their own profit are at pains to present women and girls as confident, autonomous and happily making the "choice" to be sexualised.

As with some of the other ethical dilemmas discussed above, feminists insist that they will not give up the fight for justice for women simply because their protests have been turned around and used against them. As Gill has said, the new sexual representations of women "are clearly responses to feminism". That being the case, feminists see no option but to renew their battle against the sexualisation and pornification of women and girls, and continue meeting the challenges head on.

Challenging the speech of other women

Another ethical dilemma for feminist activists exists in the philosophical differences among women who call themselves feminists. To criticise publicly the speech and actions of feminists who hold a different view to one's own is to play directly into the hands of the male-dominated power elite and their tactic of "divide and conquer". On the other hand, when women are heard defending what some call "woman-hating practices" such as pornography and prostitution, radical feminists see no option but to speak out.

In the early years of Second Wave feminism, there existed a taboo against criticising other women publicly. Men and male institutions were the enemy, and women who supported them were seen to be simply ignorant of their own oppression. As women supporters of woman-hating practices became more vocal and militant, however, that attitude began to change. Not speaking out against other women was costing the movement too much, as discussed in some detail in Chapter Five. Revisiting the words of Renate

Klein, not speaking out was "contributing to invisibilising ... years of radical feminist work" (2002, p. 12). Realising that some women were colluding with mainstream power-brokers to silence the voices of radical feminists, a decision was taken to challenge the views of other women publicly whenever those views were seen to be destructive of women.

As feminist activists continue to speak those words which have been rendered unspeakable, it is imperative that they take the ethical implications of their decision very seriously. As discussed above, the determination of feminists to speak through the silencing may have a detrimental effect on some individual women and, for that reason, the decision to speak ought to be taken, in each instance, only after careful consideration of all the possible repercussions.

Implications for the speaker

There are ethical implications, also, for the speaker/activist herself in terms of her motives, her analysis of situations, and the tactics she chooses to use, as well as the effect her activism will have on herself and her relationships. The dilemma can be expressed in an overall sense as the cost of speaking out versus the cost of not speaking out. The following analyses that dilemma under four headings: fighting unwinnable battles; standing in judgement of others; ensuring one's speech is fair speech; and considering the cost of not speaking.

Fighting unwinnable battles

There is a view that only fools choose to go into battle knowing that they will lose. The battle for women's rights is one such battle. Every generation of feminists in recent times has fought for a fairer deal for women, but still the battle has not been won. Susan Faludi declared in 1991 that it was due to a process she called "backlash". Women work hard at gaining equality and justice, she said, and just when the goal is in sight, the tables turn and they are prevented from ever reaching their goal. Faludi describes the process:

> Woman is trapped on this ... spiral, turning endlessly through the generations, drawing ever nearer to her destination without ever arriving. Each revolution promises to be "*the* revolution" that will free her from the orbit, that will grant her, finally, a full measure of human justice and dignity. But, each time, the spiral turns her back just short of the finish line. Each time, she hears that she must wait a little longer, be a little more patient—her hour on the stage is not yet at hand [1991, p. 67].

In *Backlash: The Undeclared War Against Women* (1991), Faludi traces the history of women's liberation in the United States from the mid-nineteenth century to the present and identifies four revolutions of the spiral.

- First, there was the movement which came out of the "1848 Seneca Falls women's rights convention and articulated by Elizabeth Cady Stanton and Susan B. Anthony…" (p. 69). The fight for women's suffrage was part of this.
- The second spiral started around the beginning of the twentieth century when the International Ladies' Garment Workers Union was formed in 1900. The National Women's Party which campaigned for an Equal Rights Amendment was organised in 1916; Margaret Sanger led the movement for birth control; and a kind of "feminist intelligentsia" began organising "early versions of consciousness-raising groups" (p. 70).
- The third spiral occurred in the 1940s when women were brought into the workforce to fill the vacancies left by the absence of the many men fighting the war. "In a record outpouring of legislative goodwill, the 1940s-era Congress passed thirty-three bills serving to advance women's rights" (p. 72). Women's energy was high. They joined unions and were politically active, making demands for equal pay, better child care and a general raising of the status of women.
- The fourth and final spiral began in the late 1960s and early 1970s and is now known as Second Wave feminism. The focus was on all issues related to bringing greater justice for women but, as discussed earlier, US feminists chose to place strong emphasis on the Equal Rights Amendment and reproductive rights (p. 76).

With every spiral, Faludi points out, there was a huge backlash against the leaders of the movement and against all women who wanted a greater recognition of women's abilities and contribution in every field. The "counterassault" each time was vicious until, finally, the movement subsided and the status quo appeared to be restored (pp. 66–80).

Questions which surely must be considered by feminist activists in the twenty-first century include: Is there anything to be gained by fighting unwinnable battles? Is it wise to "waste" words? Could feminists use their energy more constructively by working to support the existing patriarchal system with a view to improving it from within? Again, while such questions need to be considered, the answers have already been given. Feminist activists will continue to fight for women's rights because the battle has not yet been won. There is the realisation that the confrontation is long-term and that this particular time in history represents just one of the spirals referred to by Faludi.

Standing in judgement of others

At the very heart of the discipline of ethics is the practice of judging systems, relationships, philosophies, governments, leaders, decision-making processes and individual actors with a view to encouraging greater honesty and justice. With every protest, with every campaign against human rights abuses, social justice activists are making judgements about the attitudes and behaviour of others. Such is the nature of protest.

A dilemma for activists, including feminist activists, is the need to judge situations and people but to do it in a way that is not arrogant or abusive or violent. Regardless of how careful or diplomatic a protester may be, however, judgement of others will always attract charges of arrogance, as illustrated in the following excerpt from an opinion piece by Nicolas Rothwell in *The Weekend Australian*. Speaking with a cynical edge about social justice activists, he says:

> if you are among the enlightened and see the truth, then those who disagree with you are not just wrong but wicked ... Intelligent difference of opinion becomes impossible on a range of questions ... the most critical function of the new moralism is ... to differentiate—for purism has the particular charm of separating the moral elite from the vulgar, unenlightened crowd [2001, p. 24].

While making judgements is fraught with difficulties and open to criticisms of arrogance, purism, essentialism, and so on, protesters do, in fact, have a right to discriminate and to speak out in judgement. Liberal philosophy encourages a non-judgemental attitude. While at one level it is commendable not to be moralistic and judgemental of others, at another level, fence-sitting or not having an opinion to offer, speaks of hollowness and emptiness. Robert Fullinwider, in his essay "On Moralism", is clear on this point when he states:

> nonjudgmentalism can reflect a thorough-going critical flabbiness. The nonjudgmentalist is unwilling or unable to apply any categories of assessment to the conduct of others. Such a promiscuous non-judgmentalism that makes no distinctions among people, or such an indiscriminate tolerance that makes no objection to anything, isn't humility and generosity in action; it is mindlessness [2006, p. 13].

Activists are reminded, however, that when it is seen to be necessary to make judgements about others, it must always be done with care and humility because our "judgments of others are too easily distorted by prejudice and partiality" (Fullinwider 2006, p. 9). An understanding of one's own temperament, motives, prejudices and passions is essential for anyone who dares to sit in judgement of others. When one's protests on social issues are accompanied by careful self-scrutiny, there is much more chance that one's judgement of others will be constructive and effective.

Ensuring one's speech is fair speech

In Chapter Two, I discussed the concept of fair speech, suggesting that it involves a "greater attention to equality and justice". This being so, the first step for social justice activists intent on ensuring that their speech is fair is to open their minds to all the difficulties involved in calling for equality and justice. To expose injustice and call for justice is rarely a simple matter. For example, sometimes justice for one person can only be achieved by denying justice to another. As discussed in earlier chapters, when activists in the West fight in the name of justice for the implementation of sharia law as a way of supporting their Muslim brothers, the harsh oppression of women living under sharia law is rarely considered. In this, as in many other situations, justice is pursued at the expense of equality.

There are many examples of social activism on behalf of men which results in a denial of justice for women. Men who rape or who participate in gang-rape are often defended by lawyers who plead with the courts to consider the rapist's disadvantaged background, the fact that he was abused as a child, the stress he was experiencing at the time of the rape due to unemployment and poverty, or his ignorance of proper protocol in relation to sex. When these kinds of pleas are successful and the rapist is given a light sentence, such activists celebrate the fact that justice has been served. For the rapist's victim/s, however, the light sentence is seen as a miscarriage of justice. "Justice" for the rapist has meant injustice for his victim.

A chilling example of this phenomenon came to light in December 2007 in relation to an incident which received international media attention. Nine males pleaded guilty in an Australian court in 2005 to the gang-rape of a ten-year-old girl at Aurukun Aboriginal community. District Court Judge Sarah Bradley, who was known for her commitment to trying to keep Aboriginal men and women out of jail,[149] did not sentence any of the nine perpetrators to a term in prison.

Crown prosecutor Stephen Carter dubbed the behaviour of the gang-rapists "childish experimentation", even though three of them were legally adults (aged 17, 18 and 26). Taking his advice, Judge Bradley pronounced that the ten-year-old girl "probably agreed" to have sex with all nine of them; she proceeded to place a 12-month probation order on the six teenage perpetrators with no conviction recorded, and give the three adult perpetrators suspended jail sentences. When the attitudes and leniency of the prosecutor and judge came to the attention of the public, there was outrage not only in Australia

---

149 Aboriginal Australians comprise a disproportionate number of the men and women incarcerated in jails around the country.

but also in media reports around the world. This attempt at "justice" was seen as an absolute miscarriage of justice for the child victim and for the reputation of the Aurukun community.[150]

In addition to developing an awareness of the dilemmas involved in fighting for justice, fair speech also requires that activists have a clear understanding of their own personal agenda, as mentioned in the previous section. An honest appraisal of "one's own temperament, motives, prejudices and passions is essential". Such self-scrutiny will ensure that the activist approaches every situation with an open mind, thus reducing the potential for unenlightened dogmatism during the appraisal phase. The charge of dogmatism is often levelled at radical feminists because, when individuals, organisations and industries who profit from violence against and exploitation of women refuse to change their behaviour till required to do so by law, radical feminists have no option but to repeat their protests over and over. Unwilling to relent or water down their insistence on justice for women, they are then accused of dogmatism. The dilemma for social justice activists in any area of concern is that the alternative to the language of dogmatism seems to be the language of "choice", which, in the eyes of many radical activists, is devoid of ethical content.

The concept of choice promotes individualism, free speech, competition and an acceptance of the fact that there will be winners and losers. The winners are seen to have achieved in their own right, while the losers are seen to be entirely to blame for their own situations. The value of promoting community, equity, cooperation and situations where there are no losers is foreign to those who believe in the concept of choice.

For radical activists, there is a dilemma in steadfastly refusing to accept the doctrine of "choice", but at the same time not wanting to appear dogmatic. While most are content to err on the side of dogmatism, there is a need to ensure that one's speech does not fall short of the standards of fair speech.

Duncan Ivison, in "The Moralism of Multiculturalism", cautions activists to exercise their right of protest, their right to judge the behaviour of others, with care—and to do it intelligently. To guard against becoming dogmatic, he argues, one must strive always for a greater understanding of issues and keep one's mind open to the influence of other ideas and possibilities: "in order for our most cherished beliefs not to become dead dogma, they should remain open in principle to the challenge of other beliefs—even false beliefs—that force us to re-articulate their rationale once again". Referring to the "value and effectiveness of basic rights", Ivison emphasises the need for activists "to understand, apply and re-craft these rights to meet new circumstances and

---

150 As reported by the national broadcaster, <http://www.abc.net.au/news/stories/2007/12/10/2113896.htm>. Also Kevin Meade and Sarah Elks, "Girl Endured Six Weeks of Sex Attacks". *The Australian*, 14 December 2007.

conditions..." (2006, p. 82). Fair speech requires that activists keep up to date and ensure that the battles they fight and the tactics they use are current ones rather than throw-backs from previous times.

In summary, effective activists (including feminist activists) are those who, in their continuing fight for equality and justice, keep themselves alert to and aware of ethical dilemmas; engage in self-scrutiny so as to be clear about their own personal agenda; keep an open mind when appraising a new situation with a view to avoiding the potential for dogmatism; and make sure the battles they engage in are current battles.

Considering the cost of not speaking

Before looking at the cost of not speaking, it is important to be reminded of the cost of speaking. When one commits to speaking the unspeakable, there are always personal costs. In most cases the cost will not be as dramatic as for Mahatma Gandhi, Martin Luther King Jr, Meena (martyred leader of RAWA), Erin Brockovich or other high-profile activists, but there are nevertheless consequences to be borne.

There is the cost of being out of step with the majority of one's peers. In every society, there is the expectation that citizens will support the status quo; consequently, those who choose to dissent for whatever reason risk being shunned or ridiculed or ignored. Crucial to a person's sense of wellbeing are feelings of sameness, familiarity and belonging. When one's need to fight for justice has the effect of separating one from one's peer group and even from one's own family, an activist can develop a deep sense of loneliness.

Another cost comes with the realisation that the issues one is fighting for might never improve. The danger, when that occurs, is that hope will dissipate and despair dominate.

Then there are everyday costs such as time, energy, money and rising stress levels, all of which can cause problems for an activist's relationships. When both partners in a relationship are equally committed to social activism, there is usually an unspoken agreement about how much time, energy and money will be spent on activist pursuits. When only one partner is involved, a rift can develop and the relationship suffers.

The costs involved in speaking the unspeakable can be considerable, but those women and men committed to working to make the world a fairer place often say that the cost of not speaking would be far greater.

Radical feminists are committed to speaking the unspeakable because of their belief that not speaking, not acting, not exposing injustices against women gives the impression of—indeed, is the same as—condoning those injustices. Silence speaks volumes, as expressed in the slogan quoted by Australian feminist Betty Green: "Silence is the language of complicity ... Speaking out is the language of change."

In much of the activism by feminists around such issues as men's violence against women, fundamentalism, rape, sexual harassment, pornography, prostitution and harmful medical procedures, their commitment to fighting these injustices is so strong, and has remained strong for so long, that it becomes obvious that silence would never be an option for them. To stop speaking out would be to betray millions of women around the world—and such a cost would be too great.

Activists fighting for common sense to prevail around the issue of climate change, global warming, destruction of old-growth forests, destruction of the habitat of some of the world's most endangered species, the damming of rivers for the purposes of irrigation and so on, are of one mind about the cost of not speaking out. To remain silent on such issues would be to condone the destruction of the earth, they insist, and rob one's children and grandchildren of a future. The cost would be far too great. Those fighting against the worst features of globalisation also believe that the cost of not speaking would be far greater than the cost of speaking. If the greed of multinational companies and the insensitive policies of global trade and financial institutions were allowed to continue with no opposing voices, the result would be the total collapse of many poorer nations and the worsening of poverty and hardship for their citizens. As it is, anti-globalisation and anti-poverty activists are having some success at challenging wealthy nations and global institutions to consider the effect their policies are having and adjust their actions so that poverty will be reduced and living standards improved. Progress is slow, but they know that the cost of not speaking out would be total devastation for millions of people.

Feminist ethical analysis has found that the patriarchal assumptions dominating all activities and relationships around the world are implicated in the injustices evident at every level. It is for this reason that feminists can be found in the front line of every battle for justice, fighting alongside their brothers around issues of global warming, poverty and violence. Although men have not been as keen to join their sisters in the battle for justice for women in areas often designated as "women's issues", there is evidence that that is changing. The implementation of Amnesty International's project against violence against women, together with the White Ribbon Day initiative, are positive signs that men are beginning to acknowledge that they too have a responsibility to play their part in making the world a safer place for women.

Keeping in mind the need for thorough ethical evaluation of one's decision to continue speaking through the silencing, as discussed above, feminist activists express the need, also, to have a clear picture of the current status of feminism coupled with an understanding of where feminism as a global movement is headed into the future. Those concerns form the basis of the discussion in the final chapter.

FEMINIST SPEECH IN THE TWENTY-FIRST CENTURY 7

The task radical feminists have set for themselves in the twenty-first century is to be alert to the tactics of silencing and commit to speaking through the silencing with the deliberate aim of defying and disrupting those forces intent on violating, subordinating and excluding women. The business of this final chapter is to explore the issue of feminism's fitness for the task.

Although there is solid evidence that feminism in Western countries is ready and able to meet the challenge (a point I will discuss in some detail soon), it is in non-Western countries that a rise in feminist determination and activism is most obvious. In the West, the feminist agenda has been seriously curtailed for more than a decade. The elevation of the mainstream by the forces of economic and political conservatism has seen a strong push to silence dissenting feminist voices and wind back of many of feminism's hard-won gains. As a result, rather than enjoying the freedom to push on and make progress toward greater equality and justice for women, valuable feminist energy has to go into revisiting battles already won in the 1980s and 1990s with the aim of simply holding the line.

Feminism in non-Western settings

In many non-Western countries, where it is often dangerous—or at least counter-productive—to claim the title feminist, the work of feminism is being led by courageous and determined groups of women. While it is, of course, not possible to list all the projects initiated by feminists in all non-Western countries, I draw attention to five examples of the important international work being done to defy and disrupt systems harmful to women and push for a greater degree of equality and justice.

In Africa, feminists from many countries are determined that their voices will be heard around a variety of issues which fundamentally affect women: HIV/AIDS, genital mutilation, poverty, fundamentalism in all its forms, violence, rape, tokenism and the exclusion of women from social and political decision-making. In recent years, African feminists have been concerned about the watering down of feminist demands by the African women's movement. Consequently, in November 2006, the first African Feminist Forum was held in Accra, Ghana, hosted by the African Women's Development Fund (AWDF).

In a report on the forum, L. Muthoni Wanyeki, a political scientist based in Nairobi, Kenya, explained that the adoption of "gender mainstreaming as the key strategy to advance African women's human rights" has resulted in the silencing of feminist perspectives. "While there exists a growing body of feminist theory and African feminist scholarship, it is rare that such scholarship informs the analysis and strategies of the African women's movement", she said. The aim of the African Feminist Forum was to "bring together self-identified African feminists to critically explore where, from its analysis and strategies, the African women's movement is headed" (Wanyeki 2006).

Bene Madunagu, general coordinator of Development Alternatives for Women in a New Era (DAWN), said in an interview with Rochelle Jones that the forum was important for three reasons.

> It was the first time ever that African feminists came together with that name in their own space to formally create and own a feminist network on the African continent ... The second ... reason was the adoption of the Charter of Principles for feminist organising in Africa, articulated by African feminists themselves and based on experiences in the African continent.
>
> The third reason ... [was that invitees were made to understand ahead of time] that each person intending to be a part, must be comfortable in publicly self-defining herself as a feminist, that is, "no feminist buts", with a willingness to sign-on to the charter.[151]

"The Charter of Feminist Principles for African Feminists" is a strong, comprehensive document setting out principles for feminist activism into the future. The six themes of the charter, endorsed by all 120 participants, are:

1. Naming ourselves as feminists.
2. Our understanding of feminism and patriarchy.
3. Our identity as African feminists.
4. Individual ethics.
5. Institutional ethics.
6. Feminist leadership.[152]

---

151 Jones 2006. See also African Women's Development Fund 2006.
152 See the full content of the Charter at <http://www.isiswomen.org/index.php?option=com_content&task=view&id=780&Itemid=80#up>.

An introduction to the Charter of Feminist Principles found on the TradewindsGhana website reveals the strength and determination of those feminists who attended the forum:

> With this Charter, we reaffirm our commitment to dismantling patriarchy in all its manifestations in Africa. We remind ourselves of our duty to defend and respect the rights of all women, without qualification. We commit to protecting the legacy of our feminist ancestors who made numerous sacrifices, in order that we can exercise greater autonomy.[153]

The work of African feminists at the beginning of the twenty-first century is an inspiration to feminists around the world. Even though the task ahead of them is huge, they are determined that they will not be silenced.

The Revolutionary Association of the Women of Afghanistan (RAWA) is another such group of feminists. Established in Kabul by female Afghan intellectuals in 1977, RAWA continues today as a strong voice against the human rights abuses perpetrated against women and girls by successive fundamentalist regimes. In the beginning, RAWA's objective was to "involve an increasing number of Afghan women in social and political activities aimed at acquiring women's human rights and contributing to the struggle for the establishment of a government based on democratic and secular values in Afghanistan". Before long RAWA expanded its programme to include involvement in "education, health and income generation as well as political agitation". Looking to the future, RAWA members express a determination to continue speaking the unspeakable in Afghanistan, Pakistan, and throughout the Muslim world. Their pledge is to continue the fight against the "criminal policies and atrocities" committed by ultra-fundamentalist leaders and, in particular, against "their incredibly ultra-male-chauvinistic and anti-woman orientation". Summing up the association's intention to continue their courageous work into the future, they say:

> Whenever fundamentalists exist as a military and political force in our injured land, the problem of Afghanistan will not be solved. Today RAWA's mission for women's rights is far from over and we have to work hard for establishment of an independent, free, democratic and secular Afghanistan. [RAWA n.d.]

Another group of feminist women working to "strengthen women's individual and collective struggles for equality and their rights" is Women Living Under Muslim Laws (WLUML). With offices in the United Kingdom, Senegal and Pakistan, WLUML "is an international solidarity network that provides information, support and a collective space for women whose lives

---

153 <http://tradewindsghana.com/v1/?menuId=23315&linkId=23322>.

are shaped, conditioned or governed by laws and customs said to derive from Islam" (WLUML n.d.). On their website they expose the repression of women by religious fundamentalists wherever it occurs. For example, in January 2008 they published an open letter by the Women's Autonomous Movement of Nicaragua, announcing "the increased presence of fundamentalists attacking feminists for defending the human rights of women". When Zoilamerica Narvaez exposed the sexual abuse she suffered from her stepfather, the current president of Nicaragua, the Network of Women against Violence rose up to support her. The National Association for Human Rights, "an organization sponsored by the Catholic right wing and the Secretary of the Episcopal Conference" laid charges against nine of the "well-known leaders of the women's movement of Nicaragua", accusing them of various criminal acts. All nine women are named on the WLUML website, where a call went out to international women's and feminist movements as well as human rights activists around the world to express solidarity with the accused women, who face time in jail if found guilty (WLUML 2008).

Members of WLUML take opportunities to speak at World Social Forums and other global events with the aim of getting their message out to those who lean toward supporting fundamentalist Muslim regimes and the establishment of sharia law in Western countries. Their message is that the central intent of sharia law and the aim of those who administer it is to deprive women of their human rights, and therefore it must be resisted at all costs.

Kyrgyzstan is another example of a country where feminists are fighting hard for women's basic human rights. One of the previous Soviet Union republics, Kyrgyzstan is said to have a strong civil society but Human Rights Watch has reported an increasing tendency on the part of the Kyrgyz government to "disrupt the work of the nongovernmental community and intimidate human rights activists". Most of the NGOs and human rights organisations are led by women, many of whom have reported harassment by law-enforcement agencies and members of the State Committee for National Security.

Two important campaigns are being waged by human rights defenders in Kyrgyzstan. One is a general campaign called "Let us Defend Freedom, Dignity, and the Personal Inviolability of People in Kyrgyzstan" and the other aims to get women into politics. The first was launched on 5 July 2007 by civil rights activists, who immediately drew up a list of activists who had suffered harassment at the hands of the authorities. In an article on the Eurasianet website, Janyl Chytyrbaeva drew attention to some of the incidents:

> Among those on the list is Valentina Gritsenko, the chairwoman of the nongovernmental organization Spravedlivost [Justice] in the southern Jalal-Abad Province, who has been persecuted for more than a year for her efforts to disclose information about the alleged torture of a pregnant woman by a local policeman …
>
> Arzykan Momuntaeva, the director of the regional office of the Coalition For Democracy and Civil Society, was arrested along with several other activists …
>
> … prominent civil society leaders Asia Sasykbaeva and Cholpon Jakupova, among others, were questioned several times by the security officials without a lawyer being present [Chytyrbaeva, 2007].

In addition to raising awareness about harassment of human rights activists, courageous women in Kyrgyzstan are actively pursuing justice for women on issues ranging from property rights to bride-kidnapping and insist that women's human rights must be dealt with by governments as a matter of urgency.

The other campaign, aimed at breaking the tradition of electing all-male parliaments, is being organised by the Forum of Women's NGOs of Kyrgyzstan. Women constitute only 5 per cent of local government bodies and 0 per cent of the national parliament. Nurgul Djanaeva, president of the Forum of Women's NGOs, explains that the campaign, which began in May 2007, aims to prepare 50 women to stand as candidates in the 2010 parliamentary elections. Women's NGOs are aware, she says, that there are few cases in the world, if any, "when long-term (at least two years) cooperation with massive preparatory long-term work was done by women's NGOs with and for group of women-candidates for posts" (Djanaeva 2007).[154] In order to ensure that women's concerns will be addressed in parliament in the future, the campaign aims to mobilise women to offer themselves as candidates and provide training and support all the way through to the election and beyond. The plan of the Forum of Women's NGOs is to "create women-leaders" and make "long-term women's movement investment in them". The training is two-pronged: "capacity building to win elections and capacity building to work for women later when they are in their posts". Djanaeva says:

> the main idea is that women themselves through women's NGOs start shaping future political behavior of women-MPs. Forum of Women's NGOs of Kyrgyzstan hopes that after 2010 parliamentary elections in Kyrgyzstan women win seats, women will bring people's and women's agenda into Parliament [2007].

---

154 Emily's List is a similar organisation operating very successfully in the US since 1985 <http://www.emilyslist.org/about/>, and in Australia since 1996 <http://www.emilyslist.org.au/about_us/about_us.asp>.

Another example of feminists in non-Western countries mobilising to bring about greater equality and justice for women is the work of Pacific Islander women. The problems being confronted in many island nations include: men's violence against women, sexual assault of women and girls, sexual harassment, trafficking for sex, inheritance rights, torture and murder of women following accusations of witchcraft and the dominance of men in the political arena. Women are also at the forefront of the battle against the build-up of military forces in the Pacific region and the call for a nuclear-free Pacific.

Feminists in Fiji have displayed a strong and persistent determination to gain justice for women and children in their country. The Family Law Bill which was "unanimously passed by the Lower House of Parliament on 14th October 2003" represented thirteen years of work by the Fiji Women's Rights Movement (FWRM), the Regional Rights Resource Team, the Fiji Women's Crisis Centre and others. The coordinator of FWRM, Virisila Baudromo, explained that the legislation would provide "a level playing field for women and men" and place the rights of the child at the centre (WLUML, 2003a).

Working closely with the FWRM was the Regional Rights Resource Team. Fiji Law Reform Commissioner, P. Imrana Jalal, and her colleagues on the team worked tirelessly to prepare the legislation, explain the legal ramifications of the new bill to the Fijian people (Jalal 2003) and respond to misrepresentations and criticisms by the Fiji Methodist Church and others. The passing of the Family Law Bill was a victory for feminists and other human rights activists in their efforts to bring about a more just society.

Another victory for women's rights in Fiji came with the approval by cabinet on 5 January 2008 of the "National Policy on Sexual Harassment in the Workplace under the Employment Relations Promulgation". Again, this was the result of years of consistent advocacy on the part of the FWRM and others working for women's human rights in Fiji.[155]

Focusing attention on the Pacific region as a whole, it must be said that one of the strengths of Pacific Islander feminist activists is their ability and willingness to connect with each other, identify common issues, draw on the power that comes from organising as a bloc and offer support to each other in the various struggles. Another strength comes from their knowledge of global and regional bodies able to assist and their willingness to work with them: United Nations bodies, Development Alternatives for Women in a New Era (DAWN), Pacific Women's Information Network, Global Fund for Women, AusAID and many others.

All centres are particularly strong in their fight against violence against women. The Fiji Women's Crisis Centre publishes a monthly newsletter on behalf of the Pacific Women's Network Against Violence Against Women. The

---

155 <http://lyris1.spc.int/read/messages?id=56701>.

May 2007 issue of *Pacific Women Against Violence* reported on International Women's Day activities organised throughout the region with the theme "Ending Impunity for Violence Against Women". Shamima Ali, coordinator of the Fiji Women's Crisis Centre, drew on research done by the centre when she spoke to a large crowd at a breakfast on International Women's Day in Auckland, New Zealand: "Violence against women and children is prevalent throughout the Pacific region across all ethnic and socio-economic groups. FWCC's national research on domestic violence and sexual assault found that 80 percent of survey respondents had witnessed violence in their home" (Ali 2007, p. 1).

In the Solomon Islands, the Family Support Centre workers conducted workshops on domestic violence at Rove prison. The biggest event in the Solomons was the International Women's Day march in Honiara organised by the Family Support Centre, when hundreds of women marched through the streets claiming "No acceptance of violence against women and girls".

The Leitana Nehan Women's Development Agency in Bougainville conducted a five-day gender awareness and human rights workshop for twenty-eight participants in North Bougainville in conjunction with International Women's Day. The Cook Islands Women Counselling Centre Punanga Tauturu conducted a four-day workshop on gender awareness, violence and child abuse on the island of Mauke to mark International Women's Day.[156]

The activism on behalf of women in many Pacific Island nations is being led by women's NGOs as well as by women's divisions within government (in those countries where such national machinery is in place).

Feminism in Western countries

The commitment and energy demonstrated by feminists in Africa, Afghanistan, Pakistan, Kyrgyzstan, the Pacific Islands and many other non-Western nations inspire Western feminists, who struggle to be heard in a strengthened and determined backlash patriarchy. What is the situation of the feminist movement in the West in these early years of the twenty-first century? Most feminists agree that an understanding of the current situation is crucial if Western feminists are to speak effectively through the silencing. In the remainder of this chapter, I will discuss the current status of Western feminism and what feminist speech will be into the twenty-first century.

---

[156] All of these activities were reported in the May 2007 newsletter. See Fiji Women's Crisis Centre 2007.

The current status of Western feminism

Since the late 1980s several theories have been advanced by feminist researchers and commentators about the status of feminism today. While there is no end to claims by detractors that feminism is dead, there is much evidence to support the contention that it is alive and well and continuing its work for women. Most feminists would admit, however, that the activities and influence of this once powerful social movement have been seriously curtailed in recent years. We will explore some of the theories floated by feminist commentators: backlash; abeyance; underground operations; diaspora; and virtual space.

Backlash theory

The best-known and most widely accepted of all the theories about the present situation of the feminist movement is that proposed by Susan Faludi in *Backlash: The Undeclared War Against Women* (1991). As mentioned in Chapter Six, Faludi identified several spirals of women's activism since the mid-nineteenth century and the counter-assault or backlash which followed each time with the purpose of putting the movement down and restoring the status quo. The backlash against the movement which has come to be known as Second Wave feminism is evident in the media, the speeches of politicians, the theories of academics and, in some cases, the words of feminists themselves.

In her introductory chapter, Faludi draws attention to the message repeated over and over by the media in the late 1980s and early 1990s. In their effort to paint the feminist movement in a negative light, their message was:

> You may be free and equal now, ... but you have never been more miserable.
>
> ... Professional women are suffering "burn-out" and succumbing to an "infertility epidemic". Single women are grieving from a "man-shortage". The *New York Times* reports: childless women are "depressed and confused" and their ranks are swelling. *Newsweek* says: unwed women are "hysterical" and crumbling under a "profound crisis of confidence". The health advice manuals inform: high-powered career women are stricken with unprecedented outbreaks of "stress-induced disorders", hair loss, bad nerves, alcoholism, and even heart attacks [Faludi 1991, pp. 1–2].

More recently, the media's preferred backlash tactic is that of silencing. Articles about feminists, when they are mentioned at all, usually represent them as self-centred, self-absorbed women, while opinion pieces by feminists are more often than not rejected. Marches and demonstrations by women (feminist and non-feminist) are sometimes ridiculed,[157] sometimes given cursory attention[158] and often ignored altogether.

Politicians, too, have added their voices to the backlash. Margaret Thatcher proclaimed that the days when women's rights were "demanded in strident tones" should be gone forever because "The battle for women's rights has been largely won" (Faludi 1991, p. 1). When Prime Minister John Howard came to power in Australia in the mid-1990s, one of his early proclamations was that women in the public service would no longer be called "Ms". He made no secret of the fact that he was determined to get rid of "politically correct" feminist language and return Australia to the days when women were women and relationships between women and men were as they had always been.

In academic circles, the backlash could be clearly seen with the rise to prominence of postmodernism in the late 1980s and the declaration that there was no longer any need to focus on inequalities and injustices. The work of the social movements of the 1960s and 1970s was said to be over. Liberation movements calling for justice on the basis of sex, race and sexual orientation were curiosities from the past. The focus was on complicated theories expressed in jargon-laden language rather than on people's everyday lives or on the need for activism to bring about a greater degree of justice and equity. As discussed in Chapter Five, many feminists employed at universities became besotted with postmodernism and joined in the backlash against feminism.

In addition to the feminists who turned to postmodernism, other feminists —perhaps confused by the West's dramatic turn toward conservatism, perhaps disappointed that the women's movement they had devoted their lives to seemed to be disintegrating—deserted the cause and lent their voices to the backlash. Betty Friedan, one of the founders of Second Wave feminism, disappointed many when she began speaking about the loneliness caused by women's new-found independence. She warned that "women now suffer from a new identity crisis", new problems "that have no name" (Faludi 1991, p. 2). Naomi Wolf, much respected for *The Beauty Myth* (1990), joined in the chorus in *Fire with Fire* (1993), saying that women's equality had been won

---

157 In the 1980s, one group of women marching on International Women's Day in one of Australia's regional cities was referred to by a journalist as a gathering of "old boiler hens".

158 In the year 2000, the World March of Women organised a huge march in New York city attended by an estimated 40,000 to 60,000 women from many countries around the world. Traffic was held up for hours as police lined the streets to allow marchers safe passage to deliver millions of signatures to Kofi Annan, then Secretary-General of the United Nations, demanding the elimination of poverty and of violence against women throughout the world. This spectacular demonstration of women's solidarity and strength warranted only a brief paragraph (40 words) and a small picture on one of the more insignificant pages of the newspaper. *New York Times Metro*, 18 October 2000, p. B5.

and it was time for feminists to stop talking about the ways in which women are victimised and begin focusing on the power women now have to work with men as equals. There was now no more need for feminism.

Faludi's theory of backlash plausibly explains the feminist movement's virtual disappearance from society's radar. Indeed, my emphasis in this book on the silencing of women through violence, subordination and exclusion supports the backlash theory throughout.

Abeyance theory

Another major theory about the status of the feminist movement since the late 1980s uses the term "abeyance". According to Verta Taylor in her article "Social Movement Continuity: The Women's Movement in Abeyance" (1989), abeyance theory or social movement continuity theory challenged the traditional view held by social movement theorists that "new" social movements "seemingly emerged out of nowhere", representing a sudden shift away from the status quo (p. 761). The traditional idea was that movements rise to ascendancy and then die out, with the possibility of being born again as a totally new movement some time in the future. This was replaced by the idea that, after a period of resurgence, movements do not die but, rather, continue simmering under the surface making ready for the next breakthrough or turning point in "movement mobilization". Taylor spoke of the women's movement of the 1960s and 1970s as a "resurgent challenge with roots in an earlier cycle of feminist activism that presumably ended when suffrage was won". Abeyance is defined by Taylor as "a holding process by which movements sustain themselves in nonreceptive political environments and provide continuity from one stage of mobilization to another" (p. 761).[159]

According to this theory, the feminist movement of today is a movement in abeyance. Taylor explains that "abeyance" was first used by Ephraim Mizruchi (1983) to describe a process of social control whereby societies are able to contain and integrate dissidents who are a potential threat to the status quo. Abeyance structures absorb marginal groups by providing enough opportunities for them to feel they are making an impact, while at the same time restraining them "from potentially more disruptive activities" (p. 762). Taylor takes the concept a step further by focusing on the potential for social change inherent in social movement abeyance organisations. Describing the process, she says:

---

[159] For more on social movement continuity theory, see: Freeman 1975, 1979; Evans 1979; Gusfield 1981; Rupp 1982; Rupp and Taylor 1987; Staggenborg 1988, 1989; and Taylor 1989b.

> As a movement loses support, activists who had been most intensely committed to its aims become increasingly marginal and socially isolated ... a movement in abeyance becomes a cadre of activists who create or find a niche for themselves. Such groups may have little impact in their own time and may contribute, however unwillingly, to maintenance of the status quo. But, by providing a legitimating base to challenge the status quo, such groups can be sources of protest and change [p. 762].

Feminists in a period of abeyance, then, are committed to maintaining a holding pattern, scaled down, retrenched, hibernating, having little impact in their own time, even contributing to the maintenance of the status quo, but preparing the ground for the next upsurge in feminist activism. Taylor suggests three ways that feminists in abeyance perform the function of preparing the ground: "through promoting the survival of *activist networks*, sustaining a repertoire of *goals and tactics*, and promoting a *collective identity* that offers participants a sense of mission and moral purpose" (p. 762, emphasis in the original). Abeyance theory has provided an explanation for many committed feminists who have been frustrated by a "nonreceptive political and social environment" (p. 762) which has existed in the West since the 1980s.

Following the discussion among feminist social movement theorists, Taylor's version of the concept of abeyance appears to have been accepted by various other feminist scholars without question. It does, after all, make sense of an otherwise frustrating and puzzling situation for committed feminists struggling to understand the general loss of interest in women's human rights. Gisela Kaplan, writing in 1996 about the history of Australia's feminist movement, spoke of the 1990s as a time for reflection and auditing (p. 194). Sarah Maddison, in an online article about young feminists, "Bombing the Patriarchy or Just Trying to Get a Cab: Challenges Facing the Next Generation of Feminist Activists", argued that "young activists are performing an essential task for the movement's maintenance by sustaining the ideologies and networks that will be necessary for another strong wave of feminist activism to emerge". She spoke about "keeping open a political space that 'belongs' to feminism" so that that space can be readily taken up again when the opportunity arises for a different form of feminist activism (2002).

Feminists generally accept that the movement needs to be maintained and sustained in difficult times, and that the task of all feminists, young and old, is to build foundations, continue their research and sustain their networks. But many feminist activists express the view that there is something sadly lacking in such a picture of the feminist movement in the twenty-first century. Abeyance terms such as holding pattern, preparing the ground, holding the fort and keeping open a political space all paint a picture of inaction, and inaction inadvertently supports the status quo.

Responding to Taylor's work on abeyance theory, Traci Sawyers and David Meyer present a more detailed interpretation of the status and role of feminists in times of movement decline in their 1999 article "Missed Opportunities: Social Movement Abeyance and Public Policy". They suggest that a movement in abeyance actually has three component parts and that Taylor's model only addressed one of them. They identify the three parts as "*marginalization*; *co-optation*; and *depoliticization*".

As a movement declines and moves into a period of abeyance, the first thing that happens is that dissidents are marginalised, that is, they are "forced so far to the edges of mainstream politics that they no longer engage meaningfully with institutional political decision-makers or mainstream discourse; they are then relatively easy to repress or ignore". Radical activists then "sharpen their rhetoric, further eschew conventional politics, and turn inward". Such disengagement with mainstream policies and politics "while nurturing ideology and identity" is what Taylor described as abeyance (Sawyers and Meyer 1999, p. 193).

Many radical feminists today could be said to fit this first category: marginalised, turned inward, nurturing ideology and identity, preparing the ground for the next surge of feminist activism. One seriously negative element for feminists in this category, however, is the potential for the widening of divisions between individuals and groups as passions seek an outlet. Exclusion from engagement with broader political and social decision-making processes combined with a focus on nurturing one's own feminist ideology and identity has at times caused feminists to take the fight to each other. While the overscrutinising of each other's politics, petty in-fighting and serious criticism of one's sisters may give one a personal sense of superiority, it is no less than disastrous in terms of movement fragmentation.

The second component part of a movement in abeyance, according to Sawyers and Meyer, is cooptation. All feminists who reject marginalisation have the choice of allowing themselves to be coopted by mainstream forces. Individuals and organisations who choose to be coopted may continue to identify as feminists but "limit their operational goals to those achievable without structural reform and their tactics to less disruptive, more conventional activities" (Sawyers and Meyer 1999, p. 193). Many liberal feminists in the West have chosen this path, and they are usually rewarded by the media and governments as women who are pushing at the boundaries of mainstream while locating themselves firmly within it.

The third component of a movement in abeyance is said to be depoliticisation, where once committed activists change their tactics to those of "protest without politics". In an era of movement decline, depoliticisation can occur in one of two ways: by changing one's focus from collective and political activism to the pursuit of individual and personal development; or by turning one's attention to other political movements as they begin their rise to prominence, for example, the movement against globalisation, the peace movement, the environment movement or the queer movement. Those who were once feminist activists are depoliticised in relation to a declining feminist movement and re-politicised in relation to other movements. Sawyers and Meyer sum up this section of their article by saying that the retrenchment of the feminist movement "was characterized by radical feminists in abeyance; institutional feminists engaged with the state in pursuit of less comprehensive goals; and, de- or re-politicized feminists struggling in different movements or alone" (1999, p. 194).

For radical feminists, important questions need to be considered: To what degree are "retrenchment and abeyance" inevitable? Is feminism completely at the mercy of what appear to be natural forces of decline and fragmentation? Do feminists have the power to minimise decline or shorten periods of abeyance?

Although the decline of social movements is generally presented as inevitable, it is important to remember that their "ebb and flow doesn't just happen. It's engineered" (McLellan 2007, p. 13). Sawyers and Meyer expressed a similar view when they said that "just as successful mobilization is a combination of agency and environment so is decline and abeyance" (1999, p. 202). They are not implying that Second Wave feminists could have stopped the decline altogether because there are socio-political factors at work. Rather, they are making the point that activists have agency. Even though backlash forces have engineered the decline of the feminist movement in the West, it is important that feminists do not see themselves as completely powerless. Opportunities arise regularly and feminists are urged to be ready to "take advantage of them through political engagement". In addition to watching and being ready for opportunities as they present themselves, feminists during a period of abeyance can also "play a role in creating and expanding their own opportunities" (p. 202). Sawyers and Meyer stress the need for unity and engagement. Unity does not mean consensus but, rather, "unity of purpose" and genuine willingness to work together. Engagement with the social and political processes of the day is imperative if feminists are to respond to opportunities as they arise and also create new opportunities to speak and act on behalf of women.

A study of the concepts of abeyance and backlash is imperative for those feminists struggling to understand the status of feminism today. Both are major social movement theories which offer the kinds of analyses necessary as background to feminist activism in the twenty-first century. The following theories are closely related. Indeed, underground operations theory, diaspora theory and virtual space theory are all attempts to explain in more concrete terms the situation of abeyance caused by backlash.

Underground operations theory

The idea of feminism as an underground operation is described by Mary Fansod Katsenstein as "unobtrusive mobilization". In her 1990 article "Feminism within American Institutions: Unobtrusive Mobilization in the 1980s", she said:

> Marches, protests, and demonstrations are now infrequent, press coverage is decreased, much of the drama is gone. Yet consciousness of continued gender inequalities has not abated ...
>
> [These] have been succeeded by a process of what might be termed unobtrusive mobilization inside institutions. Occurring inside institutions of higher education, foundations, the social services, the media, the professions, the armed forces, the churches—inside the core institutions of American society and the American state—unobtrusive mobilization by women now drives second-wave feminism ahead into the 1990s [pp. 27–8].

Despite sustained attempts to "delegitimate ideologies of feminism" in the United States during the 1980s, she says, "gender consciousness (awareness of and opposition to gender inequality) continues to grow" (p. 30). Some women, Katzenstein explains, prefer not to identify as feminist in an attempt to separate themselves from what they see as an obligation to "subscribe to a requisite set of views on particular subjects" (p. 30n) but are, nevertheless, working for women's rights inside institutions.

Another form of underground operations could be described as guerilla tactics, where feminist activists engage in subversive acts while being careful not to be caught. So-called adult magazines on sale in newsagents are sometimes targeted by feminists armed with stickers which say: "This offends women" or "This degrades all women". As they browse in the magazine department, they surreptitiously attach stickers to the offending publications. Similarly, there is much anecdotal evidence of women deliberately turning offending magazines around or burying them behind other less offensive publications so that, for a time at least, the exploitation of women's bodies is not immediately on display.

In the United States a group calling itself Tennessee Guerilla Women has a mission statement and goals that place it in the category of virtual space theory rather than underground operations theory, but its members still have a view of themselves as working underground to bring about a more just society. On their website they explain that they "are working to mobilize a very large state-wide internet-based community of politically active women" to achieve certain goals for women and the most vulnerable in society (Tennessee Guerilla Women n.d.).

Diaspora theory

Diaspora theory is similar to underground operations theory in referring to the mobilisation of feminists within institutions. The difference is that feminists in the diaspora do not attempt to be unobtrusive. In the absence of a vibrant collective feminist movement, committed feminists are working individually or in small groups to achieve the aims of equality and justice for women. Those who maintain the rage and continue to speak out in mainstream institutions such as universities, the media, politics, government bureaucracies and the arts know that they are less likely to be promoted and less likely to be asked for their opinions than those who choose to remain underground, but they prefer to be part of the diaspora, alert and ready to speak out regardless of the personal cost.

By far, the majority of diaspora feminists are found working in NGOs, in particular, women's services such as health, domestic violence, sexual assault services and women's refuges. In the 1970s, when feminist trail-blazers convinced governments to fund a variety of women's services, feminists moved into those areas hoping to make a difference for women. In every Western nation, there are government-funded women's services scattered throughout, mostly staffed by committed feminist activists. The attraction for many activists in the 1970s and 1980s was that an important part of the brief handed to them by funding bodies was advocacy. Democratic governments wanted to hear from the most disadvantaged groups in their society and invited NGOs to advocate on their behalf. As discussed in Chapter Four, that situation changed with the rise of ultra-conservative governments in the 1990s to the extent that, in many countries, NGOs were prevented from speaking out and advocating on behalf of those who used their services and were restricted to caring roles only.

There is hope that, at the end of the first decade of the twenty-first century when conservative regimes are no longer in control in the United Kingdom, Australia, Spain and the United States, the proper democratic function will be restored to NGOs. Those members of the feminist diaspora who have continued advocating for women during the conservative years, in spite of the fact that their activism placed their particular NGO in jeopardy, are hopeful that they will be able to support women more openly in the future.

Virtual space theory

Virtual space is seen by many feminist activists as the way of the future. More and more feminists are creating blogs as a way of communicating with each other and the online world. Indeed, in 2006 Kira Cochrane wrote that the estimated number of feminist blogs was around 240,000 and admitted that the true figure could be much higher. Also, feminists of all ages are involving themselves in feminist email discussion lists. Some have designed and created websites devoted to feminist pursuits. Feminists are also making good use of the internet by presenting opinion pieces for publication online.[160]

The view expressed in a radio interview by Australian social commentator Hugh Mackay, that many activists are now "making their point in cyberspace rather than marches and demonstrations" (ABC Radio National, 26 January 2008), raises an interesting question. Cyberspace certainly does afford feminists and other human rights activists unlimited freedom to say all that they want to say, but is such a limited arena effective in terms of getting one's message across to those who have the power to make the changes being called for? In the West politicians, spin doctors, business leaders and advertisers use the internet, mobile phones and other technologies when they want to reach young people with their propaganda, but one wonders how many of them actually look at sites and blogs in an attempt to find out what young people are thinking and how they are coping with day-to-day life.

Activists of all ages—feminists, Indigenous women and men, dissidents in every area—have turned to virtual space because they have been systematically excluded from the mainstream media and other arenas controlled by the power elite. Such a situation must suit those in power because, if protests and criticisms can be contained in virtual space, dissidents will offer no challenge in the real world. The question for feminists is: Should feminist activists give up the fight to have a voice in maintream media so easily and restrict themselves to virtual space? The answer surely is that virtual space is but one space in which feminist voices will be heard.

Feminist speech into the future

Feminist activists are determined that the unspeakable will be spoken. While there seems to be no need for discussion or argument on that point, there is much discussion, writing, division, arguing over the shape and sound of feminist speech in the twenty-first century. There is little doubt that feminist speech will continue into the future and come from both non-radical and radical voices. It will still be true that non-radical feminists will be more readily accepted and more easily coopted by mainstream and that attention will be given, in particular, to those who speak the words the power elite want to hear.

---

160 Examples of blogs are: <http://allecto.wordpress.com>; <http://thefword.org.uk/blog/index>; <http://sazziesblog.blogspot.com>; <http://spinningspinsters.wordpress.com>; <http://dis-senter.livejournal.com>; <http://witchywoo.wordpress.com>.
International email lists include CATW (Coalition Against Trafficking in Women) and GSN (Global Sisterhood Network), and Australian lists include f-agenda, CATWA and elsa. For a selection of radical feminist websites, see the References list.
Examples of feminist contributions to opinion writing are Women's Forum Australia, <http://www.womensforumaustralia.org>. Also <http://www.onlineopinion.com.au>; <http://www.abc.net.au/unleashed/>.

Non-radical feminist voices
In the non-radical sector of feminism, there will continue to be several streams committed to highlighting issues of sexual freedom, equality, the environment and poverty.

The first stream comprises liberal women who are proud advocates of pornography and prostitution and who make it known that they support the increasing sexualisation of women and girls through fashion and advertising. It goes without saying that their voices are readily heard and relayed through the mainstream media, where they are erroneously touted as "the voice of feminism" because their speech serves to support the agenda of male-focused societies in relation to women.

The second stream comprises liberal women who are more interested in battles involving leadership, employment and inclusion of women in corporate boardrooms, political inner circles, the military and international decision-making bodies. This stream of non-radical feminist voices always has more difficulty getting the attention of the media or politicians than do the sexual liberals because they often make demands which have the potential to upset the status quo. When governments feel compelled to give some ground in an attempt to appease feminists, however, it is usually the demands of this stream which receive attention. It was through the efforts of this group of liberal feminists in the past that much was achieved for women in the West and they will continue to be a valuable part of the feminist endeavour into the future.

The third stream of non-radical feminists comprises those who have worked tirelessly to raise issues of concern in relation to the environment. Sometimes called eco-feminists, they campaign (often alongside men) to raise the alarm about global warming, to save forests from decimation by the timber industry, to protect animals from cruel and destructive practices, to preserve the habitats of endangered species, and so on. The invaluable work of eco-feminists will continue to be part of feminism's impact into the future.

The fourth stream comprises those feminists who work for the elimination of poverty worldwide. In the main, they are proudly socialist feminists who agitate against the attitudes and practices of international trade and finance organisations and against the exploitative workplace practices of certain companies and industries. Often at the forefront of the anti-globalisation and union movements, feminists emphasising the need to eliminate poverty by sharing wealth nationally and globally will continue to be an important part of the feminist movement.

Radical feminist voices

In the radical feminist sector, there will continue to be loud and persistent protest against all the practices which demean and subordinate women. Also, there is no doubt that the mainstream tactics of silencing discussed in Chapter Three will continue to be used against them. As is evident in the present, neither the backlash nor the abeyance of the feminist movement will deter feminists committed to fighting for justice for women. Strong, courageous feminist voices will continue to speak through the silencing, highlighting and protesting about violence against women in all its forms, the sexual exploitation of women and girls and the exclusion of women from inner circles where real power is exercised and decisions of national and international import are made.

The process recommended by leaders in the field of feminist ethics (mentioned in the Introduction) will continue to be followed: total engagement, appraisal, reflection, protest and action.

Total engagement

Recognising that the feminist movement at the beginning of the twenty-first century is, in mainstream terms, a movement in abeyance, radical feminists refuse to accept that decline and invisibility are inevitable. In line with the view expressed by Sawyers and Meyer that abeyance is due to "a combination of agency and environment" (1999, p. 202) they, as agents working for a more just society, are determined to continue to engage with the world as it is. It is understood that, without total engagement, effective action will not be possible.

Social and political engagement enables one to respond to opportunities as they arise. For example, feminists of all persuasions were quick to seize on the opportunity to protest early in 2008 against Australia's newly elected Labor government led by Kevin Rudd when nine middle-class, middle-aged white men, one Indigenous man and one white woman were chosen to serve as the steering committee charged with the task of choosing 1000 people to attend the government's 2020 Summit to discuss ten critical problems facing the nation.[161] The almost total exclusion of women and Indigenous people sent shockwaves through the feminist community because it signalled that the new government, who feminists believed would value and demonstrate equality and fairness, might not be very different in terms of inclusiveness from the previous conservative government.

---

161 For details of the 2020 Summit, see <http://www.australia2020.gov.au/>.

Engagement with social and political processes enables feminists to take advantage of opportunities to protest, to formulate their protests accurately and effectively, to raise awareness, and to demonstrate their support of justice for women and other disempowered groups.

By recognising and engaging with social and political processes, feminists can create new opportunities as well as expand in new ways the work they are already doing. Total engagement involves keeping up to date with current issues and responding in contemporary ways. Radical feminists of all ages will continue their commitment to such comprehensive engagement into the future.

Appraisal and reflection

Radical feminist activists have always demonstrated a reliance on solid feminist analysis and research as the basis for their action, and this will not change. The word appraisal is used here because it is the word most often used in literature about ethics, but it can also be called analysis.

Ethical reflection and subsequent protests and action depend on one's appraisal of situations of injustice. Appraisal involves the defining of a problem, examination of all relevant historical data, loyalties and pressures, and a clear analysis of the roots of oppression.

Definition of the problem

In an overall sense, feminist ethicists have consistently defined the problem requiring attention as that of the subordinate status of women in all societies around the world. Beginning with the lived experiences of women, they claim that the many injustices suffered by women are due to the subordinate position assigned to them by men in power. Such a definition is aimed at unmasking the dominant ideology which still attempts to portray the dominant/subordinate relationship between men and women as somehow natural. Feminism's definition of the overall problem is an affront to those with a stake in maintaining the status quo, and for that reason it is important to acknowledge that "the act of defining a problem is a political act" (Robb 1987, p. 213).

By defining the problem in this way, feminists in every generation intentionally question the very foundations of patriarchy. It is not surprising, then, that feminism is fiercely resisted and attacked with every spiral of protest and activism.

Appraisal of and reflection on individual situations of injustice, too, must be approached in the same way as that for women's overall situation, that is, appraisal and reflection must begin with a clear definition of the problem.

Historical data

In appraising either the overall situation of women or the impact on women of one particular incident, feminist ethicists have always been aware of the need for an historical perspective. Feminist historians have pointed out that women, their experiences and achievements, were largely omitted from historical accounts nationally and internationally, and they have delved into archives to find and bring to light the writings of women in every generation in an attempt to right that wrong. Ethical appraisal of, and decisions about, any issue must involve past, present and future perspectives. Data from the past and the present will always be helpful in informing decisions about feminist protest and action to bring about a better future for women.

Loyalties and pressures

Appraisal of a situation also involves an analysis of loyalties, that is, who owes what to whom. Loyalties are often deliberately hidden and, as such, are difficult to identify, but information about loyalties is crucial if one is to understand overt and covert dynamics. On the international stage, leaders of nations are engaged in either pressuring or being pressured by other leaders through political manoeuvres, incentives, bribes, threats and promises. On the national stage, political games and power plays often take precedence over the need to make decisions for the good of the people. Feminists are aware that, whenever something or someone has to be sacrificed for the sake of a politician's "loyalties", the sacrificial lamb is often a woman, women's freedom, or funding for women's services.

Carol Robb draws attention to another kind of loyalty feminist ethicists need to be aware of in their appraisal of situatons pertaining to women. Whenever human rights activists, politicians or other leaders make decisions affecting women, she says, one needs to ask oneself "whether loyalty to women as women is operative". She goes on: "It is not sufficient to espouse justice for women solely or even primarily as a means to achieve justice for the underdeveloped, a racial or ethnic group, or a nationality". Feminist ethicists need to engage in "a continuing search for the relationship between loyalty to women and loyalty to other oppressed groups" (1987, p. 215) but, at the same time, be alert to the possibility of women being used or sacrificed in the pursuit of other loyalties.

Analysis of the roots of oppression

In addition to developing a clear definition of a problem and involving oneself in analysing loyalties and pressures, thorough ethical appraisal also requires an analysis of the roots of oppression. Where one locates the roots of oppression will influence one's ethical reflection and affect one's decisions about methods of protest and action.

As defined in the Introduction, there have always been differing categories of philosophical thought within feminism. Such differences in philosophy are largely influenced by one's view about where the roots of women's oppression are located. Liberals continue to believe that lack of equality between the sexes is the problem. Socialists posit a combination of class differences and gender differences as the problem. Some postmodern feminists reject the idea that there is a problem of oppression. Radical and political feminists locate the roots of women's oppression in the deliberate subordination and exclusion of women by dominating male forces domestically and globally. In order for individual feminists to be effective, they need to be clear about their own analysis of the roots of oppression.

When feminist ethical appraisal of individual situations of injustice begins with a definition of the problem, takes into account historical data, loyalties and pressures, and clearly analyses the roots of women's oppression, the ground is ready for protest and action. Thorough appraisal of unjust situations leads one to conclusions which Barbara Ehrenreich described as "jarring and disturbing at the same time that they are liberating" (1978, p. 3). In many instances, awareness of the situation of women is disturbing but the fact that an activist has the knowledge and will to protest is liberating.

Protest

For a radical feminist, the existence of injustice demands protest and action or, in the words of Barbara Ehrenreich writing about both Marxism and feminism: "There is no way to have a Marxist or feminist outlook and remain a spectator. To understand the reality laid bare by those analyses is to move into action to change it" (1978, p. 3). There is no doubt that feminist protest and action will continue into the future. Armed with accurate information from a thorough appraisal and analysis of each situation of injustice, feminist protests will continue to be heard.

For protests to be effective, they need to be focused. Feminist activists must refuse to be diverted by false claims, false promises, misrepresentations or criticisms. Also, protests need to be both rational and emotional. Neither emotional outbursts alone nor the stating of cold, rational facts will command the same attention as the facts supported by genuine emotion. The timing of protests is also important. Sometimes a protest needs to be voiced immediately, taking the opportunity as soon as an injustice presents itself, while on other occasions, protests are more effective when time is taken to get it right.

Action

Often the only form of action needed is the raising of one's voice in protest. Any form of activism, including voicing protests, needs to be well organised. The purpose of ethical action is to command the attention of those who have the power to make changes and influence them to take the kind of action needed. The preferred methods of activism will continue to be public demonstrations, marches, rallies, dramatic presentations, letter writing and opinion pieces. The methods afforded by the internet will continue to grow in popularity: blogs, online opinion pieces, online petitions and email discussion groups.

The goal of feminist ethics is the transformation of societies and situations where women are harmed through violence, subordination and exclusion. When such injustices are evident now and in the future, radical feminist activists will continue their work of protest and action following careful appraisal and reflection.

Conclusion

The systematic silencing of women is one of the great tragedies of history. Throughout this book, I have demonstrated that the democratic principle of freedom of speech, so closely guarded by members of the power elite in all democracies, is in fact a right accorded only to the powerful. Members of disempowered groups are denied the right to speak and be heard. Dissenting voices, including the voices of feminist activists, are among those whom Arundhati Roy referred to as the "preferably unheard". The silencing is deliberate and the tactics of silencing are many and varied. For speech to be called free, it must be free for all—and it must be fair.

REFERENCES

All web links are correct at time of printing.

An Abuse, Rape and Domestic Violence Aid and Resource Collection. 2006. "DANGER! Separation Violence". <http://www.aardvarc.org/dv/sepviolence.shtml>.

African Women's Development Fund. 2006. "First Ever African Feminist Forum held in Accra". <http://www.awdf.org/pages/nletter_detail.php?issue=11&id=64>.

Age. 2007. "Heffernan's Gibe 'Hurt Australian Women'". <http://www.theage.com.au/news/national/heffernans-gibe-hurt-australian-women/2007/05/04/1177788348405.html>.

Akhter, Farida. 1992. *Depopulating Bangladesh*. Dhaka: Narigrantha Prabartana.

—— 1995. *Resisting Norplant: Women's Struggle in Bangladesh Against Coercion and Violence*. Dhaka: Narigrantha Prabartana.

Albrechtsen, Janet. 2005. "I Raped Her, Sir, but My Culture Made Me Do It". *The Australian*. 9 November. <http://www.leightonsmith.co.nz/?s=Topics&id=5135>.

—— 2006. "Heed the PM's Call for Women's Rights". *Australian*. 6 September. <http://www.muslim-refusenik.com/news/the-australian-2006-09-06.html>.

Ali, Ayaan Hirsi. 2006. *The Caged Virgin: An Emancipation Proclamation for Women and Islam*. New York: Simon & Schuster.

Ali, Shamima. 2007. "Ending Impunity for Violence". *Pacific Women Against Violence*. Vol 11, no. 7, May.

Amnesty International. 2001. *Crimes of Hate, Conspiracy of Silence: Torture and Ill-Treatment Based on Sexual Identity*. 16 April. <http://web.amnesty.org/library/Index/engACT400162001?OpenDocument&of=THEMES\SEXUAL+ORIENTATION>.

—— 2004. "It's in Our Hands: Stop Violence Against Women". <http://www.amnesty.org/en/library/info/ACT77/001/2004/>.

Andrews, Lori. 1986. "My Body, My Property". *Hastings Centre Report*. pp. 28–37.

—— 1988. "Alternative Modes of Reproduction". In *Reproductive Laws for the 1990s: A Briefing Handbook*. Newark: Women's Rights Litigation Clinic, Rutgers Law School.

Arditti, Rita, Renate Duelli Klein and Shelley Minden, eds. 1984. *Test-Tube Women: What Future for Motherhood?* London and Boston: Pandora Press.

Australian Bureau of Statistics. 1996. *Women's Safety Australia*. <http://www.abs.gov.au/Ausstats/abs@.nsf/7d12b0f6763c78caca257061001cc588/b62deb3ac52a2574ca2568a900139340!OpenDocument>.

—— 2002. *Crime and Safety Survey*. <http://www.abs.gov.au/AUSSTATS/abs@.nsf/allprimarymainfeatures/F50CC9985653BB76CA25715A001C9053?opendocument>.

Australian Council of Trade Unions. 2005a. "ACTU Pushes to Lift Pay By 4% For Workers on Minimum Wage". 21 September. <http://www.actu.asn.au/public/campaigns/minimumwages/minwage05mr.html>.

—— 2005b. "Families Worse off Under Individual Contracts: PM Is Wrong, Again". 24 September. <http://www.actu.asn.au/public/campaigns/workandfamily/families_worse_off.html>.

—— 2006. "Low-Paid Deserve Reward for Their Effort: ACTU Submission to the 'Fair Pay Commission'". 28 July. <http://www.actu.asn.au/public/campaigns/minimumwages/ACTU-Submission.html>.

Australian Government. 2009. *Time for Action: The National Council's Plan for Australia to Reduce Violence against Women and their Children, 2009–2021*. Commonwealth of Australia, Canberra. <http://www.ofw.fahcsia.gov.au/reducing_violence/national_plan/index.htm>.

Australian Law Reform Commission. 1994. *Equality before the Law: Women's Equality*. Canberra: Commonwealth of Australia Report No. 69, Part I. <http://www.austlii.edu.au/au/other/alrc/publications/reports/69part1/>.

Barry, Kathleen. 1995. *The Prostitution of Sexuality: The Global Exploitation of Women*.
    London: New York University Press.
Bell, Diane and Gloria Jones, eds. 2007. *All about Water: All about the River*.
    A symposium of many voices and many views, Strathalbyn Town Hall. 13 April.
    <http://www.stoptheweir.com/index.php?option=com_content&task=view&id=122&Itemid=1] >.
Bell, Diane and Renate Klein, eds. 1996. *Radically Speaking: Feminism Reclaimed*.
    North Melbourne: Spinifex.
Bell, Diane and Topsy Napurrula Nelson. 1989. "Speaking about Rape is Everyone's Business".
    Women's Studies International Forum. Vol. 12, no. 4.
Bell, Shannon. 1994. *Reading, Writing and Rewriting the Prostitute Body*.
    Bloomington and Indianapolis: Indiana University Press.
Bhandari, Neena. 2006. "Australia: 'Debt Relief, Better Than Aid'".
    Inter Press Service News Agency. 16 May.
    <http://www.ipsnews.net/news.asp?idnews=33244>.
Bolton, Sue. 2005. "Howard's Lies on Industrial Relations 'Reforms'". *Green Left Weekly*. 20 July.
    <http://www.greenleft.org.au/back/2005/634/634p9.htm>.
Bonisteel, Mandy and Linda Green. 2005. "Implications of the Shrinking Space for Feminist
    Anti-Violence Advocacy". Paper presented at the Canadian Social Welfare Policy
    Conference, Forging Social Futures. Fredericton, NB.
    <http://www.ccsd.ca/cswp/2005/bonisteel.pdf>.
Brownmiller, Susan. 1999. *In our Time: Memoir of a Revolution*. London: Aurum Press.
Bunch, Charlotte. 2002. "Whose Security?". *The Nation*. 23 September.
    <http://www.wworld.org/crisis>.
Burgi, Noelle and Philip Golub. 2000.
    "The States We Are Still in", *Le Monde diplomatique*, April:
Butler, Judith. 1993. *Bodies that Matter: On the Discursive Limits of "Sex"*.
    New York and London: Routledge.
Campbell, Matthew. 2005.. "Interview: Matthew Campbell meets Rania al-Baz –
    Testimony of a Broken Face". *Sunday Times*. 16 October.
    <http://www.timesonline.co.uk/article/0,,2092-1827346,00.html>.
Campbell, Tom. 1994. "Rationales for Freedom of Communication". In Tom Campbell and
    Wojciech Sadurski, eds. *Freedom of Communication*. Aldershot: Dartmouth.
Cannon, Laura. 2005. "Compassion: A Rebuttal of Nussbaum". In Barbara S. Andrew, Jean
    Kelle, and Lisa H. Schwartzman, eds. *Feminist Interventions in Ethics and Politics*.
    Lanham, MD: Rowman & Littlefield. pp. 97–110.
Caputi, Jane. 2004. "Cuntspeak: Words from the Heart of Darkness".
    In Stark and Whisnant, eds. 2004. pp. 362–85.
Cass, Deborah. 1994. "Through the Looking Glass: The Right to Political Speech in Australia".
    In Tom Campbell and Wojciech Sadurski, eds. *Freedom of Communication*.
    Aldershot: Dartmouth. pp. 179–98.
Castellanos, Angela. 2007. "Colombian Women in Times of War". Paper delivered at the
    International Feminist Summit, Townsville, Australia. 17–20 July.
Charlesworth, Hilary. 2003. "What's Law Got To Do with the War?".
    In Raimond Gaita, ed.. *Why the War was Wrong*. Melbourne: Text. pp. 35–60.
Chavis, Melody Ermachild. 2004. *Meena: Heroine of Afghanistan*. London: Bantam.
Child, Jennie. 2003. Review of report by Patricia Hayes, "Taking It Seriously:
    Contemporary Experience of Sexual Harassment in the Workplace".
    <http://www.aifs.gov.au/acssa/pubs/newsletter/n4.html#sexharass>.
Chomsky, Noam. 1989. *Necessary Illusions*. Boston: South End Press.
—— 1991a. *Deterring Democracy*. London: Verso.
—— 1991b. *Media Control: The Spectacular Achievements of Propaganda*.
    New York: Seven Stories. Reprinted 1997, 2002.

—— 1992. *Chronicles of Dissent: Interviews with David Barsamian*.
   Monroe, ME: Common Courage Press.
—— 1999. *Profit over People*. New York: Seven Stories.
—— 2003. *Hegemony or Survival: America's Quest for Global Dominance*.
   New York: Henry Holt and Co.
Chytyrbaeva, Janyl. 2007. "Kyrgyzstan: Women Activists Report Increasing Harassment".
   EurasiaNet Partner Post. 8 May.
   <http://www.eurasianet.org/departments/insight/articles/pp080507.shtml>.
Clark County Prosecuting Attorney's Office, Indiana. n.d. "Fast Facts on Domestic Violence".
   <http://www.clarkprosecutor.org/html/domviol/facts.htm>.
Clarke, D.A. 2004. "Prostitution for Everyone: Feminism, Globalisation, and the 'Sex' Industry".
   In Stark and Rebecca Whisnant, eds. 2004. pp. 149–205.
Clarke, Tony and Maude Barlow. 1997. *The Multilateral Agreement on Investment and the Threat to Canadian Sovereignty*. Toronto: Stoddart Publishing.
Cochrane, Kira. 2006. "The Third Wave – At a Computer near You". *Guardian*. 31 March.
   <http://www.guardian.co.uk/world/2006/mar/31/gender.uk>.
Cohn, Carol. 1993. "Wars, Wimps, and Women: Talking Gender and Thinking War".
   In Miriam Cooke and Angela Woollacott, eds. *Gendering War Talk*.
   Princeton, NJ: Princeton University Press. pp. 227–46.
Cohn, Carol and Cynthia Enloe. 2003. "A Conversation with Cynthia Enloe:
   When Feminists Look at Terrorists, 'Boring Men', and International Politics".
   Signs: Journal of Women in Culture and Society. Vol. 28, no. 4.
Conway, Doug. 2009. "Australia to Launch Anti-Poverty Push". *Age*, 18 May.
   <http://news.theage.com.au/breaking-news-national/australia-to-launch-antipoverty-push-20090518-bbej.html>.
Conway, Janet. 2007. "Transnational Feminisms and the World Social Forum:
   Encounters and Transformations in Anti-globalization Spaces".
   Journal of International Women's Studies. Vol. 8 no.3 April. pp. 49–70.
   <http://www.bridgew.edu/SOAS/jiws/April07/Conway.pdf>
Corea, Gena. 1985. *The Mother Machine: Reproductive Technologies from Artificial Insemination to Artifician Wombs*. New York: Harper and Row.
Corea, Gena, ed. 1987. *Man-Made Women: How New Reproductive Technologies Affect Women*.
   Bloomington: Indiana University Press. Originally published 1985. London: Hutchinson.
Crabbe, Maree. 2007. "Young People Duped by Culture of Degrading Sexual Attitudes".
   Age. 8 November <http://www.onlineopinion.com.au/view.asp?article=6633>.
Daly, Mary. 1973. *Beyond God the Father: Toward a Philosophy of Women's Liberation*.
   Boston: Beacon.
—— 1979. *Gyn/Ecology: The Metaethics of Radical Feminism*. London: The Women's Press.
   Originally published 1978. Boston: Beacon.
—— 1984. *Pure Lust: Elemental Feminist Philosophy*. London: The Women's Press.
de Ishtar, Zohl. 2005. *Holding Yawulyu: White Culture and Black Women's Law*.
   North Melbourne. Spinifex.
Deen, Thalif. 2005. "Iraqi Women May Lose Basic Rights Under New Constitution".
   Inter Press Service. 23 July. <http://www.ipsnews.net/print.asp?idnews=29609>.
Dines, Gail, Bob Jensen and Ann Russo. 1997. *Pornography: The Production and Consumption of Inequality*. New York: Routledge.
Djanaeva, Nurgul. 2007. Response to "Pakistani Women in Politics".
   International Knowledge Network of Women in Politics. 5 May.
   <http://www.iknowpolitics.org/node/1900>.
Dodson, Patrick. 2007. "Pat Dodson: Whatever Happened to Reconciliation?".
   In Jon Altman and Melinda Hinkson, eds. *Coercive Reconciliation: Stabilise, Normalise, Exit Aboriginal Australia*. Melbourne: Arena Publications.
   <http://www.arena.org.au/coercive_order.pdf>.
Dowrick, Stephanie. 2004. *Free Thinking*. Sydney: Allen & Unwin.

Dworkin, Andrea. 1979. *Pornography: Men Possessing Women*. New York: Pedigree Books. 1981, London: The Women's Press.
—— 1987. *Intercourse*. New York: Free Press and Macmillan.
—— 1988. *Letters from a War Zone*. London: Secker and Warburg.
—— 1990. "Women-Hating Right and Left". In Leidholdt and Raymond, eds.1990. pp. 28–40.
—— 1996. "Pornography and Women's Human Rights". Paper delivered at the Violence, Abuse and Women's Citizenship Conference, Brighton UK. 10 November. <http://www.andreadworkin.com/audio/ViolenceAbuseWomensCitizenshipM.mp3>.
—— 1998. *In Harm's Way: The Pornography Civil Rights Hearings*. Cambridge, MA: Harvard University Press.
—— 2004. "Pornography, Prostitution, and a Beautiful and Tragic Recent History". In Stark and Whisnant, eds. 2004. pp. 137–45.
Dworkin, Andrea and Catharine MacKinnon. 1988. *Pornography and Civil Rights: A New Day for Women's Equality*. Minneapolis: Organizing Against Pornography.
Easteal, Patricia. 1994. *Voices of the Survivors*. North Melbourne: Spinifex.
Eddy, Fanny Ann. 2004. "Testimony by Fanny Ann Eddy at the United Nations Commission on Human Rights. Item 14 – 60th Session, UN Commission on Human Rights". <http://hrw.org/english/docs/2004/10/04sierra9439.htm>.
Ehrenreich, Barbara. 1978. "What is Socialist Feminism?". In *New American Working Papers on Socialism and Feminism*. Chicago: National Office, p. 3.
Eisenstein, Zillah. 2004. *Against Empire: Feminism, Racism and 'the' West*. London and New York: Zed Books. North Melbourne: Spinifex.
—— 2007. *Sexual Decoys*. London and New York: Zed Books. North Melbourne: Spinifex.
Enloe, Cynthia. 2000. *Bananas, Beaches and Bases: Making Feminist Sense of International Politics*. Los Angeles: University of California Press. Originally published 1989. London: Pandora
—— 1993. *The Morning After: Sexual Politics at the End of the Cold War*. Berkeley: University of California Press.
—— 2000. *Maneuvers: The International Politics of Militarizing Women's Lives*. Berkeley: University of California Press.
—— 2004a. *The Curious Feminist: Searching for Women in a New Age of Empire*. Berkeley: University of California Press.
—— 2004b. "Duelling Masculinities" (Book Review). *Women's Review of Books*. 1 September. Vol. 21, no. 12. p. 10.
—— 2007. *Globalization and Militarism: Feminists Make the Link (Globalization)*. Lanham, MD: Rowman & Littlefield.
Evans, Sara. 1979. *Personal Politics: The Roots of Women's Liberation in the Civil Rights Movement and the New Left*. New York: Knopf.
Faludi, Susan. 1991. *Backlash: The Undeclared War Against Women*. London: Chatto & Windus.
Farley, Melissa. 2005. "Unequal". 30August. <http://action.web.ca/home/catw/readingroom.shtml?x=81265>.
—— 2007. *Prostitution and Trafficking in Nevada: Making the Connections*. San Francisco: Prostitution Research and Education.
——, ed. 2004. *Prostitution, Trafficking, and Traumatic Stress*. New York: Routledge.
Fergus, Lara. 2004. "Making Rights a Reality: The Human Rights Approach to Stopping Violence against Women". <http://www.aifs.gov.au/acssa/pubs/newsletter/n4.html#rights>.
—— 2005. "Trafficking in Women for Sexual Exploitation". *Aware: Newsletter of the Australian Centre for the Study of Sexual Assualt*. June. <http://www.aifs.gov.au/acssa/pubs/briefing/b5.html>.
Ferguson, Sarah. 2009. "Code of Silence". *Four Corners*. ABC television. 11 May.

Fiji Ministry of Information. 2008. "Fiji Cabinet Approves National Policy on Sexual Harrassment in the Workplace". 5 January <http://lyris1.spc.int/read/messages?id=56701>.
Fiji Women's Crisis Centre. 2007. *Pacific Women Against Violence*. May. Vol 11, no. 7.
Firestone, Shulamith. 1970. *The Dialectic of Sex: The Case for Feminist Revolution*. London: The Women's Press. Reprinted 1979.
Frantz, Laurent B. 1962. "The First Amendment in the Balance". *Yale Law Journal*. Vol. 71. p. 1424.
Freeman, Jo. 1975. *The Politics of Women's Liberation*. New York: David McKay.
—— 1979. "Resource Mobilization and Strategy: A Model for Analyzing Social Movement Organization Actions". In M. Zald and J. McCarthy, eds. *The Dynamics of Social Movements*. Cambridge, MA: Winthrop. pp. 167–89.
French, Marilyn. 1992. *The War Against Women*. London: Penguin.
Friedan, Betty. 1963. *The Feminine Mystique*. New York: Penguin.
Friedman, Marilyn. 1987. "Care and Context in Moral Reasoning". In Eva Kittay and Diana T. Meyers, eds. *Women and Moral Theory*. Totowa, NJ: Rowman and Littlefield. pp. 190–204.
Fullinwider, Robert K. 2006. "On Moralism". In C.A.J. Coady, ed. *What's Wrong with Moralism?* Malden, MA: Blackwell. pp. 5–20.
Gatens, Moira. 1996. *Imaginary Bodies: Ethics, Power and Corporeality*. London and New York: Routledge.
Gaze, Beth. 1994. "Theories of Free Speech, Pornography and Sexual Equality". In Tom Campbell and Wojciech Sadurski. *Freedom of Communication*. Aldershot: Dartmouth.
Gaze, Beth and Melinda Jones. 1990. *Law, Liberty and Australian Democracy*. North Ryde, NSW: Law Book Company.
Gelber, Katharine and Adrienne Stone, eds. 2007. *Hate Speech and Freedom of Speech in Australia*. Sydney: Federation Press.
Gill, Rosalind. 2003. "From Sexual Objectification to Sexual Subjectification: The Resexualisation of Women's Bodies in the Media". *Feminist Media Studies*. Vol. 3, no. 1. pp. 99–106. <http://monthlyreview.org/mrzine/gill230509.html>.
—— 2007. *Gender and the Media*. Cambridge: Polity.
Gilligan, Carol. 1982. *In a Different Voice: Psychological Theory and Women's Development*. Cambridge, MA: Harvard University Press.
Gilmore, Kate. 2004. Address at the Australian launch of the *Stop Violence Against Women* campaign, Parliament House, Canberra. 8 March.
Government of Tasmania. 2003. "Pathways: How Women Leave Violent Men". Hobart: Government of Tasmania.
Griffin, Susan. 1981. *Pornography and Silence*. London: The Women's Press. Reprinted 1988, New York: Harper and Row.
Grosz, Elizabeth. 1994. *Volatile Bodies: Toward a Corporeal Feminism*. Bloomington and Indianapolis: Indiana University Press; Sydney: Allen and Unwin.
Grosz, Elizabeth and Elspeth Probyn, eds. 1995. *Sexy Bodies: The Strange Carnalities of Feminism*. London and New York: Routledge.
Gusfield, Joseph R. 1981. "Social Movements and Social Change: Perspectives of Linearity and Fluidity". In Louis Kriesberg, ed. *Research in Social Movements, Conflict and Change*. Vol. 4. Greenwich, CT: JAI Press. pp. 317–39.
Harvie, Betsy A. 2002. "Regulation of Advocacy in the Voluntary Sector: Current Challenges and Some Responses". Prepared for the Advocacy Working Group. January. <http://www.ginsler.com/documents/advocacy_regulation.pdf>.
Hawthorne, Susan. 2002a. *Wild Politics: Feminism, Globalisation and Bio/diversity*. North Melbourne: Spinifex.
—— 2002b. "Fundamentalism, Violence and Disconnection". In Hawthorne and Winter, eds 2002. pp. 339–59.

—— 2003. "The Australia–United States Free Trade Agreement".
Arena Magazine. February–March. No. 63. pp. 29–32.
—— 2004a. "The Political Uses of Obscurantism: Gender Mainstreaming and Intersectionality".
Development Bulletin. No. 89. pp. 87–91.
—— 2004b. "Research and Silence: Why the Torture of Lesbians is Invisible". Collected Papers and Presentations. *Proceedings of Women's Studies Association Conference* (NZ), Massey University, Palmerston North. pp. 64–72.
—— 2004c. "The Torture of Lesbians: Where Is the Outcry?" *Reproductive Rights Newsletter.* Vol. 82, no. 2. pp. 12–14.
—— 2005a. "The Invisible Torture". *Arena Magazine.* August–September. No. 78. p. 10.
—— 2005b. "Not on Anyone's Program: Lesbian Refugees and the Torture of Lesbians". Paper delivered at a Conference on *Hopes Fulfilled or Dreams Shattered.* Centre for Refugee Research, University of New South Wales, Sydney, 25 November.
—— 2007. "The Silences Between: Are Lesbians Irrelevant?"
Journal of International Women's Studies. Women's Bodies, Gender Analysis, and Feminist Politics at the Fórum Social Mundial. April. Vol 8, no. 3. pp. 125–38.
<http://www.bridgew.edu/SoAS/jiws/April07/Hawthorne1.pdf>.
Hawthorne, Susan and Bronwyn Winter, eds. 2002.
September 11, 2001: Feminist Perspectives. North Melbourne: Spinifex.
Hayes, Patricia. 2003. "Taking It Seriously: Contemporary Experience of Sexual Harassment in the Workplace". <www.rwh.org.au/casa>.
Herman, Edward and Noam Chomsky. 1988. *Manufacturing Consent: The Political Economy of the Mass Media.* New York: Pantheon. Toronto: Random House. Reprinted 2002.
hooks, bell. 1987. "Feminism: A Movement to end Sexist Oppression".
In Anne Phillips, ed. *Feminism and Equality.* Oxford: Basil Blackwell, p. 62.
—— 1989. *Talking Back: Thinking Feminist, Thinking Black.* Boston: South End Press.
Huggins, Jackie et al. 1991. *Women's Studies International Forum.* Vol. 14, no. 5. p. 506.
Huggins, Jackie. 1994. "A Contemporary View of Aboriginal Women's Relationship to the White Women's Movement". In Grieve, Norma and Ailsa Burns, eds. *Australian Women: Contemporary Feminist Thought.* Melbourne: Oxford University Press. pp. 70–79.
Hughes, Donna. 1999. *Pimps and Predators on the Internet – Globalizing Sexual Exploitation of Women and Children.* <http://www.uri.edu/artsci/wms/hughes/pprep.htm>.
—— 2004. "The Use of New Communication and Information Technologies for Sexual Exploitation of Women and Children". In Stark and Whisnant, eds. 2004. pp. 38–55.
Hughes, Patricia. 2004. *Enough.* North Melbourne: Spinifex.
Human Rights Watch. 2005. "Maid to Order". 6 December.
<http://www.hrw.org/en/reports/2005/12/06/maid-order>.
—— 2006. "South Africa: Murder Highlights Violence Against Lesbians". 1 March.
<http://hrw.org/english/docs/2006/03/02/safric12753.htm>.
Hutchings, Kimberly. 1999. "Feminism, Universalism and the Ethics of International Politics".
In Vivienne Jabri and Eleanor O'Gorman, eds. *Women, Culture, and International Relations.* Boulder, CO: Lynne Reinner. pp. 17–38.
International Feminist Journal of Politics. 2002. "Forum: The Events of 11 September 2001 and Beyond". Vol. 4, no.1. <http://www.ingentaconnect.com/content/routledg/rfjp/2002/00000004/00000001/art00006>.
Iraqi Women's Movement. 2005. "Iraqi Women's Movement Appeal". 16 July.
<http://www.whrnet.org/fundamentalisms/docs/action-iraq-law-0507.html>.
Itzin, Catherine, ed. 1992. *Pornography. Women, Violence and Civil Liberties.*
Oxford: Oxford University Press.
Ivison, Duncan. 2006. "The Moralism of Multiculturalism".
In C.A.J. Coady, ed. *What's Wrong with Moralism?* Malden, MA: Blackwell. pp. 71–84.
Jabri, Vivienne. 2004. "Feminist Ethics and Hegemonic Global Politics".
Alternatives: Global, Local, Political. June. Vol. 29, no. 3. 1 pp. 265–84. Lynne Rienner.

Jaggar, Alison. 1989. "Feminist Ethics: Some Issues for the Nineties".
   Journal of Social Philosophy. Spring–Fall. Vol. XX, nos 1–2.
—— 1992. "Feminist Ethics". In Lawrence Becker with Charlotte Becker, eds.
   Encyclopedia of Ethics. New York: Garland. pp. 361–70.
Jaggar, Alison M. and Paula Rothenberg Struhl. 1978. *Feminist Frameworks: Alternative Theoretical Accounts of the Relations between Women and Men*.
   New York: McGraw–Hill.
Jalal, P. Imrana. 2003. "Why Fiji Needs a Family Law Bill". *Fiji Times*, 18 November.
   <http://www.rrrt.org/page.asp?active_page_id=141>.
Jeffreys, Sheila. 1990a. *Anti-climax: A Feminist Perspective on the Sexual Revolution*.
   London: The Women's Press. 1991. New York: New York University Press.
—— 1990b. "Sexology and Antifeminism". In Leidholdt and Raymond, eds. 1990. pp. 14–27.
—— 1993a. "Butch and Femme: Now and Then". In Lesbian History Group.
   Not a Passing Phase: Reclaiming Lesbians in History, 1840–1985.
   London: The Women's Press. Originally published 1989.
—— 1993b. *The Lesbian Heresy: A Feminist Perspective on the Lesbian Sexual Revolution*.
   North Melbourne: Spinifex.
—— 1996. "Return to Gender: Post-modernism and LesbianandGay Theory".
   In Bell and Klein, eds. 1996.
—— 1997. *The Spinster and Her Enemies: Feminism and Sexuality, 1880–1930*. New edn.
   North Melbourne: Spinifex.
—— 1999. "Globalizing Sexual Exploitation: Sex Tourism and the Traffic in Women",
   Leisure Studies. No. 18. pp. 179–96.
—— 2000. "Challenging the Child/Adult Distinction in Theory and Practice on Prostitution",
   International Feminist Journal of Politics. Vol. 2, no. 3. pp. 359–79.
—— 2005. *Beauty and Misogyny: Harmful Cultural Practices in the West*. London: Routledge.
—— 2009. *The Industrial Vagina: The Political Economy of the Global Sex Trade*.
   London: Routledge.
Jhappan, Radha. 1996. "Post-Modern Race and Gender Essentialism or a Post-Mortem of Scholarship". *Studies in Political Economy*. No. 51. p. 25.
—— 2002. "The Equality Pit or the Rehabilitation of Justice". In Ngaire Naffine, ed.
   Gender and Justice. Aldershot: Ashgate Dartmouth. pp. 169–216.
Johnston, Jill. 1973. *Lesbian Nation: The Feminist Solution*.
   New York: Touchstone, Simon & Schuster.
Jones, Rochelle. 2006. "The African Feminist Forum".
   <http://www.icae.org.uy/eng/voicesrising208.html#afri>.
Joseph, Ammu and Kalpana Sharma, eds. 2003. *Terror, Counter-Terror: Women Speak Out*.
   London and New York: Zed Books.
Kaplan, Gisela. 1996. *The Meagre Harvest: The Australian Women's Movement 1950s–1990s*.
   St. Leonards, NSW: Allen & Unwin.
Katzenstein, Mary Fainsod. 1990. "Feminism within American Institutions: Unobtrusive Mobilization in the 1980s". *Signs: Journal of Women in Culture and Society*.
   Vol. 16, no. 1. pp. 27–54.
Kingston, Margo. 2004. *Not Happy, John: Defending our democracy*. Camberwell, Vic.: Penguin.
Klein, Renate, ed. 1989. *Infertility: Women Speak Out about Their Experiences of Reproductive Medicine*. London: Pandora.
—— 2002. "When Silence is not Golden: the radical feminist dilemma of not criticising other feminists". Paper presented at Townsville International Women's Conference, 3-7 July.
   <http://www.austdvclearinghouse.unsw.edu.au/Conference%20papers/TIWC/KleinRenate.pdf>.
Kristof, Nicholas D. 2005. "Another Face of Terror". *New York Times*. 31 July.
   <http://topics.nytimes.com/top/opinion/editorialsandoped/oped/columnists/nicholasdkristof/index.html?offset=60&&&>.

Kurup, K. Balachandra. n.d. "Community Management in Rural Water Supply through the Development of Natural Springs". International Water and Sanitation Centre. Community Water Supply Management. Case Study. <http://www2.irc.nl/manage/manuals/cases/natsprings.html>.

Lake, Marilyn. 1999. *Getting Equal: The History of Australian Feminism.* Sydney: Allen & Unwin.

Langton, Rae. 1994. "Speech Acts and Unspeakable Acts". In Tom Campbell and Wojciech Sadurski, eds. *Freedom of Communication.* Aldershot: Dartmouth. pp. 95–129.

—— 1997. "Pornography, Speech Acts, and Silence". In Hugh LaFollette, ed. *Ethics in Practice: An Anthology.* Cambridge, MA: Blackwell, pp. 338–49.

Law Council of Australia. 2006. "Recognition of Cultural Factors in Sentencing". 10 July. p. 11. <http://www.lawcouncil.asn.au/get/submissions/2425538720.pdf>.

Leidholdt, Dorchen A. 2003. "Demand and the Debate". Coalition against Trafficking in Women. October. <http://action.web.ca/home/catw/readingroom.shtml?x=53793>.

Leidholdt, Dorchen and Janice G. Raymond, eds. 1990. *The Sexual Liberals and the Attack on Feminism.* New York: Pergamon Press.

Lewis, Stephen. 2005. *Race against Time: Searching for Hope in AIDS-ravaged Africa.* Melbourne: Text.

Lieven, Anatol. 2003. "A Trap of Their Own Making". *London Review of Books.* 8 May. Vol. 25, no. 9. <http://www.lrb.co.uk/v25/n09/liev01_.html>.

Lippmann, Walter. 1921. *Public Opinion.* London: Allen & Unwin. Reprinted 1932.

Lorde, Audré. 1984a. "Grenada Revisited: An Interim Report". In Lorde.1984b. pp. 176–90.

—— 1984b. *Sister Outsider: Essays and Speeches by Audre Lorde.* Freedom, CA: Crossing Press Feminist Series.

Lyons, Miriam. 2005. "Taxing Times for Outspoken Charities". *New Matilda.* 29 June. <http://www.newmatilda.com/home/articledetail.asp?ArticleID=737>.

Machina, Tina. 1996. "Sisters of Mercy". In Monika Reinfelder, ed. *Amazon to Sami: Toward a Global Lesbian Feminism.* London: Cassell. pp. 118–29.

MacKinnon, Catharine A. 1986."Pornography as Sex Discrimination." *Law and Inequality: A Journal of Theory and Practice.* Vol. 38, no. 4.

—— 1987. *Feminism Unmodified: Discourses on Life and Law.* Cambridge, MA: Harvard University Press.

—— 1989a. *Towards a Feminist Theory of the State.* Cambridge, MA: Harvard University Press.

—— 1989b. "Pornography: Not a Moral Issue". In Renate Duelli Klein and Deborah Lynn Steinberg, eds. *Radical Voices: A Decade of Feminist Resistance from Women's Studies International Forum.* Oxford: Pergamon. pp. 143–68.

—— 1990. "Liberalism and the Death of Feminism". In Leidholdt and Raymond, eds. 1990. pp. 3–13.

—— 1993. "Turning Rape into Pornography: Postmodern Genocide". *Ms Magazine.* July–August. pp. 24–30.

—— 1994a. "Equality and Speech". In MacKinnon. 1994b. pp. 49–78.

—— 1994b. *Only Words.* London: HarperCollins.

Maddison, Sarah. 2002. "Bombing the Patriarchy or Just Trying to Get a Cab: Challenges Facing the Next Generation of Feminist Activists". *Outskirts Online Journal.* No. 10. <http://www.chloe.uwa.edu.au/outskirts/archive/volume10/maddison>.

—— 2004. "Silencing Dissent". *Australia Institute Newsletter.* June. No. 39.

Maddison, Sarah, Richard Denniss and Clive Hamilton. 2004. "Silencing Dissent: Non-government Organisations and Australian Democracy". Australia Institute Discussion Paper No. 65. June. <http://www.tai.org.au/

Mandela, Nelson. 2000. Lecture at the British Museum. 16 November. <http://www.globalissues.org/TradeRelated/FreeTrade/Criticisms.asp#SimplisticIdeologyRhetoricversusReality

—— 2003. *Independent* (Cape Town). 30 January.

—— 2005. *The Weekend Australian,* 5–6 February.

Manji, Irshad. 2003. *The Trouble with Islam: A Muslim's Call for Reform in Her Faith.*
  Milsons Point, NSW: Random House.
Mann, William C. 2005. "Gang-raped Pakistani woman brings fight to U.S.".
  The Namibian. 10 November. <http://www.namibian.com.na/index.php?id=28&tx_ttnews%5Btt_news%5D=19212&no_cache=1>.
Manne, Robert, ed. 2005. *Do Not Disturb: Is the Media Failing Australia?*
  Melbourne: Black Inc.
Marchand, M. and A. S. Runyan, eds. 2000. *Gender and Global Restructuring.*
  London: Routledge.
Marohasy, Jennifer. 2003. "Myth and the Murray: Measuring the Real State of the River Environment". *IPA Backgrounder*, December. Vol. 15, no. 5.
  <http://www.ipa.org.au/publications/449/myth-and-the-murray-measuring-the-real-state-of-the-environment/pg/2>.
Mason-Grant, Joan. 2004. *Pornography Embodied: From Speech to Sexual Practice.*
  Lanham, MD: Rowman & Littlefield.
Matsuda, Mari J. et al. 1993. *Words That Wound: Critical Race Theory, Assaultive Speech, and the First Amendment* (New Perspectives on Law, Culture, and Society).
  Boulder, CO: Westview.
Matsuda, Mari J. 1989. "Public Response to Racist Speech: Considering the Victim's Story".
  Michigan Law Review. Vol. 87. pp. 2320–81.
McLellan, Betty. 1995. *Beyond Psychoppression: A Feminist Alternative Therapy.*
  North Melbourne: Spinifex.
—— 2002. "Another Feminist Response to the Terrorist Attacks". In Hawthorne and Winter, eds. 2002. pp. 78–80.
—— 2003. "'No Place to call 'Home': A Feminist Ethical Inquiry into Women's Place in Today's Masculinist World". Paper delivered at *Activating Human Rights and Diversity Conference.* Byron Bay, NSW. 1–4 July.
—— 2006. "Indigenous Women's Health". In *Queensland Women's Health Network News.*
  December. <http://www.qwhn.asn.au
—— 2007. "Feminism: A Spent Force or Still a Force to Be Reckoned With?"
  Paper delivered at the International Feminist Summit, Townsville, Qld. 17–20 July.
  <http://www.feministagenda.org.au/IFS%20Papers/Betty2.pdf
Mendelson, Wallace. 1962. "On the Meaning of the First Amendment: Absolutes in the Balance". *California Law Review.* December. Vol. 50, no. 5. pp. 821–8.
Mill, John Stuart. 1999. *On Liberty.* New York: Bartleby.com (online books).
  First published 1869. London: Longman, Roberts & Green.
Miller, Benjamin F. and Claire Brackman Keane. 1987. *Encyclopedia and Dictionary of Medicine, Nursing, and Allied Health,* 4th edn. Philadelphia: W. B. Saunders.
Mizruchi, Ephraim H. 1983. *Regulating Society.* New York: Free Press.
Moghadam, Valentine M. 1999. "Revolution, Religion and Gender Politics: Iran and Afghanistan Compared". *Journal of Women's History.* Vol. 10, no. 4. pp. 172–95.
—— 2002. "Women, the Taliban, and the Politics of Public Space in Afghanistan".
  In Hawthorne and Winter, eds. 2002. pp. 260–84. Originally published 2002.
  Women's Studies International Forum. Vol. 25, no. 1.
—— 2005. *Globalizing Women: Transnational Feminist Networks.*
  Baltimore: Johns Hopkins University Press.
Moon, Katharine H.S. 1999a. *Sex among Allies: Militarized Prostitution in U.S.–Korea Relations.* New York: Columbia University Press.
—— 1999b. "South Korean Movements against Militarized Sexual Labor".
  Asian Survey. March–April. Vol. 39, no. 2. pp. 310–27.
Moraga, Cherrie and Gloria Anzaldua. eds. 1981. *This Bridge Called My Back: Writings by Radical Women of Color.* Watertown, MA: Persephone Press.
Moreton-Robinson, Aileen. 2000. *Talkin' Up to the White Woman: Indigenous Women and Feminism.* Brisbane: University of Queensland Press.

——, ed. 2004. *Whitening Race: Essays in Social and Cultural Criticism.*
    Canberra: Aboriginal Studies Press.
Morgan, Robin. 1996. "Light Bulbs, Radishes, and the Politics of the 21st Century".
    In Bell and Klein, eds. 1996.
—— 2002. "New York City: The Day After". In Hawthorne and Winter, eds. 2002. pp. 9–13.
Morton, Nelle. 1985. *The Journey is Home.* Boston: Beacon.
Moser, Caroline and Fiona Clarke, eds. 2001. *Victims, Perpetrators or Actors?*
    Gender, Armed Conflict and Political Violence. London: Zed Books.
Mouzos, Jenny. 2004. "Women's Experiences of Male Violence: Findings from the Australian
    Component of the International Violence Against Women Survey (IVAWS)".
    In *Australian Domestic Violence Clearinghouse Newsletter.* December. No. 20.
    <http://www.austdvclearinghouse.unsw.edu.au/Publications.htm#Newsletters>.
Msimang, Sisonke. 2003. "HIV/AIDS, globalisation and the international women's movement".
    Gender and Development, Vol. 11, No. 1 (May). pp. 109–13.
    <http://www.jstor.org/pss/4030702>.
Mulroney, Jane. 2003. "Australian Statistics on Domestic Violence".
    Australian Domestic and Family Violence Clearinghouse.
    <http://www.austdvclearinghouse.unsw.edu.au/PDF%20files/Statistics_final.pdf>.
Myron, Nancy and Charlotte Bunch, eds. 1975. *Lesbianism and the Women's Movement.*
    Baltimore: Diana Press.
Naffine, Ngaire, ed. 2002. *Gender and Justice.*
    International Library of Essays in Law and Legal Theory. Aldershot: Ashgate/Dartmouth.
Nasreen, Taslima. 2005. "Taslima Nasreen – My Story". 21 June.
    International Humanist and Ethical Union. <http://www.iheu.org/node/1535>.
Nawa, Fariba. 2002. "Demanding to Be Heard, 14 November 2001".
    In Hawthorne and Winter, eds. 2002. pp. 176–8.
Nicholson, Brendan and Gary Hughes. 2003. "Attack on Covert Project for IPA". *Age.* 10 August.
    <http://www.theage.com.au/cgi-bin/common/popupPrintArticle.pl?path=/articles/2003/
    08/09/1060360555284.html>.
Norman, Amy. 2005. *Dancing with the Devil.* North Sydney: Random House.
—— 2006. *Living with the Devil.* London: John Blake Publishing.
Oberin, Julie. 2001. "Women Silenced on Violence". Panel presentation on Responding to
    Emerging Issues. WESNET National Committee at Australia's Inaugural Domestic
    Violence and Sexual Assault Conference. Gold Coast, Qld. 5–7 September.
    <http://wesnet.org.au/document/women-silenced-violence>.
O'Gorman, Eleanor and Vivienne Jabri. 1999. "Locating Difference in Feminist International
    Relations". In Vivienne Jabri and Eleanor O'Gorman, eds. *Women, Culture, and
    International Relations.* Boulder, CO: Lynne Reinner. pp. 1–15.
O'Keefe, Derrick. 2005. "Seven Questions". *Seven Oaks: a Magazine of Politics, Culture and
    Resistance.*15 March. <http://www.sevenoaksmag.com/questions/55.html>.
O'Neill, Onora. 2002. *A Question of Trust.* Cambridge: Cambridge University Press.
O'Tuama, Seamus. 2002. "Key Players or Cameos: Science and Technology Policy and
    Customers, Stakeholders and Citizens". Political Studies Association Annual Conference
    Papers. <http://www.psa.ac.uk/journals/pdf/5/2002/otuama.pdf>.
Organization of Women's Freedom in Iraq. 2008. "A statement by organization of Women's
    freedom in Iraq – abroad representative on International Women's Day (8 March)".
    <http://www.equalityiniraq.com/index.php?option=com_content&view=article&id=59:a-
    statement-by-organization-of-womens-freedom-in-iraq--abroad-representative-on-
    international-womens-day-8-march&catid=38:press-release&Itemid=57 >.
Oxfam. 2003. "Time to Make Trade Fair in 2003". <http://www.maketradefair.com/en/index.
    php?file=18072002163823.htm>.
Partnerships Against Domestic Violence. 2000. "Reshaping Responses to Domestic Violence",
    Final Report. Canberra: Commonwealth of Australia.
Pelly, Michael. 2009. "Heeding Society's Lessons". *Weekend Australian.* 16–17 May. p. 19.

Penberthy, David. 2009. "Budget Has Interest but Sex Has Currency". *Weekend Australian*. 16–17 May. p. 26.
Penelope, Julia. 1990. *Speaking Freely: Unlearning the Lies of the Fathers' Tongues*. New York: The Athene Series. Pergamon.
Pettman, Jan Jindy. 2004. "Feminist International Relations After 9/11". *Brown Journal of World Affairs*, Winter–Spring. Vol. X, no. 2. pp. 85–96.
Plibersek, Tanya. 2006. "Mind What You Say or You'll Lose Your Funding". *Sydney Morning Herald*. 12 July. <http://www.onlineopinion.com.au/view.asp?article=4688>.
Pretnar, Bojan. 1990. "The European Communities and the Meaning of Patents and Trademarks for Developing Countries". *Patinova '90: Strategies for the Protection of Innovation. Proceedings of the First European Congress on Industrial Property Rights and Innovation*. Madrid: Kluwer Academic Publishers and Deutscher Wirtschaftsdienst. pp. 249–53.
Queensland Government. 1999. *The Aboriginal and Torres Strait Islander Women's Task Force on Violence Report*. Brisbane: The State of Queensland.
Rashid, Ahmed. 2000. *Taliban: Militant Islam, Oil and Fundamentalism in Central Asia*. New Haven: Yale University Press.
Raymond, Janice G. 1986. *A Passion for Friends: Toward a Philosophy of Female Affection*. London: The Women's Press.
—— 1994. *Women as Wombs: Reproductive Technologies and the Battle over Women's Freedom*. North Melbourne: Spinifex. Originally published 1993. San Francisco: Harper.
—— 2005. "Sex Trafficking is Not 'Sex Work'". *Conscience*. Spring. Vol. XXVI, no. 1. <http://action.web.ca/home/catw/readingroom.shtml?x=74355>.
Raymond, Janice G., Renate Klein and Lynnette Dumble. 1991. *RU486: Misconceptions, Myths, and Morals*. Cambridge, MA: Institute on Women and Technology, MIT; North Melbourne: Spinifex.
Rebick, Judy. 2005. *Ten Thousand Roses*. Toronto: Penguin.
Redgold, Spiderlily. 2007. "Sappho had a Party and ...". Paper presented at the International Feminist Summit, Townsville. 17-20 July. <http://www.feministagenda.org.au/IFS%20Papers/Spiderlily2.pdf>
Rehn, Elisabeth and Ellen Johnson Sirleaf. 2003. *Women, War, Peace – The Independent Experts' Assessment on the Impact of Armed Conflict on Women and Women's Role in Peacebuilding*. New York: UNIFEM.
Reinfelder, Monika. 1996. "Persecution and Resistance". In Monika Reinfelder, ed. *Amazon to Sami: Toward a Global Lesbian Feminism*. London: Cassell. pp. 11–29.
Revolutionary Association of the Women of Afghanistan (RAWA). 2002a. "Let Us Struggle Against War and Fundamentalism and for Peace and Democracy!" 8 March. In Hawthorne and Winter, eds. 2002. pp. 232–42.
—— 2002b. "Statement on the US Strikes on Afghanistan". In Hawthorne and Winter, eds. 2002. pp. 95–6.
———. n.d. "About RAWA". <http://www.rawa.org/rawa.html>.
Rich, Adrienne. 1979. *On Lies, Secrets, and Silence: Selected Prose, 1966–1978*. New York: W. W. Norton. Reprinted 1980, London: Virago.
Robb, Carol S. 1987. "A Framework for Feminist Ethics". In Barbara Hilkert Andolsen, Christine E. Gudorf and Mary D. Pellauer, eds. *Women's Consciousness Women's Conscience: A Reader in Feminist Ethics*. San Francisco: Harper & Row. pp. 211–33. Originally published 1985. Minneapolis: Winston.
Rose, Hilary. 1988. "Victorian Values in the Test-Tube: The Politics of Reproductive Science and Technology". In Michelle Stanworth, ed. *Reproductive Technologies: Gender, Motherhood and Medicine*. Minneapolis: University of Minnesota Press.
Rothwell, Nicolas. 2001. "Wholly Holier than Thou". *Weekend Australian*. July 14.
Rowland, Robyn. 1992. *Living Laboratories. Women in Reproductive Technologies*. Bloomington: Indiana University Press. Sydney: Pan Macmillan.

Roy, Arundhati. 2004a. "Do Turkeys Enjoy Thanksgiving?" *The Hindu*, 18 January.
<http://www.hindu.com/2004/01/18/stories/2004011800181400.htm>.
—— 2004b. "Peace and the New Corporate Liberation Theology". City of Sydney Peace Prize Lecture. 3 November. <http://www.abc.net.au/rn/bigidea/stories/s1232956.htm>.
Rozario, Santi. 1997.
"The Feminist Debate on Reproductive Rights and Contraception in Bangladesh".
<http://www.hsph.harvard.edu/Organizations/healthnet/SAsia/repro/rozario1.html>.
Rundle, Guy. 2005. "The Rise of the Right". In Manne, ed. 2005. pp. 28–49.
Rupp, Leila J. 1982. "The Survival of American Feminism".
In R. H. Bremner and G. W. Reichard, eds. *Reshaping America*.
Columbus: Ohio State University Press. pp. 33–65.
Rupp, Leila J. and Verta Taylor. 1987. *Survival in the Doldrums: The American Women's Rights Movement, 1945 to the 1960s*. New York: Oxford University Press.
Rush, Emma and Andrea La Nauze. 2006a. "Corporate Paedophilia: Sexualisation of Children in Australia". Australia Institute Discussion Paper No. 90. October.
<http://www.tai.org.au/documents/downloads/DP90.pdf>.
—— and ——. 2006b. "Letting Children be Children. Stopping the Sexualisation of Children in Australia". Australia Institute Discussion Paper No. 93. December.
<http://www.tai.org.au/documents/downloads/DP93.pdf>.
Sadurski, Wojciech. 1994. "Racial Vilification, Psychic Harm and Affirmative Action" in Campbell, T, & Sadurski, W, (eds), *Freedom of Communication*, Dartmouth: Aldershot, pp. 77–94.
—— 1999. *Freedom of Speech and Its Limits*. Law and Philosophy Library.
Vol. 38. Dordrecht, The Netherlands: Kluwer Academic Publishers.
Santiago, Mari. 2004. "Building Global Solidarity through Feminist Dialogues".
<http://www.isiswomen.org/pub/wia/wia2-04/mari.htm>.
Sawer, Marian. 2003. "Down with Elites and Up with Inequality: Market Populism in Australia". *The Drawing Board: An Australian Review of Public Affairs*. Symposium: Elitist anti-elitism. 27 October. <http://www.australianreview.net/digest/2003/10/sawer.html>.
—— 2005. "Gender Equality in the Age of Governing for the Mainstream". *United Nations Division for the Advancement of Women (DAW)*. Theme: "The Role of National Mechanisms in Promoting Gender Equality and the Empowerment of Women: Achievements, Gaps and Challenges". 29 November–2 December 2004. Rome.
<http://polsc.anu.edu.au/EP.4-sawer.pdf>.
Sawyers, Traci M. and David S. Meyer. 1999. "Missed Opportunities: Social Movement Abeyance and Public Policy". *Social Problems*. May . Vol. 46, no. 2. pp. 187–206.
Schauer, Frederick. 1982. *Free Speech: A Philosophical Enquiry*.
Cambridge: Cambridge University Press.
Schwartzman, Lisa H. 2005. "A Feminist Critique of Nussbaum's Liberalism: Toward an Alternative Feminist Methodology". In Barbara S. Andrew, Jean Keller and Lisa H. Schwartzman, eds. *Feminist Interventions in Ethics and Politics*. Lanham, MD: Rowman & Littlefield. pp. 151–65.
Scutt, Jocelynne. 1983. *Even in the Best of Homes: Violence in the Family*.
Ringwood, Vic.: Penguin.
—— ed. 1988. *The Baby Machine: Commercialisation of Motherhood*.
Carlton, Vic.: McCulloch Publishing.
—— 1990. "Woman as Property: Prostitution, Pornography and Sexist Advertising".
Keynote speech at Women's Studies Summer Institute, Deakin University,
Geelong, Vic. Reprinted in Jocelynne Scutt. 1994. *The Sexual Gerrymander*.
North Melbourne: Spinifex. pp. 165–79.
Sere, Adriene. 2004. "Sex and Feminism: Who Is Being Silenced?"
In Stark and Whisnant, eds. 2004. pp. 269–74.

Shah, Anup. 2008. "Structural Adjustment—A Major Cause of Poverty". Global Issues.
<http://www.globalissues.org/article/3/structural-adjustment-a-major-cause-of-poverty>.
Sheehan, Paul. 2006a. "A Shameful Silence on Women's Rights". *Sydney Morning Herald*. 24 July.
<http://www.smh.com.au/articles/2006/07/23/1153593209660.html>.
—— 2006b. *Girls Like You: Four Young Girls, Six Brothers and A Cultural Timebomb*.
Sydney: Pan Macmillan.
Sher, George. 1987. *Moral Philosophy: Selected Readings*.
New York: Harcourt Brace Jovanovich.
Shiva, Vandana. 2000. *Stolen Harvest: The Hijacking of the Global Food Supply*.
Cambridge, MD: South End Press.
Soros, George. 2002. "The Will to Act Can Save Global Financial System". *Business Day*
(Johannesburg). 4 October.
SourceWatch. 2003. "Institute of Public Affairs".
<http://www.sourcewatch.org/index.php?title=Institute_of_Public_Affairs>.
—— n.d. "IPA targets non-government organisations".
<http://www.sourcewatch.org/index.php?title=Institute_of_Public_Affairs/IPA_targets_non-government_organisations>
Spallone, Patricia and Deborah L. Steinberg, eds. 1987.
Made to Order: The Myth of Reproductive and Genetic Progress.
Oxford and New York: The Athene Series, Pergamon Press.
Spender, Dale. 1980. *Man Made Language*. London: Routledge and Kegan Paul.
Staggenborg, Suzanne. 1988. "Consequences of Professionalization and Formalization in the
Pro-Choice Movement". *American Sociological Review*. Vol. 53. pp. 585–606.
—— 1989. "Stability and Innovation in the Women's Movement: A Comparison of Two
Movement Organizations". *Social Problems*. Vol 36. pp. 75–92.
Stanton, Elizabeth Cady. 1898. *The Women's Bible*. New York: European Publishing Co.
Stanworth, Michelle, ed. 1988. *Reproductive Technologies: Gender, Motherhood and Medicine*.
Minneapolis: University of Minnesota Press.
Stark, Christine and Rebecca Whisnant, eds. 2004. *Not For Sale: Feminists Resisting Prostitution
and Pornography*. North Melbourne: Spinifex.
Stiglmeyer, Alexandra, ed. 1994. *Mass Rape: The War Against Women in Bosnia–Herzegovina*.
Trans. Marion Faber. Lincoln: University of Nebraska Press.
Strang, Heather. 1996. "Children as Victims of Homicide. Trends and issues in
Crime and Criminal Justice". Australian Institute of Criminology. No. 53.
<http://www.aic.gov.au/publications/tandi/tandi53.html>.
Su, Julie. 1997. "El Monte Thai Garment Workers: Slave Sweatshops".
In Ross, Andrew, ed., *No Sweat: Fashion, Free Trade, and the Rights of Garment Workers*.
London: Verso.
Sullivan, Mary Lucille. 2004. "Can Prostitution Be Safe? Applying Occupational Health
and Safety Codes to Australia's Legalised Brothel Prostitution".
In Stark and Whisnant, eds. 2004.
—— 2006. *Making Sex Work: A Failed Experiment of Legalised Prostitution*.
North Melbourne, Spinifex.
Summers, Anne. 2003. *The End of Equality: Work, Babies and Women's Choices in 21st Century
Australia*. Milsons Point, NSW: Random House.
Svirsky, Gila. 2004. "Working to Break the Silence". 6 June.
<http://wworld.org/programs/middleEast.asp?ID=441>.
Swanson, David. 2006.
"Sweat Shop Workers Tour US Colleges That Sell Their Products". 26 February.
<http://www.zmag.org/content/showarticle.cfm?SectionID=19&ItemID=9804>.
Taft, Angela. 2002. "Violence against Women in Pregnancy and after Childbirth: Current
Knowledge and Issues in Health Care Responses". Issues Paper 6.
<http://www.austdvclearinghouse.unsw.edu.au/Publications.htm>.

Tankard Reist, Melinda. ed. 2009. *Getting Real: Challenging the Sexualisation of Girls*. North Melbourne: Spinifex.

Taylor, Verta. 1989a. "Social Movement Continuity: The Women's Movement in Abeyance". *American Sociological Review*. October. Vol. 54. pp. 761–75.

—— 1989b. "The Future of Feminism: A Social Movement Analysis". In Laurel Richardson and Verta Taylor, eds. *Feminist Frontiers II*. New York: Random House. pp. 473–90.

Tennessee Guerilla Women. n.d. "Mission, Goals".
<http://www.tnguerillawomen.org/pages/mission.html>.

Thobani, Suneri. 2003. "War Frenzy". In Joseph and Sharma, eds. 2003. pp. 90–9.

Thompson, Denise. 2001. *Radical Feminism Today*. London: Sage.

Tinkner, J. Ann. 2001. *Gendering World Politics*. New York: Columbia University Press.

—— 2002. "Feminist Perspectives on 9/11". *International Studies Perspectives*. Vol. 3, no. 4. p. 336.

Tong, Rosemarie. 1993. *Feminine and Feminist Ethics*. Belmont, CA: Wadsworth Publishing.

—— 2003. "Feminist Ethics". *Stanford Encyclopedia of Philosophy*.
<http://plato.stanford.edu/entries/feminism-ethics/>.

Toohey, Paul. 2005. "Age of Contempt". *Bulletin*. 17 August.
<http://bulletin.ninemsn.com.au/bulletin/site/articleIDs/65DFAC188739076DCA25705E0004A183>.

Turpel, Mary Ellen. 1993. "Patriarchy and Paternalism: The Legacy of the Canadian State for First Nations Women". *Canadian Journal of Women and the Law*. Vol. 6. pp. 179–80.

Victorian Community Council Against Violence. 2003. *Family Violence Database*,
<http://www.vccav.vic.gov.au>.

Volokh, Eugene and David Newman. 2003. "In Defense of the Slippery Slope". Legal Affairs. March–April. <http://www.legalaffairs.org/issues/March-April-2003/>.

Wanyeki, L. Muthoni. 2006. "The African Feminist Forum: Beginnings".
<http://www.isiswomen.org/index.php?option=com_content&task=view&id=780&Itemid=80#up>.

Watkins, Kevin. 2002. "Trade, Globalisation and Poverty Reduction: Why the Rules of the Game Matter". Paper presented at Seminar on World Trade and Poverty, Carnegie Endowment for International Peace. Washington, DC. 2 July.
<http://www.maketradefair.com/en/assets/english/Kevin_Watkins_Carnegie.pdf>.

Whisnant, Rebecca. "Confronting Pornography: Some Conceptual Basics". In Christine Stark and Rebecca Whisnant. 2004. *Not For Sale: Feminists Resisting Prostitution and Pornography*. North Melbourne: Spinifex. pp. 15–27.

Whitworth, Sandra. 2004. *Men, Militarism and UN Peacekeeping: A Gendered Analysis*. Boulder, CO: Lynne Rienner.

Wilkinson, Sue and Celia Kitzinger. 1996. "The Queer Backlash". In Bell and Klein, eds. 1996.

Winter, Bronwyn. 2001. "Fundamental Misunderstandings: Issues in Feminist Approaches to Islam". *Journal of Women's History*. Spring. pp. 9–41. Followed by comments from Valentine Moghadam, Riffat Hassan and Margot Badran, with a reply from the author, pp. 42–57.

—— 2002. "Who Will Mourn on October 7?" In Hawthorne and Winter, eds. 2002. pp. 360–71.

Wolf, Naomi. 1990. *The Beauty Myth*. London: Chatto and Windus.

——1993. *Fire with Fire: The New Female Power and How It Will Change the 21st Century*. London: Chatto & Windus.

Wolfe, Leslie R. 2004. "Fighting the War against Sexual Trafficking of Women and Girls". In Stark and Whisnant. 2004. pp. 419–26.

Women Living Under Muslim Laws. 1997. "Women's Rights in the Current Political Backdrop of Afghanistan". Afghan Women's Network. September.
<http://www.wluml.org/english/publistheme.shtml?cmd[23]=c-1-Militarisation>.

—— 2003a. "Fiji: Family Law Bill Passed". 27 October.
<http://www.wluml.org/english/newsfulltxt.shtml?cmd%5B157%5D=x-157-23006>.

—— 2003b. "In Search of Justice, Human Rights and a Just Peace".
Feminist International Radio Endeavor (FIRE) and WLUML. October 2003.
—— 2005. "WLUML Statement to the World Social Forum – Appeal Against Fundamentalisms", 21 January
<http://wluml.org/english/newsfulltxt.shtml?cmd[157]=x-157-103376>.
—— 2008. "Nicaragua: Feminists under Attack by Fundamentalist Forces". 7 January. <http://www.wluml.org/english/newsfulltxt.shtml?cmd[157]=x-157-559677>.
—— n.d. "About WLUML". <http://www/wluml.org/english/about.shtml>.
Women's Electoral Lobby. 1999. <http://www.wel.org.au/issues/releases/9903prea.htm>.
Women's Safety After Separation. n.d. <http://www.ncsmc.org.au/wsas/welcome.htm>.
Women's Services Network (WESNET). 2004a.
"Women and Children Out in the Cold Again". Media release. 27 October.
<http://www.wesnet.org.au/publications/MediaReleases/041027MediaRelease.htm>.
—— 2004b. "Facts and Figures on Domestic Violence in Australia".
<http://www.wesnet.org.au/publications/0405DVFactsandFigures.htmv
—— 2006. "New Survey Again Proves that Women Bear the Brunt of Domestic Violence".
Media release. 24 August.
<http://www.wesnet.org.au/publications/MediaReleases/060824MediaRelease.htm>.
Woodley, Emma. 2005. "Women and Power: Ethical Issues".
Paper delivered at the Contemporary Voices Workshop, Magnetic Island, Qld. 8–10 July.
World Health Organization. 2002. *World Report on Violence and Health: Summary*.
Geneva: World Health Organization Office of Publications.
World March of Women. 2000. *Changing the World Step-by-Step: Mosaic in Tribute to Women's Struggles World-wide*. 2000. Canada: World March of Women in the year 2000 – Fédération des femmes du Quebec.
—— 2004. Women's Global Charter for Humanity, Supporting document 1:
"The Charter – Another Way To March".
<http://www.marchemondiale.org/en/charter3.html>.
Young, Iris Marion. 1990. *Justice and the Politics of Difference*.
Princeton, NJ: Princeton University Press.
Zalewski, Marysia. 1995. "Well, What Is the Feminist Perspective on Bosnia?"
International Affairs. Vol. 71, no. 2. pp. 339–56.
Zalewski, Marysia and Jane Parpart, eds. 1998. *The "Man" Question in International Relations*.
Boulder, CO: Westview Press.
Zipper, Juliette and Selma Sevenhuijsen. 1988.
"Surrogacy: Feminist Notions of Motherhood Reconsidered". In Stanworth, ed. 1988.

SELECTION OF RADICAL FEMINIST WEBSITES

Coalition Against Trafficking in Women, Australia, <http://www.catwa.com>
Coalition Against Trafficking in Women, International, <http://www.catwinternational.org>
Coalition for a Feminist Agenda, <http://www.feministagenda.org.au>
Feminist International Network of Resistance to Reproductive and Genetic Engineering,
<http://www.finrrage.org>
Hands off our Ovaries, <http://www.handsoffourovaries.com>
RadFemSpeak, <http://radfemspeak.net/>
The Fury: Australian Radical Feminism, <http://radfemspeak.net/the-fury>

INDEX

2020 Summit, 150, 158, 236
9/11: after, 15, 126, 133, 158; and fear, 136; responses to, 14

A

abeyance: theory of, 226, 228–31, 236
Aboriginal and Torres Strait Islander Commission (ATSIC): abolished, 156
Aboriginal, 50, 119, 156, 158, 167, 191, 215; traditional law, 119–21
abortion, 48, 78, 143, 181, 204; access to, 80, 202
abuse of women, 73, 84, 92–9, 164, 177, 181, 193; as integral to men's sport, 94–6; by military personnel, 92–4
accountability, 132; to government, 144–8, 151; to the public, 145
action, 3, 6, 9, 29, 33, 36, 46, 50, 66, 69, 71, 93–4, 115, 130, 134, 142, 152, 155, 161, 163, 169, 172, 181, 185n, 188n, 201, 211, 218, 236–40
advocacy, 115; curbing, 129, 144, 146, 150–2; on behalf of marginalised groups, 144, 233
Africa, 53, 56, 88, 106, 107, 117, 134, 186, 194; and HIV/AIDS 195; feminism in 219–21
African American, 186–92
Amnesty International, 74, 77, 79, 87–8, 218
Anthony, Susan B., 2, 7, 186, 202, 213
anti-discrimination legislation, 62
anti-globalisation: activists 78, 123, 161, 218; movement, 19, 160–1, 235
anti-pornography ordinance, 5
anti-racism, 78, 119–21
appraisal, 6, 181, 216, 236, 237–9, 240
Austin, J.L., 68–70
Australian Bureau of Statistics, 74, 148, 207n
Australian Law Reform Commission, 62–4

B

backlash, 43, 50, 104, 212–13, 225, 226–8, 231, 236
Barry, Kathleen, 6
Bell, Diane, 116, 130n, 142–3, 184–5, 187n
Bonisteel, Mandy, 115, 140, 144n, 145, 147, 150
Brownmiller, Susan, 202–4
Bunch, Charlotte, 12, 19, 171–3

Bush, George W., 15, 54, 79, 80, 91, 102, 108, 126, 127, 131, 133, 136, 194

C

Campbell, Matthew, 86
Campbell, Tom, 28, 29–32, 33
Carson, Donna, 85
Cass, Deborah, 6
censorship, 17, 31, 65, 69, 123, 183n
children overboard affair, 132, 134–5
choice, 8, 11, 40, 52, 96, 138, 139, 140, 145, 148, 153, 164, 168, 172, 174, 175, 178, 181–2, 203, 211, 216, 230
Chomsky, Noam, 38, 124, 125, 126, 130, 131, 133, 134, 135, 136, 137, 152, 154
civil rights, 5, 33, 66, 180, 222
Clarke, De, 138
Coalition Against Trafficking in Women (CATW), 94, 234n
CODEPINK, 159
consent: age of, 204, manufacture of, 125
consultation, 157, 191; managed, 140, 144, 148, 149–50
control, 9, 20, 31, 36, 38, 44, 53, 55, 59, 76, 77–8, 83, 91, 97, 101, 123–5, 126, 127, 130, 135, 137, 146, 152, 161, 164, 182, 207, 228, 233, 234
Coomaraswamy, Radhika, 93
cooptation, 21, 230
cultural inclusiveness, 105, 119–21
cultural solidarity, 105, 116–19

D

Daly, Mary, 3, 7, 142
de Ishtar, Zohl, 187n, 189
decision-making, 31, 37, 39, 154, 210, 214; exclusion from, 5, 13, 64, 73, 103, 118, 140, 219, 230
democracy, 49, 59, 60, 89, 123, 125, 131, 144, 145, 150, 151, 155, 161, 169, 223; crisis of, 152, 154; definitions of, 36–41; free speech and, 23, 28, 35, 36–41
depoliticisation, 141, 143, 230, 231
disablement: silenced by, 70, 71–3, 200, 209
discrimination, 18, 50, 63, 66, 67, 68, 77, 79, 104, 110, 157, 158; positive, 48, 63, 157
disengagement, 83, 230
disruption, 21, 23, 144, 219, 222, 228, 230

dissent, 1, 3, 17, 18, 20, 21, 23, 30, 37n, 40, 79, 100, 102, 103, 123–62, 196, 199, 200, 217, 219, 240
Dodson, Patrick, 157, 158
domination, 7, 9, 12, 16, 22, 79–80, 116–7, 143, 161n, 176, 177; and subordination, 7, 12, 66; structures of, 21, 100, 101; systems of, 191–2
Dowrick, Stephanie, 167–8
Dworkin, Andrea, 5, 6, 15, 33, 61, 64, 66, 67, 68, 77, 180, 184

E

Easteal, Patricia, 86
Ehrenreich, Barbara, 239
engagement, 6, 11, 21, 175, 230, 231, 236
Enloe, Cynthia, 14, 15, 100, 101, 103
environmentalists, 60, 129, 139, 160
equal opportunity, 62, 70, 77, 80, 141, 164, 202, 204, 210
equal rights, 27, 91
Equal Rights Amendment, 202, 213
equality, 2, 5, 8, 10–12, 18–19, 23, 27, 29, 31, 32, 36, 37n, 47–8, 50, 58–62, 66–7, 70, 77–9, 80, 83–4, 94, 96, 100, 104, 118, 119, 139–40, 157, 164, 166, 178, 180–1, 202–4, 205, 206, 209, 212, 215, 217, 219, 221, 224, 227, 233, 235, 236, 239; approaches to, 62–5, 73; argument for, 29, 32–5, 41, 51, 57
equity, 8, 55, 59, 60, 61, 80, 216, 227
ethics, 6, 8, 47, 132, 185n, 237; feminist, 6–9, 9–12, 12–16, 21, 23, 101, 199–200, 201–12, 212–17, 218, 229, 236, 237–40 *see also* feminist ethics
exclusion, 4, 5, 10, 12–13, 15–16, 17, 21, 23, 40, 60, 64, 73, 79–80, 83, 84, 100–5, 150, 151, 169, 203, 219, 228, 230, 236, 239, 240; effects of, 103–5; of lesbians, 171.
exploitation, 12, 34, 60, 94, 113, 114, 123, 155, 178, 210, 216, 232, 236

F

fair speech, 1, 5, 9, 17, 23, 28, 51–80, 199, 212, 215–17; compared with fair trade, 58–61; concept of, 61; context for, 51–2;
fair trade, 17, 23, 51; compared with fair speech, 58–61
FairWear, 112, 114
Faludi, Susan, 212, 213, 226, 227, 228
fear, 1, 2, 31, 76, 85, 103, 111, 124, 132, 133, 135–7, 143, 186, 208

feminism, 1, 3, 5, 6, 18, 67, 83, 136, 139, 142, 143, 155, 164, 165, 167, 172, 175, 176–7, 180, 181, 182, 193, 200, 204, 210–11, 218, 219, 239; and CALD women, 192–6; and Indigenous women, 186–92; and lesbians, 171–5; and radicals, 176–85; attack on, 182–4; definitions of, 18–22; in non-Western settings, 219–25; in Western countries today, 225–34; nineteenth-century, 1, 6; non-radical, 235; of dissent, 1, 102; reclaimed, 184–5; Second Wave, 3, 5, 18, 92, 154, 163, 168, 180, 203, 206, 211, 213, 227; future of, 199–240; twenty-first century, 1, 6, 225
feminisms, 18, 20
feminist, 1, 3, 4, 5, 6, 7n, 12–16, 18–19, 19–22, 23, 27, 40, 43, 45, 48, 49, 60, 83, 92, 94, 96, 100–1, 105, 112, 114n, 116, 119, 121, 123, 136, 137, 141, 142, 143, 147, 149, 150, 154, 158, 161, 163–4, 169, 199, 200, 201–11, 212–18; argument for equality, 29, 32–5, 41, 51, 57, 61, 64; criticism of 165–8; movement, 104, 154–6, 168, 171; speech in twenty-first century, 219–40; theory on free speech, 61–80; token 102–3
feminist ethics, 1, 6–9, 21, 101, 199, 218, 236, 237, 238, 239, 240; and international relations, 12–16; current debates in, 10–12;
Feminist International Network of Resistance to Reproductive and Genetic Engineering (FINRRAGE), 181–2
Feminist Ordinance against Pornography, 5–6, 33, 61, 66, 180–1
Fergus, Lara, 15, 74, 77
Firestone, Shulamith, 176
free speech, 1, 4, 5, 12, 17, 23, 27–50, 57–8, 61, 62, 64–73, 216; and democracy, 36–41; and harm, 65–73; and power, 41–9; arguments for 29–35; compared with free trade, 52–8; for all 17, 49–50
free trade, 17, 23, 51, 52–7, 58, 59–60, 130; and pornography 98–9; and prostitution 97–8; compared with free speech, 52–8
freedom, 15, 32, 52–7, 58, 60, 77, 78, 88, 89, 109–10, 123, 130–1, 139, 144, 156, 159, 164, 194, 202, 204, 209, 219, 222, 234, 235, 238; limitations on, 61; of choice, 182; of movement, 78, 110

freedom of speech, 1, 5, 16, 17, 27, 28, 31, 32–4, 36–8, 51, 58, 64, 65, 69, 123, 196, 199, 240; as universal right, 1, 17, 33, 34, 51, 199; democratic principle of, 5, 17, 28, 41, 51, 240
French, Marilyn, 138
fundamentalism, 12, 13, 14, 16, 23, 64, 73, 77–9, 84, 89, 92, 121, 218, 219

G

G8, 106–8
gang-rape, 14, 87, 96, 165, 167, 215
 see also rape
Gaze, Beth, 6, 64, 66–7, 73
gender, 8, 11, 13n, 15, 16, 19, 50, 62–3, 78, 80, 88, 100, 116, 148, 168, 203, 210, 220, 225, 232, 239; postmodern use of, 20, 142–3, 175, 178, 179
General Agreement on Tariffs and Trade (GATT), 42
Gill, Rosalind, 210–11
Gilligan, Carol, 7–9, 10, 11
Gilmore, Kate, 77
globalisation, 5, 12, 13, 15, 17, 19, 41–2, 52, 53–4, 56–7, 58–9, 78, 83, 112–14, 123, 160–1, 218, 231, 235
Green, Betty, 217
Green, Linda, 115, 140, 144, 145, 147, 150
grief, 44–5
Griffin, Susan, 96–7

H

harm, 58, 63, 64, 74,164, 168, 181, 183, 218, 219, 240; of pornography, 65–8, 180; of prostitution, 94, 98–9; of sexualisation, 99
hate speech, 34, 51, 57, 58, 68, 69–70
Hawthorne, Susan, 14, 15, 41–2, 48, 52, 77, 87–8, 89, 137, 141–2, 161n, 175
Herman, Edward, 125
heterosexual, 7, 84, 89, 168, 171–3, 174, 176; privilege 172
HIV/AIDS, 106, 195, 219
hooks, bell, 11, 191
Howard, John, 27, 43, 44, 46, 47, 80, 91, 115, 126–7, 128–30, 132, 134, 140–1, 145, 146n, 147–8, 149, 150–1, 153, 154, 157–8, 160, 165–6, 194, 227; lies, 132–5, 153
Huggins, Jackie, 116–17, 190–1
Hughes, Donna, 6
Hughes, Patricia, 85

human rights, 16, 20, 27, 31, 47–8, 57, 77, 78, 88, 91, 93, 94, 105, 106, 110, 112, 116, 118, 119, 126, 158, 185, 195, 214, 221–3, 224–5, 229, 234, 238; law, 64n; theory, 74
Human Rights Watch, 89, 109

I

imperialism, 11, 12, 60, 176, 194, 196
Indigenous women, 16, 23, 116–17, 139n, 156–7, 163, 167, 169, 171, 186–92, 196, 234
individual rights, 31–2
inequality, 5, 11, 12, 16, 18–19, 27, 33, 34, 51–2, 53, 54–5, 57–8, 61–2, 63–5, 66, 72–3, 83–4, 99, 143, 176, 183, 232
injustice, 32, 57, 58, 74, 83, 87, 109, 117, 119, 141, 154–5, 156, 168, 185, 199, 206, 215, 217, 218, 227, 237, 239, 240
Institute of Public Affairs, 126, 128–30, 145–6
International Monetary Fund, 42, 47, 57, 60, 106
international relations, 1, 9, 12–16, 103, 133
Itzin, Catherine, 6, 15, 64, 67

J

Jabri, Vivienne, 16, 21, 100, 101–2
Jaggar, Alison, 7, 8, 9, 18–19, 176
Jeffreys, Sheila, 6, 15, 97–8, 143, 172, 173–4, 183
Jhappan, Radha, 10–12
judgement, 73, 119, 163, 169, 185n, 212, 214
justice, 1, 6, 7–8, 10–12, 14n, 23, 31, 35, 40, 47, 49, 50, 51, 55–6, 58–60, 61, 65, 73, 80, 83, 104, 115, 119, 121, 123, 139–41, 143, 152, 157, 158, 161, 164, 165, 168–70, 173, 176, 180, 184–5, 194, 201, 204, 205, 211, 212–13, 214, 215–17, 218, 219, 223, 224, 227, 233, 236, 237, 238–9

K

Kapululangu Aboriginal Women's Association, 189
Kaplan, Gisela, 229
Kingston, Margo, 35n, 126–7, 146n
Klein, Renate, 7n, 142–3, 177, 181–2, 184–5, 212

L

La Nauze, Andrea, 99
Lake, Marilyn, 204
Langton, Rae, 6, 62, 64, 68–72, 200

language, 3, 31, 47, 48, 52, 54, 69, 104, 105, 114, 124, 128n, 140–1, 157, 171, 178, 216, 217, 227; as tool of control, 137–143; as tool of propaganda, 130, 135–43; of corporate governance, 114–15, 138–9, 148; of post-modernism, 141–3, 190; of war, 138
Leidholdt, Dorchen, 15, 182–3
lesbians, 7, 10, 11, 19, 23, 51, 137, 139, 141, 143, 163, 168, 169, 176, 179, 183, 186, 196; feminists, 171–3; rejected by heterosexual feminists, 171–3; separatism, 173–5; torture of, 87–9; violence against, 84, 87–9
Lewis, Stephen, 100, 104, 106–7
lies, 29, 46–8, 101, 104, 132–4, 135, 136, 155, 159; by John Howard, 46–7, 134–5, 153–4
Lorde, Audre, 4, 136, 186–8
loyalties, 237, 238–9

M

MacKinnon, Catharine, 5, 6, 11, 12, 15, 21, 32–5, 41, 49, 57, 61–2, 64–73, 77, 79, 142, 177, 180–1, 183
Maddison, Sarah, 144–5, 149, 150, 151, 229
Make Poverty History, 59, 106–7
Mandela, Nelson, 53, 56, 59
manipulation, 167, 170; of the mind, 44, 123–4, 135, 161
Manne, Robert, 127
Marchiano, Linda, 71–2
marginalisation, 12, 59, 141, 143, 144, 150, 228–9, 230
market, 35, 52–3, 55–6, 60, 92, 115, 128–30, 138–41, 144, 161; fundamentalism, 16, 77–8, 89, 91–2
Marketplace of Ideas, 29–32, 34, 123n
masculinities, 14, 15, 101
Mason-Grant, Joan, 6, 69n
Matsuda, Mari, 64, 69
McLellan, Betty, 16, 104, 164n, 190, 231
media, 17, 29, 35, 38, 41, 43–5, 46, 47, 48, 52, 84, 92, 94n, 102, 111, 123, 129, 135, 143, 145, 148, 155, 156, 159, 165–8, 179, 184, 185, 199, 210–11, 215–16, 226, 230, 232, 233, 234, 235; and propaganda, 124–8
Meyer, David, 230–1, 236
migrants, 117, 137, 141, 158, 194; domestic workers, 109–12, 114, 194
militarism, 12, 13, 14, 15
Mill, John Stuart, 7, 8, 30, 65

minorities, 10, 23, 37n, 51, 64, 70, 119, 127, 141, 156–8, 163, 183n, 199
misinterpretation, 199
misrepresentation, 52, 155, 165–8, 184, 185, 199, 200–1, 224, 239
Moghadam, Valentine M., 14, 15n, 20, 90
Moreton-Robinson, Aileen, 190
Morgan, Robin, 14, 22
Morton, Nelle, 3
Mott, Lucretia, 1, 202
Movements, 20, 59, 78, 106, 139, 143, 154, 185, 227, 228–31; anti-globalisation, 19, 160–1, 233; anti-poverty, 19; environment, 160–85; fair trade, 58; feminist/women's, 1, 3, 6, 18, 20, 54, 79, 80, 83, 91, 104, 116, 154–6, 163–4, 168, 171, 172–5, 176, 180–1, 183–4, 187, 190, 191, 192–3, 194, 195, 202–4, 211, 213, 218, 220, 222–5, 225–9, 231, 233, 236; fragmentation of, 230; peace, 159; racial minorities, 156–8, 185; trade union, 144, 150n, 152–4, 233
Msimang, Sisonke, 195
multiculturalism, 139, 158, 166, 216
Murray River, 129–30
Murray-Darling Basin, 129
Myron, Nancy, 171–3, 176

N

nationalism, 44–5
Nawa, Fariba, 102, 118
neoliberalism, 17, 18, 20, 52, 54–5, 56, 100, 101, 128–30, 139, 142, 170, 200
new class theory, 139
Non-Government Organisations (NGOs), 38, 56, 60, 73, 114n, 115, 129, 140, 144–54, 156, 161, 222–3, 225, 233
Norman, Amy, 85

O

Oberin, Julie, 147–8
O'Neill, Onora, 146
Organisation of Women's Freedom in Iraq, 78
outworkers, 114, 194

P

Partnerships Against Domestic Violence, 76
Patriarchal Universe of Discourse, 4
peace activists, 15–16, 46, 103, 118, 123, 159, 161
Penelope, Julia, 4

pornography, 4, 5, 6, 15, 33–5, 48, 51, 58, 61, 64–5, 65–73, 77, 79, 92, 96–9, 103, 155, 164, 177, 178, 183–4, 185n, 202, 203, 210, 211, 218, 235; and silencing, 69–73; and subordination, 68–9; Feminist Ordinance against, 5–6, 33, 61, 66, 180–1
postmodernism, 16, 19–20, 21, 142, 175, 177, 178–9, 182, 184–5, 186, 190, 196, 227, 239; language of, 141–3
poverty, 13, 15, 19, 47, 54, 57, 58–60, 91, 92, 105, 106–9, 110–14, 115, 116, 131, 141, 151, 155, 158, 161, 170, 215, 218, 219, 227n, 235
Poverty Reduction Growth Facility, 106
power, 6–7, 8, 11, 14, 16, 17, 21, 29, 32–3, 35, 36–7, 37–9, 51, 52–7, 58, 61, 64, 65, 68, 79–80, 83–4, 90, 94, 116, 119, 123, 128, 132, 134–5, 142, 143, 149, 150, 154–6, 161, 170–1, 175, 193, 196, 201, 205–6, 224, 231, 237, 238, 240; elite, 23, 28, 125, 130, 135, 137, 142, 143, 154, 159–61, 196, 199, 211, 234; exclusion from, 23, 79, 100–5, 236; imbalance, 63, 183, 203; speech and, 34–5, 41–50, 57–8, 199–200; structures of, 189–91, 207
propaganda, 67, 104, 124–35, 161, 178, 234; and fear, 135–41; and language, 141–3
prostitution, 4, 7n, 13, 15, 34, 48, 51, 64, 65, 72, 92–4, 96–9, 103, 108–9, 111, 147n, 155, 164, 177, 178, 183, 184, 185n, 193–4, 203, 210, 211, 218, 235
protest, 3, 6, 37–40, 70, 71–2, 94, 98, 103, 123, 130n, 132, 146, 156, 159, 160, 167, 190, 194, 200, 210–11, 214, 216, 229, 230, 232, 234, 236–40
public choice theory, 139–40

Q
quality of life, 51–2, 56–7, 58

R
racial vilification, 34, 51, 58, 64, 70, 110, 156–7
racism, 11, 19, 34, 78, 105, 114, 118, 157; feminism and, 186–92, 193–6
radical feminism, 1, 5, 6, 11–12, 13, 18, 19, 20, 21–2, 23, 40, 65, 67, 73, 83, 92, 96, 105, 116, 119, 142, 143, 164, 165, 168–70, 175, 176, 186–92, 194, 196, 199, 200–1, 211–12, 216, 217, 219, 230–1, 234–7, 239–40; silencing of, 176–85

rape, 4, 13, 34, 35, 48, 64, 65, 66, 71, 73, 86–9, 103, 110–11, 116, 117, 119–21, 137, 138, 147, 164, 167, 171, 177, 180, 183, 188, 194, 202, 203, 208, 210, 215, 218, 219; as subordinating tactic, 14, 68; by sportsmen, 94–5; date, 71; in marriage, 177–8, 205; of "comfort women", 92–4; of lesbians, 87–9 *see also* sexual abuse
Raymond, Janice, 7, 15, 45, 174, 182, 183
Reagan, Ronald, 125–6, 131, 136, 138, 152
Rebick, Judy, 204–5
refusal, 71–2, 79
reproductive technologies, 7, 177, 178, 181–2, 183
resistance, 37, 60, 88, 116, 144, 181, 183
Revolutionary Association of the Women of Afghanistan (RAWA), 14, 89–90, 217, 221
Rice, Condoleezza, 15, 80, 102, 134
Rich, Adrienne, 3, 171–2, 186–90
Robertson, Boni, 117, 191
roots of oppression, 18; analysis of 237–9
Roy, Arundhati, 14, 47–8, 54–60, 106, 200, 240
Rudd, Kevin, 47, 102, 108, 115, 150, 151n, 155, 156n, 157n, 158, 236
Rundle, Guy, 127
Rush, Emma, 99

S
Sadurksi, Wojciech, 64, 69–70
Sawer, Marian, 139–41, 165
Sawyers, Traci, 230–1, 236
Schauer, Frederick, 31–2, 36, 40, 65
Scutt, Jocelynne, 6, 182, 205
Second Wave feminism, 3, 4, 5, 18, 83, 92, 104, 154, 163, 168, 180, 203, 206, 211, 213, 226–7, 231, 232
self-determination, 3, 12, 28, 31–2, 33, 58
Seneca Falls, 1, 213
separatism, 172, 173–5
Sere, Adriene, 6
sex tourism, 193
sexism, 11, 18–19, 34, 67, 117, 176, 186, 188n, 190–1, 193, 210
sexual abuse, 13, 14, 51, 58, 67, 68, 71, 73, 74, 75–6, 86, 87, 89, 92–4, 94–6, 102, 109, 114n, 118, 137, 140, 143, 193, 222, 224, 225, 233; of children, 48, 86, 89, 150, 188, 206 *see also* rape
sexual harassment, 4, 11, 73, 77, 87, 109, 111, 117, 165, 202, 218, 224

sexual liberals, 177, 182–3, 235
sexualisation, 209, 210–11, 235; of children, 99, 209, 211, 235
Sharia Law, 78, 91, 194, 215, 222
Shiva, Vandana, 15, 41, 53, 59, 91
SIEV 4, 135
silence, 3–4, 5, 12, 17, 23, 37, 48, 51, 57–8, 61, 62, 64–72, 73, 84, 87–9, 89–92, 94, 97, 105, 108–9, 114, 114, 117, 118, 121, 123, 137, 142–3, 145, 147–8, 150, 151, 155, 157–8, 161, 163–4, 165, 167–8, 169, 170–1, 185, 187, 191, 195, 196, 199, 212, 217, 219, 221; code of, 95–6; not an option, 201
silencing, 1, 4, 5, 12–13, 17, 23, 30, 64, 70–1, 73, 79, 96–9, 104, 114, 115, 116–121, 240; accusations of, 165–8; actual, 168–96; by fundamentalism, 89–92; of dissenting voices, 17, 123–161; of ethnic minorities, 192–6; of heterosexual women, 84–7; of Indigenous women, 186–92; of lesbians, 87–9, 171–5; of radical feminists, 176–85; of women by women, 163–96; of women's voices, 81–121; perceptions of, 163–4; speaking through the, 199–218, 225; tactics of, 84–105, 105–21, 226, 236
Slippery Slope, 29, 30–1
social change, 19, 102, 228
social movements, 18, 139, 144, 154–61, 185, 226, 227, 228–31
Soros, George, 52–3
speaking, 1, 21, 23, 31, 69n, 78, 116, 142, 150, 152, 161, 167, 168, 177, 184–5, 193, 197–218, 221, 233
speech, 1, 2, 3–4, 5, 6, 12, 17, 42, 43, 48–9, 50, 211–12; access to, 41; equality and, 32, 41, 64–73; fair, 9, 17, 23, 51–80, 215–17; feminist, 200, 201, 206, 219–40; free, 12, 16, 17, 23, 27–50, 57–8; racist, 69; rendered unspeakable, 200, 212; robbed of, 39, 73, 200; victims of, 1, 51, 58, 171
speech acts, 32, 34, 62, 64, 68–9, 199
Spender, Dale, 3–4
Stanton, Elizabeth Cady, 1, 2, 7, 202, 213
Structural Adjustment Programmes, 56–7, 106

subordination, 2, 4–5, 7, 9, 12, 13, 14–15, 21, 23, 33, 34, 51–2, 58, 61–2, 63–5, 65–67, 83–4, 91, 96, 116, 117, 123, 137, 168, 175, 203, 207, 219, 228, 236, 237, 239–40; by pornography, 68–9, 72, 73–7, 79, 96, 155; sexual, 201, 209–11
Sullivan, Mary, 15, 98, 194n
Svirsky, Gila, 118–19
sweatshops, 105, 112–14, 194

T
Taylor, Verta, 228–30
terrorism, 13, 14, 15, 126n, 133, 139; domestic, 12
see also 9/11
The Australia Institute, 144–5, 149–51
Thompson, Denise, 18, 22, 116, 176–7
Tong, Rosemarie, 7–10
Trade Related Intellectual Property Rights (TRIPs), 41–2
trade unions, 60, 112–13, 123, 128, 130, 139, 144, 150n, 152–4, 161, 213, 235
transformation, 6, 20, 83, 168–9, 183, 201, 240
truth, 2, 8, 28, 34, 46, 48, 97, 126, 135, 168–9, 214; argument for, 29–31, 32, 33, 123
truth-telling, 47

U
underground operations theory, 226, 231, 232–3
unity, 231

V
violence, 4–5, 12, 13–14, 15–16, 23, 40, 48–9, 51, 54, 58, 64–5, 73–7, 79, 93, 97, 104, 108, 111, 114n, 115, 117, 118, 140, 145, 147–9, 154, 155–6, 158, 164, 165–8, 177, 178–9, 184, 188, 190–2, 193, 195, 201, 204, 205–6, 206–9, 216, 218, 219, 222, 224–5, 227n, 228, 233, 236; after separation, 207–9; and war, 138; men's sport and, 13, 94–5; pornography and, 65–8, 71; prostitution and, 97–8; silenced by, 70, 83, 84–9; subordinates women, 14, 73
virtual space theory, 226, 231–2, 233–4

W

Wanyeki, L. Muthoni, 220
war, 13–14, 15–16, 38, 42, 44, 46, 54, 70, 79, 80, 83, 89–90, 92–3, 100, 102–4, 118–19, 123, 125, 128, 131, 134, 136, 155, 159, 176, 202, 203, 210, 213, 226; language of, 138; on terror, 125–6, 131, 133; victims of, 5
Washington Consensus, 52
Watkins, Kevin, 58, 60
weapons of mass destruction, 46, 133–4
Whisnant, Rebecca, 6, 15, 33, 67
Winter, Bronwyn, 14, 15n, 89
Wolf, Naomi, 203, 205, 227
woman, 1–2, 4, 8, 14, 21, 35, 40, 71, 76, 102, 103–4, 107, 111, 116–17, 132, 147n, 150, 164, 168, 170, 173, 178, 180, 185, 188n, 191, 207–8, 212, 223, 236, 238; anti-, 77–8, 221
woman-hating, 183–4, 211
women: throughout the book; culturally and linguistically diverse, 16, 192–6; fundamentalism and, 13, 23, 64, 77–8, 79, 84, 89, 91–2, 218, 219; heterosexual, 84–7, 89, 173; Indigenous, 16, 23, 116, 117, 139n, 141, 156, 157, 163, 167, 169, 171, 186–92, 196, 234; lesbian, 87–9, 173; silencing of, 1, 5, 12, 23, 64, 81–121, 163–96; token, 80, 100, 102, 105, 118, 219
Women Against Fundamentalism, 77–8
Women in Black, 159
Women Living Under Muslim Laws, 78–9, 221–2, 224
women of color, 191, 192–3
Women's Bible, 2
Women's Electoral Lobby (WEL), 27
Women's Safety After Separation, 209
Women's Services Network (WESNET), 75, 147–8, 208
Woodbridge, Pauline, 148
Woodley, Emma, 6
Working Against Sexual Harassment (WASH), 77
World Bank, 42, 47, 57, 106, 118
World Health Organization (WHO), 74
World March of Women, 15, 54, 57, 60, 227n
World Social Forum, 19, 20, 55–6, 60, 78, 79, 121, 161, 222
World Trade Organization (WTO), 42, 52

Y

Young, Iris Marion, 12